SOULS,
BODIES,
SPIRITS

SOULS, BODIES, SPIRITS

The Drive to Abolish
Abortion Since 1973

Kerry N. Jacoby

Westport, Connecticut
London

Library of Congress Cataloging-in-Publication Data

Jacoby, Kerry N., 1962–
    Souls, bodies, spirits : the drive to abolish abortion since 1973
  / Kerry N. Jacoby.
     p.   cm.
    Includes bibliographical references and index.
    ISBN 0–275–96044–7 (alk. paper)
    1. Pro-life movement—United States—History. 2. Abortion—United
States—History. I. Title.
    HQ767.5.U5J324 1998
    363.46'0973—dc21   97–33700

British Library Cataloguing in Publication Data is available.

Library of Congress Catalog Card Number: 97–33700
ISBN: 0–275–96044–7

First published in 1998

Praeger Publishers, 88 Post Road West, Westport, CT 06881
An imprint of Greenwood Publishing Group, Inc.

Printed in the United States of America

(∞)™

The paper used in this book complies with the
Permanent Paper Standard issued by the National
Information Standards Organization (Z39.48–1984).

10 9 8 7 6 5 4 3 2 1

Copyright Acknowledgments

The author and publisher gratefully acknowledge permission for use of the following
material:

Excerpts from *Revival: Principles to Change the World* by Winkie Pratney (copyright © 1983)
and *Operation Rescue* by Randall Terry (copyright © 1988) are used by permission of the
publisher, Whitaker House, 30 Hunt Valley Circle, New Kensington, PA 15068.

Contents

Acknowledgments

It is probably impossible to adequately recognize all the people who have contributed to making this book possible. Some of them are well-known to me, while others simply appeared at the right place at the right time, anonymous strangers whose last-minute interventions enabled me to do what seemed beyond possibility before I met them. Although I will attempt here to express my gratitude, if there are those who are left out, I hope they will be gracious and forgiving, recognizing my omissions as the product of a brain subject to the absentmindedness of being nine-and-a-half-months pregnant. Of course, it goes without saying that all those who contributed are known to the One who will reward them best and that any mistakes in the text are my responsibility alone.

My gratitude goes to Purdue University and those with whom I entered its Ph.D. program. There are many with whom I have shared classrooms, living rooms, bar benches, and endless cups of coffee, and all helped me in one way or another to refine my thought processes, my writing, and my patience—and especially my rapport with the all-important computer. Special thanks go to Doug and Debbie for sticking it out all the way to the end, to Loretta for being there with me when we first realized it might be possible to move into the professional world someday after all, and to Joanne for endless hours of keeping me from thinking about whether or not I would ever get this done.

Thanks, too, go to my committee members, Lyn Kathlene, Harry Targ, Cheryl Oreovicz—and Susan Curtis for so graciously and helpfully stepping into the breach at a crisis point. Very special thanks to Len Neufeldt, who made sure everything got done on time, and to his lovely wife, Mera, for just doing her job and making my life easier because of it.

This book could never have even been begun without the day-to-day efforts of the clerical staff in the Political Science Department and the calm professionalism of the ladies at Printing Services, who never complained about my messy paperwork or my last-minute mailing requests. For all their patience, and especially for the beyond-the-call-of-duty support from Barbara Bergner and Theresa Walker, I will be eternally grateful.

Naturally, there could be no book on activism without the willingness of the activists themselves to take their time and energy to participate. To all who did so, I am most thankful, although most are anonymous to me. Special thanks go to those in Wichita and Buffalo who overcame their skepticism of academics to give me a few minutes of their time, especially Karen Swallow Prior, Johnny Hunter, Tom and Linda Hall, Jim Phillips, Donna and Mark, and Frank Lowinger. Additional thanks go to those whose generosity of time, spirit, and space made the Buffalo trip possible—Mark Roy, Roy and Rosie Walls, Vic and Jewell Miller, Jerry and Verna Mae Boshart, Robert Weiss, and "Saint" Jane Denton. In addition, I am most grateful to Patti Lukis, her family, and her employer for graciously making way for me during a busy day and providing me a chance to witness fetal development at a wide variety of stages through ultrasound.

All good wishes, prayers, and thanks go, as well, to the faith communities that have been there for me during this laborious process: the good people of the Lafayette Mennonite Fellowship, who helped me to start asking the right questions, and to Pastor Greg Hackett, Pastor Ed Summerfield, Shelloy Mason, Jon Smith, and the family and elders of First Assembly of God of Lafayette, whose prayers and support have borne fruit in my life in countless ways over the past few years.

Finally, I would be remiss if I did not thank my wonderful family, who have provided support throughout the many stages of this project, especially my mother- and father-in-law, George and Sylvia. and my husband, David, for fitting all this into his own hectic schedule, even during Finals Week. And though they are also in the dedication, I really must make special mention again of my mom and dad, Neal and Carolyn, for their uncomplaining grace in providing free babysitting; their contribution, when all is said and done, probably made this process less stressful than anything else could have.

Introduction

As 1994 came to a close, two telling events with implications for the American entity calling itself the "pro-life movement" took place. On November 8, 1994, the Republican party became the majority party in both the House of Representatives and the Senate. For abortion opponents, the massive power shift in Congress was doubly sweet, for it represented the fruits of at least a decade of tireless labor. As the National Right to Life (NRL) Committee and the *National Review* were quick to point out, the results for pro-life candidates were not apparently affected by party affiliation:

> Big tent Republicans, like-minded pundits, and all others still calling for the GOP to abandon its pro-life stand should chew on the following election results: not a single pro-life governor or member of Congress of either party was defeated by a pro-choice challenger; pro-life challengers defeated 28 House and 2 Senate incumbents; of the 48 races for open House seats, pro-lifers took 34; of the 11 new senators, all but one are pro-life; and of the 26 percent of the electorate who said, according to a Wirthlin Group post-election survey, that the abortion issue affected the way they voted, two-thirds backed

abortion foes while only one third voted for pro-choice candidates.[1]

It seemed, for the moment at least, that pro-life legislators were coming
into their own.

Shortly thereafter, a second, more sinister, shade of abortion's loyal
opposition showed its colors. John Salvi III was arrested as the alleged
shooter in two slayings of abortion clinic employees. Salvi was neither a
leader nor much of an activist. He was a student hairdresser with strong
opinions on the issue of abortion. The women he killed were neither
abortionists nor the type of strident activists he could have confronted
outside the clinic where the lines of battle are usually drawn. They were
receptionists, doing the same clerical job done by millions of women,
pro-life and pro-choice, across America.[2]

These two events—so close in time, yet so far apart on the spectrum
of political activity—are not just moments of history. They are also indicators of the state of the current controversy and oracles as to what
may lie ahead. The abortion abolition enterprise is at a crossroads. After
decades of work, prayer, struggle, failure, and triumph, it finally seems
to some as though their viewpoint is and will continue to be strongly
represented in both houses of Congress, the state legislatures, and local
governments. After a 1992 election when pro-choice forces claimed to
have decisively won the debate, the 1994 midterm elections seemed to
fulfill the predictions of the NRL legislative committee's 1992 winter conference. There NRL members reminded the audience that the question
of slavery was once thought closed, as well—until Lincoln rolled back
the tide not long after the Dred Scott decision appeared to have pronounced the final word on the personhood of slaves.

And, yet, with victory finally seeming possible, there remain individuals and groups calling themselves "pro-life" who have simply given
up on elections, laws, and patient deliberation. Paul Hill (convicted killer
of a Florida abortionist) and John Salvi speak for a generally silent but
desperate minority, people whose agony over the massive number of
abortions performed in this country drives them to acts that others—
even others who agree with them politically and profess deep spiritual
pain over the issue—could never contemplate. Randall Terry, founder of
the direct-action group Operation Rescue, is fond of saying, "If you believe abortion is murder, start acting like it." Yet, even Operation Rescue
officially rejects the "justifiable homicide" theory advanced by Hill and
Salvi.

While the pro-life speakers featured on the television talk shows
would prefer the movement be seen as represented by the quiet dignity
of long-time Illinois congressman Henry Hyde, pro-choice speakers
claim that the rhetoric common among their opposition leads logically

to actions such as those of Hill and Salvi. Yet most who oppose abortion are neither congressmen nor terrorists. Even most of those who take the time to be activists are ordinary citizens, fighting for a cause they genuinely believe in. It is the goal of this book to bring realism and a human face back to the public perception of the abortion abolition activist.

To examine the activists with a narrow focus would not do justice to the activists or the issue. For the oddity of abortion is the fact that it is not a single issue at all. Rather, it is a complex web of many connected, competing, and conflicting issues of American life, held together at the center by a real act that is devastating in its symbolic implications. Although, as a noun, "abortion" signifies an act or a procedure, the word stands for much more in the minds of the American public. More than a simple act, it is as well an *issue*, a *debate*, a *question*—even, to some (including the Supreme Court), a *right*. When one says "abortion," one is only rarely speaking solely of the act of terminating a pregnancy. The multiple meanings of "abortion" and the Pandora's box of political and social questions it opens make it difficult to discuss the actions of its activists with any single focus. Even, as here, if we only examine one side of the issue, to be fair to the subjects, honest about the issue, and comprehensive in the exploration, it is necessary to expand our vision and go beyond traditional ways of thinking about complex cultural issues. Thus, this book uses three distinct approaches to obtain the fullest possible picture.

For quite some time, abortion abolitionists were rarely studied in their own right. The opinions on abortion were tossed into the mix of "conservatism" with other social concerns of the time, and the complexities of the anti-abortion position were rarely explored, except in reference to their "inconsistency" when compared with abolitionists' positions on other issues. The issue of abortion, in general (both in academia and in popular discourse), was often shouted about but rarely discussed.

Except in their own advocacy literature, the available information about the abolitionists has been somewhat lacking in sensitivity to its subjects, their assumptions, and their place within the larger culture. This book seeks to provide a comprehensible introduction to those who passionately oppose abortion, tracing the abolition effort as it has evolved from 1973 to its current state, and formulating a framework for studying it as it moves into the twenty-first century. Rather than merely reporting public opinion, it provides a window into the heart and soul of the abortion abolitionist. It is hoped that, in studying the history told in these pages, we will be able not only to observe and to analyze, but also to listen and to more fully understand why the abolitionists act and think as they do, and particularly why they appear to be so different from those who oppose them.

As we approach the millennium, Americans still have not come to terms with the political and moral implications of terminating nascent human life. New technologies developed in the past two decades have only made the long-term picture more murky, the issues and answers more ambiguous. Questions surrounding conception and death—the poles between which we seek to define life—have not become more easily resolved, but more complex. Physician-assisted suicide, fetal tissue transplant research, new forms of contraception, and experimental abortifacients such as RU-486—even possibilities once found only in the realm of science fiction, such as in-vitro fertilization and, most recently, cloning—have strained the capacities of scientists and ethicists alike. Creating life only to destroy it, as happens as a byproduct of in-vitro fertilization and cloning, has become not only common in scientific research, but deeply troubling to the conscience of the American public. Yet those procedures are astronomically rare in comparison with the more than 4,000 abortions believed to be performed daily—and which remain both unsettling and controversial to the average American.

Abortion, as an act and as an issue, complicates the deepest questions we can ask ourselves as human beings—about life, rights, responsibility, religion, and autonomy. The public image of the abortion debate, however, has largely ignored the complexities, focusing instead on painting the simplest picture of each side and the least reflective summary of the issues involved. In the public eye, both pro-choice activists and abortion abolitionists are represented largely in caricature. The wild-eyed feminist and the fire-breathing fundamentalist have their slight basis in reality, but ignore the sincerity that each side brings to the debate and the human characteristics and honest passion that drive both. On an issue so complex, so important, and so controversial, the American public deserves better.

This book is meant to flesh out one-half of that cartoon—the image of the abortion abolitionist. It presents the abolitionists in the context of their own historical reality, their belief systems, and the American culture as they see it. By seeking to understand abolitionism in its incarnations as a moral crusade, a social movement, and an adjunct phenomenon to religious revivalism, we can better see the tapestry that is abolitionism—a multifaceted, many-hued portrait of light and dark, patience and passion.

It is not my expectation to change anyone's mind about the issue of abortion; in the free marketplace of ideas in a democratic republic, men and women of good conscience may disagree on matters of importance. It is, rather, my hope that an open-minded examination of the growth and development of this enterprise will move us beyond the politics of name-calling and stereotyping, and toward a renewed understanding of activists as people.

We may never come to a point at which abortion abolitionists will relinquish their contention that abortion is a moral evil. We may never come to a point at which abortion rights activists agree with that contention. Let us hope, however, that someday we may come to an understanding that both should be seen as men and women of good conscience whose deeply held convictions profoundly influenced American political discourse.

Between the democratic process and bloody vigilantism lie myriad forms of political action. This book seeks to present not only those extremes, but also an accurate picture of the vast majority of those who have, in one way or another, played a part in this great American drama that is still running after more than a quarter of a century. In these pages, the reader will find portraits of abortion abolitionists distinct from the common stereotype. From the rank-and-file ordinary people who pray and fast and sing on the lawn of the abortionist, to pro-life feminists and major political operatives—here they stand, defined in their own words.

If the debate over abortion is becoming, as James Davison Hunter indicates, a "culture war," the people in these pages are the soldiers who are fighting that war every day, on battlegrounds as diverse as academic classrooms and abortion clinics themselves. The voices of the warriors in this struggle are compelling; they are ordinary voices speaking the extraordinary language of America's political heart. The reader is admonished to remember—lest we are tempted to take too lightly opinions with which we disagree, facts we instinctively wish to deny, and spokespeople we consider less than pedigreed—that these are the men and women on the front lines of the conflict. These are the feet that tread the picket lines, the hands folded in prayer—or clenched into fists—that line the barricades, the hands that pull the ballot levers.

These are the activists.

They have earned, at the least, our thoughtful attention.

NOTES

1. "This Week," *National Review* 46 (December, 1994): 12.

2. Salvi was convicted of the crimes but died in prison while awaiting a response to the appeal of his sentence.

CHAPTER 1

Abortion and Its Discontents

On January 22, 1973, the U.S. Supreme Court handed down a ruling that would have far-reaching implications. Rather than putting an end to the debate over legalized abortion, the decision in *Roe v. Wade* stimulated a long-term counterattack from what is now loosely termed the "pro-life movement." The importance of abortion in political affairs has risen and fallen over time, depending on the prevailing political culture. In the 1990s, however, the issue is both relevant and volatile.

Its relevance can be seen in its persistence as a topic of opinion research. Despite years of practice, professional pollsters still cannot give a precise reading of how many Americans are on each side of the debate. Both sides claim to have a majority, but that "majority" has never been stable. As Gallup and Castelli have observed, "slight differences in the wording of questions produce wide differences in response" (Gallup and Castelli, 1989: 167).

What does seem clear is that those who have strong feelings on the subject are almost evenly divided (with 33% of the population identified as strong supporters of anti-abortion efforts and 36% identified as strong opponents), according to those researchers (Gallup and Castelli, 1990: 172). Two years later, a *Time*/CNN poll, conducted on August 19–20, 1992, found that 49% of respondents agree that "A woman should be able to get an abortion no matter what the circumstances." However, 48% believe either that "abortion should be legal only in certain circumstances" or that "abortion should be illegal in all circumstances" (Morrow, 1992: 24).

Yet abortion has not always fared so well in the eyes of the American public. Its acceptance has come only after a long history of shadows and shame. How this seismic shift in respectability came about, however, depends largely on who you ask. The history of abortion comes in two flavors: the preservationist (favored by pro-choice forces and most academics) and the abolitionist (favored by pro-life groups and individuals, and only recently and occasionally apparent in the academic world). According to the preservationists, abortion was in widespread practice in the United States from the founding until the 1860s. At that point, newly professionalizing physicians turned public opinion to their advantage and succeeded in criminalizing abortion in nearly every state. There followed a long and gradual struggle to decriminalize abortion, which achieved small successes from time to time, finally coming to fruition with the 1973 *Roe* decision, which righted constitutional wrongs by recovering and preserving the right of reproductive choice.

A look into the abortion abolitionist literature, however, tells a far different story. Although this history will be explored in more detail throughout this work, it should be noted here that abortion abolitionists reject the preservationist reading of abortion history. Relying on religious history and, as Condit (1990) notes, constructing a "heritage tale" in marked contrast to the laissez-faire version of abortion history favored by the other side, abortion abolitionists reach into antiquity to depict a struggle of good versus evil that is eons old.

This version of history maintains that, although abortion has been legal at times, it has never been viewed by civilized people as a positive good, until recently. Its continued practice through history is a sign not of the need for such a procedure, but of the fallenness of humankind and the relentlessness of human cruelty. Abolitionist history argues that public opinion—not the physicians' need to solidify their professional position—caused the shift in abortion law that effectively criminalized the procedure nationwide by 1900. The "reform" movement of the twentieth century identified by Lader, Luker, and others is seen by abolitionists as a surge of selfishness that ended in a catastrophically mistaken decision by the Supreme Court. The results of that decision, according to this history, range in direct relation to it from 35 million abortions since 1973 to a general moral breakdown of the social order in America. According to this reading, the story is not complete. No matter how long it takes, abortion foes maintain, there will come a time when abortion will once again be abolished.

Whichever historian one reads, they all seem to agree on some of the more recent facts. Long before *Roe*, the groundwork was being laid for a large-scale shift in American abortion law. As early as 1954, in *Medicine and Morals*, Joseph Fletcher was arguing for a change in the expectations for therapeutic abortion. Fletcher, perhaps best known for his later development of "situational ethics," argued that there were certain instances in which nonphysical circumstances rendered abortion the most humane and spiritually correct choice for a pregnant woman. In *Situation Ethics*, Fletcher, an Episcopal professor of social ethics, outlines a general theory of ethics based on his interpretation of Christian *agape* love.

In dealing with a hypothetical pregnancy resulting from rape by an insane person, Fletcher argues that the most loving solution is abortion. He states: "Even self-defense legalism would have allowed the girl to kill her attacker, no matter that he was innocent in the forum of conscience because of his madness. The embryo is no more innocent, no less an aggressor or unwelcome invader! Is not the most loving thing possible (the right thing) in this case a responsible decision to terminate the pregnancy?" (Fletcher, 1966: 39).

In 1954, Harold Rosen edited a volume of works questioning the illicit status of abortion. *Therapeutic Abortion: Medical, Psychiatric, Legal, Anthropological, and Religious Considerations* began a dialogue in the religious, legal, and psychiatric communities that would become important as the next two decades played out. Adding to the intellectual mix, in 1957, a series of essays by Glanville Williams was published, in which the noted law professor argued that the law ought to demarcate time frames during gestation within which abortion would be legally permissible. He stated:

> This, then, seems to be the short and simple solution of the problem of abortion. Let any religious sect characterize abortion as a sin if it sees fit to do so, and punish its members for this sin by censure or other ecclesiastical punishment. But whether abortion should be a crime is to be judged by worldly considerations, and the case against treating it in this way— the case against the rule established in 1803—is, after the experience of one and a half centuries, overwhelming. (Williams, 1968: 233)

The frequently invoked "rape, incest, and life of the mother" exception to abortion restrictions is largely derived from Fletcher, Rosen, and Williams. In 1959, the American Law Institute revised its Model Penal Code with regard to abortion. It proposed three defenses to the crime of abortion, which sound rather familiar to the modern ear: fetal abnormality, rape or incest, and danger to the physical or mental health of the pregnant woman.

Less than a decade and a half later, the law would change. In the intervening historical moment, the invention of the birth control pill and the next wave of the women's movement brought both contraception and abortion more fully to the consciousness of American women. The era saw the inception of social movements aimed ultimately at expanding the Constitution's de facto reach with regard to women, racial minorities, and homosexuals. Mass protest, whether seeking civil rights or opposing U.S. involvement in the Vietnamese conflict, became standard fare on Americans' television screens. New and different presidents brought new Supreme Court justices. The nation was changing on many fronts, and, at the time, abortion was relatively low on the national radar. In the early 1960s, however, a prophetic blip appeared on that radar, when the country was briefly mesmerized by the tragedy of Sherri Finkbine.

Sherri Finkbine's story was a classic tale of an idyllic life turned nightmarish by the obstinance of bureaucracy. A "Romper Room" hostess in Phoenix, Arizona, Finkbine was happily expecting her fifth child. Seeking sleep, she unwittingly ingested the fetus-deforming drug thalidomide in the form of a tranquilizer that had been prescribed for her husband by a doctor in Europe. Terrorized by reports of the "thalidomide babies" being born overseas without limbs, the Finkbines sought a therapeutic abortion.

Had it not been for Finkbine's desire to warn other women of the dangers of thalidomide, the story might have ended there quietly. Her abortion had been accepted by the hospital's board as therapeutic and all was ready. However, Finkbine called a local newspaper to tell her story. Although her identity was withheld in the initial story, the hospital administrators made the connection and canceled the abortion, filing instead in court, hoping for a favorable declaratory judgment. The court, however, refused to rule, making Sherri Finkbine a worldwide celebrity, as she and her husband considered whether to seek the abortion in Japan or Sweden. Eventually, they chose Sweden, where the abortion took place and coverage of their plight trailed off.

Sherri Finkbine's case was widely publicized, and its treatment marked a change in the way abortion was reported in the national media. For the first time, the term "fetus" displaced the words "unborn child" in general public discourse. As Condit observes, the case "mythicized the illegal abortion drama by providing a shared, real case exemplifying [for millions of Americans] their experiences in their store of conventional knowledge" (1990: 30). Sherri Finkbine's tragedy, followed quickly by the domestic scare of a rubella outbreak that threatened the well-being of many American women's unborn children, highlighted the ambiguity of American abortion law, prompting further reflection.

The latter half of the 1960s was a relatively quiet time on the abortion front, with the public political focus shifting to other issues more clearly national and international in scope. As Luker notes, "given that now it [abortion] has become one of the central moral dilemmas of our time, it is particularly hard to imagine that it took at least a decade for the moral dimensions of the debate to come to the fore" (1984: 67). Yet that is precisely what happened. For the most part, abortion activism during this period was left to public health officials, doctors, and lawyers. Because this project focuses on public activism rather than elite activity, the reader is referred to Luker, Lader, and others for this portion of the story.

By the time the *Roe* opinion appeared, there was some evidence of change in the laws of the various states. Mary Ann Glendon (1987) argues that the changes in state laws indicated an emerging trend, which, if allowed to proceed on their own, might have avoided much of the acrimony that has attended the abortion debate. Lawrence Tribe disagrees, contending that the condition of state laws in 1973 indicates instead that no substantial change was likely to take place with any deliberate speed. Today, we can never know what the states might have done, despite Glendon's optimism and Tribe's fears. Nevertheless, we can say that the *Roe* decision was largely unanticipated by the average American, and its surprise came most unpleasantly for those who would later identify themselves as "pro-life." When the Supreme Court first articulated reproductive freedom as a form of the right to privacy, the decision, as Luker notes, appeared as a "bolt out of the blue" to those who would become the beginnings of the abortion abolition enterprise.

Obviously, however, Supreme Court decisions do not just mysteriously appear; some anti-abortion activists, most notably doctors and lawyers, were alerted to the possibility of a *Roe*-style decision coming out. However, even among those who had cause to anticipate the ruling, Luker reports that the expectation was that the public would never countenance such an unthinkable decision. Until they realized that the public reaction of outrage they expected was simply not going to come they did not recognize their own need to act. Among Luker's respondents, nearly all joined the pro-life movement in 1973, and many mobilized the very day the decision was handed down. Luker describes this initial post-*Roe* mobilization as that of "the housewives."

While pro-life activists scrambled to gather together the like-minded to reverse the ruling and its effects, the Supreme Court handed down decisions reinforcing the position of abortion as a right, while honing the scope of that right. Following *Roe*, the majority ruled that it was unconstitutional for a state to require a wife to obtain her husband's consent for an abortion (*Planned Parenthood of Central Missouri v. Danforth*, 1976), invalidated a Massachusetts law requiring unmarried minors to obtain the consent of both parents before undergoing an abortion (*Bellotti v. Baird*, 1979), and struck a second-trimester hospitalization requirement as unconstitutional (*Akron v. Akron Center for Reproductive Health*, 1983). In the meantime, pro-life legislators were doing what they could to restrict abortion—most notably Henry Hyde, author of the amendments that restrict federal funding for abortion (amendments ruled constitutional in 1980, in *Harris v. McRae*).

In 1989, however, another decision changed the legal terms and the governmental focal point of the debate. *Webster v. Reproductive Health Services* gave abortion abolitionists a new avenue through which to seek an end to legal abortion; essentially, the decision in *Webster* shifted the focus of action. It preserved the right of reproductive choice per se (thus angering right-to-life activists) but backed away from the Court's sixteen-year record, declaring that the states could now, if they so chose, set the confines within which that right could be exercised (angering pro-choice forces).

The decision sent shock waves through the political landscape. Both sides reacted with rallies, marches, rhetoric, political threats, and (in some cases) physical violence. Suddenly, for abortion abolitionists, the road to victory was open. Suddenly, for abortion rights activists, reversal seemed imminent. With the *Webster* decision, the undecided public became a vital potential resource for each group. The need to lobby the public and the state legislatures overshadowed the potential advantage of arguing the best legal case. The option to restrict now lay in the domain of the state.

At the state level, the battle was already joined. The grass-roots armies on both sides had been facing off for years. In city after city, then as now, pro-life "rescuers" sat, prayed, resisted arrest, and disturbed the peace in their attempts to prevent abortions from taking place, while pro-choice advocates counterdemonstrated, dedicated to preserving abortion as a legal reproductive option. At the local, state, and national levels, supporters on both sides staged rallies, marches, debates, and sit-ins, hoping to further their cause.

Since *Webster*, abortion abolitionists have avidly pursued this avenue, and the Court has been willing to let many of the states' new regulations stand. In 1990, in *Hodgson v. Minnesota*, the Court, though rejecting a state requirement that minors give both parents forty-eight hours' notice, upheld one-parent notification. Also in 1990, in *Ohio v. Akron Center for Reproductive Health*, Ohio's twenty-four-hour, one-parent notification requirement (with judicial bypass) was ruled constitutional. Two years later, in *Planned Parenthood of Southeastern Pennsylvania v. Casey*, the Court rejected spousal notification requirements but upheld the bulk of Pennsylvania's regulatory scheme, including informed consent, a twenty-four-hour waiting period, parental consent, and specific direction as to recording and recordkeeping. Clearly, *Webster* did not represent an anomaly; rather, it signaled a significant shift toward a more state-centered philosophy of abortion regulation. As we shall see, as the twentieth century approaches, the abortion abolitionists are prepared to position themselves to take advantage of the new paradigm.

Between *Roe* and *Webster*, abolitionist forces were by no means idle. To the contrary, the issue of abortion ignited passions that immediately sparked an enduring moral crusade. Over time, the narrow religious demographics of the abolitionists expanded sufficiently to make abortion the leading issue for a multifaceted social movement. And once *Webster* had thrown the question into the domain of the states and the people, direct-action protest tactics became a prominent feature of abolition strategy. The story of this evolution is the subject of this book. In these pages, the reader will discover a history that is often overlooked and a cast of characters that is generally underexamined.

The rest of this chapter will present short outlines of the three perspectives that will be used to explore the history of the abortion abolition effort and a brief sketch of the "average" abortion abolition activist, to give the reader a sense of the terrain we will be covering. The next six chapters, in sets of two, trace the development of the abortion abolition movement through the three phases identified here. Finally, the last chapter will analyze general trends that might be important in the future and propose a new model of faith-based political action.

THREE PERSPECTIVES ON SOCIAL ACTION

While the issue of abortion is, unquestionably, a very private matter of opinion on which individuals differ sharply, much of the debate has been played out in the very public arenas of journalism, politics, education, and law. The political debate has largely been shaped by the observable behavior of competing groups. Exploring the dynamics of those groups helps us to better understand the nature of the debate and begin to explain its endurance and volatility in the American experience. This book traces the historical evolution of abolitionist efforts from their beginnings as a moral crusade through their turbulent 1980s transition to a social movement. Finally, it explores the abolitionists' current linkages to modern revivalism and suggests a new way of thinking about the larger issues of faith-based activism that can incorporate all three of these developmental stages.

The Moral Crusade

When the pro-life enterprise first awoke, it was as a moral crusade to preserve a moral and social worldview that its members believed was directly threatened by the successes of the abortion reform movement.

Moral crusades are also called "status politics" and "the politics of life-style concern." They are, as Joseph Gusfield notes, distinguishable from the activities of a social movement in goal orientation and in the characteristics of the groups whose values and welfare the group addresses. Status movements are carried by status communities rather than individuals or class groups. Gusfield identifies these communities as being identifiable subgroups within society (such as religious or ethnic groups), "with associations, institutions, and a group life akin to a subcommunity within the society" (Gusfield, 1963: 21).

Nicola Beisel sees status politics as a means by which economic or social classes (similar to Gusfield's status communities) seek to use political means to ensure the continuation of their own cultures (class reproduction). A moral crusade uses status communities as filters through which individuals enter issue-related activities, ideally becoming activists over time. The means by which individuals within a status community become mobilized to engage in activism vary from issue to issue, community to community, and individual to individual. Some status communities, such as the Catholic Church, may overtly endorse the goals of the crusading group, with elites (such as priests, bishops, cardinals, and popes) exerting authoritative pressure on members of the community to participate in or contribute to activism. In this case, official resources may be used to advance the cause, as when a percentage of the offering is dedicated on a particular Sunday to a pro-life group, an event is held to benefit a crisis pregnancy center, or the church itself provides accommodations for meetings or lectures.

More commonly, status communities serve as meeting places where like-minded individuals gather, eventually broaching the topic with each other and seeking avenues through which to exert their influence. Although the community as a whole may not formally take a position on the issue or officially sanction the activity taken by its membership, it can facilitate the formation of smaller activity-oriented groups. For example, some church members may find themselves discussing the issue and choose to form groups of community, rather than sectarian, concern.

As status groups compete for dominance in the culture of the society, they do so through symbolic (rather than instrumental) goals. Symbolic activity is a goal in itself rather than a means to a larger one. For example, while a rally or a prayer meeting has the ultimate expressed goal of influencing public opinion, the immediate goal for the participants is reached through engaging in the act itself, which bonds the membership and creates a sense of potential. Particularly in the early stages of group formation, this community-building function is vital. In the case of the abortion abolitionists, nearly a decade would pass before their activities had any evident value other than as a social bonding agent. Yet, as we shall see, the peculiar nature of the abortion issue in matters of faith and conscience made possible long periods of apparent failure, without re-ducing existing members' sense of usefulness or causing loss of mem-bership.

A moral crusade carries with it assumptions about the character of the behavior or the culture being opposed. There is an underlying under-standing that there is something inherently positive about the values that motivate crusaders that is not shared by those who oppose them. In this sense, the moral crusade becomes something larger than a debate about policy; it is a value-driven attempt to assert or reassert moral norms. The moral crusade is not a logical policy debate between equal contenders; it is viewed as a battle between positive and negative values, the out-come of which will have a significant impact on the continued stability of the social structure.

The moral crusade attempts to reestablish the social support that its values once commanded, and its primary focus is, not surprisingly, moral reform. While some actions of the crusade and the crusaders may appear overtly political, even (as when compromise is made on posi-tions) cynically so, the central motivating factor is not politics. Politics, in this formulation, is purely a means to an end, which can be extremely distressing to allies of the crusade who find themselves trapped between political efficacy and true belief. (For example, Senator Bob Smith came under some friendly fire in 1995, when he agreed to accede to Senator Arlen Specter's wishes and move the House-passed Partial-Birth Abor-tion Ban Act to the Judiciary Committee prior to a full Senate vote on the measure. Despite Senator Smith's passion for passage of the bill, his willingness to make necessary political compromise was seen as a tem-porary retreat on the issue.)[1]

The moral component in the crusade is seen by the membership as both absolute and universally applicable. In other words, no value neu-trality is permitted. One cannot, as with lesser issues of politics, hold the position that the moral offense in question is wrong for one group but might be right (or even merely not-wrong) for another. To its opponents, one of the most truly maddening aspects of the abolitionist argument is its refusal to accept situational ethics. Right is right, and wrong is wrong; and never the twain shall meet.

The Social Movement

In predicting the development of a social movement as a form of col-lective behavior, Neil Smelser posits five essential elements: the condition of the social structure must be conducive to formation of a movement; there must be an appropriate type of strain; a generalized belief must develop that explains the strain and indicates the kind of solution needed; people must be mobilized for action in the name of the generalized belief; and the efforts toward social control of the movement by authorities must reinforce or at least not undermine the movement.

In speaking of structural conduciveness, Smelser argues that collective behavior may be limited by the type of social structure within which it takes place but is not necessarily determined by it. At most, the social structure sets the bounds of possibility. For example, riots are a form of collective behavior that may occur within a total institution such as a prison, but economic boycotts are barred from being successful in such a setting (since inmates have no significant purchasing power to manipulate). Thus, for a social movement to emerge, it must do so in a place and at a time favorable to its formation—or, at the very least, not overtly hostile to it.

In the presence of a conducive (or, minimally, nonhostile) environment, social movements tend to be precipitated by some type of strain that disrupts the previously existing acceptable status quo. However, for a collective action to fulfill its potential as a social movement, it must be capable of developing and sustaining a generalized belief and indicate a solution to the perceived problem. A group that has no goals, or too many goals, quickly loses members as its lack of direction generally leads to failure and despair. In the case of a group that is consistently on the losing side of the equation, the absence of clear direction to solve the problem can retard growth, discourage new membership, and sometimes prove fatal.

Just as the right social structure is not sufficient to stimulate movement activity alone, having a generalized belief about the issue is not of much help to the embryonic social movement if members cannot or will not take action. The ease with which like-minded individuals can be motivated to act varies from issue to issue and group to group. However, it is important, no matter what the issue or the possibility of victory, for social movement organizations to persuade their membership to do *something*.

Once a social movement has jumped all of the aforementioned hurdles, it still must face the problem of social control. According to Smelser, "In certain respects, this final determinant arches over all the others" (p. 17). There are, roughly, two types of social control—preventive and reactive. Preventive social controls act to regulate the flow of social behavior in such a way as to deflect movement formation. Reactive social controls, on the other hand, operate after the fact, forming society's response to collective behavior. Both can have effects on the strategy and tactics used by movement participants, and on the overall success of the movement as a whole.

In describing an ideal life cycle for a social movement, Turner and Killian identify four stages of development: a preliminary stage of social unrest; a popular stage of unrest; formal organization; and institutionalization. The preliminary stage is characterized by "unfocused and unorganized restlessness, evidence of increasing disorder, and susceptibility to the appeals of agitators" (Turner and Killian, 1972: 253). As Wilson notes, "In common-sense terms, the reason why people organize themselves into social movements is because they are discontented with the way things are and wish to see them changed but despair of the institutionalized methods of doing so" (1973: 32). This notion of prior discontent is often used to explain the circumstances out of which social movements arise. The beginning stages of social movements appear to be similar to less organized, crowd-type activity, with individuals milling somewhat aimlessly about (whether literally or metaphorically), uncertain of exactly what is causing the discontent they are feeling. After a decade of waiting for something to happen to cause the *Roe* decision to be reversed, by the time the abortion abolition enterprise emerged as a social movement, its members were overflowing with prior discontent.

The second stage of social movement formation is characterized by the discovery of unrest, which is then given a positive focus, transforming it into "collective excitement." Social myths develop within the movement to describe and justify it. Agitators and prophets are displaced by reformers, who focus the aims of the enterprise and provide more explicit programs of reform.

In the formal organization stage, the movement becomes more organized. Its members learn to commit to stable goals and strategies, and they begin to focus on community power centers in seeking change. At this stage, statesmen become the more crucial leaders. Increases in membership, formal requirements for membership, dues structures, and diffusion of responsibilities in various levels of structure are some signs of this stage of the process. Lobbying, letter writing, and other forms of institutional pressure are all indicators of growth into this level of development.

At the institutional stage, the movement becomes established as an organic part of society. At this point, the leadership of the movement becomes largely administrative, and its primary goal becomes the continuation of its own existence. At this advanced level of development, administration becomes a central concern of the enterprise. More individuals are employed by the official groups within the movement in some administrative capacity. Grass-roots membership may become somewhat less active, participating in the movement primarily by the payment of dues and attendance of structured meetings that are hierarchically controlled by officers of the organization. In addition, there should be some evidence that the enterprise itself is working with, rather than against, the agents of government.

At all these stages, we must keep in mind that membership consists of individuals. In terms of this consideration, Mancur Olson (1965) provides both food for thought and a problem to solve. Olson develops the "rational actor" model of microeconomics, which has been incorporated into the resource mobilization school of social movement theory, to explain the choice of individuals to enter into collective behavior. Essentially, Olson argues that the central problem in voluntary organizations seeking collective benefits is that the benefits obtained are accessible to all, not only to those who do the work of the collective entity. Thus, there must be a way to overcome the "free-rider" problem—to make it more worthwhile to join than not for those who will benefit in any case.

Building on Olson, McCarthy and Zald dominated the field of social movement theory with their theory of resource mobilization. Following a market-centered economic model, they seek to explain social movement organization, primarily focusing on those that have had time enough to evolve into interest groups.

While economic theory has its uses in sociology, it of course also has its discontents. The new social movement scholars rebel against the restrictive nature of resource mobilization, arguing that its cost-benefit analysis fails to take into account the more subtle implications of human behavior. The issues considered in recent social movement theory illustrate the complexity of studying the behavior of humans in groups. The expectations of the rational actor model are uniformly applied to all actors and seem overly simplistic. That simplicity is evident even when (as here) dealing with individuals whose traditions appear to fit that model. The feminist critique of the microeconomic model as presenting a false dichotomy of reason and emotion is particularly valid in the context of the abortion abolition enterprise. Indeed, as we shall see, Jaggar's insistence that "emotions provide the experiential basis for values" (1989: 153) is helpful in explaining much that seems illogical in abolitionist thinking.

The new social movement approach also allows us greater latitude to examine issues of framing in the context of the middle years of the abortion abolition enterprise, during which regaining control of the dialogue was a central focus of the movement. Working from Snow and Benford's theory of the relationship between what they call "master frames" and cycles of protest, we will examine the ways in which abortion abolitionists sought to define the act of abortion in ways that would bring in and retain membership.

Religious Revival

Finally, the abortion debate is fraught with archetypal overtones; it draws stark and unforgiving lines of good and evil, light and dark. One faction of the abolitionist enterprise articulates apocalyptic assumptions that may only be implied by the larger group. Those who make those assumptions overt, though perhaps not in the majority, have made important contributions to the linguistic and cultural patterns of the enterprise as a whole. The religious revival approach is useful in interpreting much of the millennialist, apocalyptic, and evangelical rhetoric that arises from time to time within abolitionist literature and that is occasionally used to explain motivation inside the abolitionist camp.

Although the religious revival perspective is not generally an academic concern with regard to the abortion abolition enterprise, the frequency with which its indicators appear in abolitionist material demands that we confront its claims. This argument begins with the assumption that America is on the verge of a national Protestant religious revival. As evidence, proponents point to the growth of evangelical (and, specifically, charismatic) denominations during the 1980s. This growth is seen as the sign of a more sweeping phenomenon yet to come, a revival on the order of the Great Awakenings.

While moral crusaders press on in the knowledge of their absolute correctness, hoping for victory, those who exhort their followers in the language of religious revival present the certainty of loss in the political and social arena, in the absence of the supernatural event they predict. Moreover, the claims made by these authors are distant enough from normal political discourse to place them outside the reach of the social movement perspective. Where social movement leaders trade in pragmatic politics, sometimes compromising an ideal to gain a slight victory, the authors from whom this perspective now emanates evidence little concern for the outcome of any given political skirmish.

Although religious revival is a generally unpredictable event, best described after the fact, the expectation of such an occurrence that weaves through abortion abolition literature has certain consequences for those who would study this enterprise. Those who act under this expectation behave in unusual ways when they enter the political arena; to the uninitiated, their rhetoric often appears nonsensical and their actions bizarre. Yet an understanding of how they view the issue of abortion in a theological revivalistic context can help us better comprehend their participation in the abortion abolition enterprise.

As Finke and Stark have noted, " 'Great Awakenings' are perhaps the most dominant theme in all general histories of American religion" (1992: 87). Religious revival is characterized by spontaneous and voluntary commitment of previously nonreligious individuals to a strong and demanding spiritual discipline, and the recommitment of previously lukewarm religious individuals to the same. In a sense, religious revival is a form of mass conversion and reconversion that is noticeable in its impact on the social and political culture of the society surrounding it. Although the religious explanation for the emergence of revival is the hand of God and the power of the Holy Spirit descending upon a particular locality, sociologists identify revival by the individuals most closely identified with it and its apparent exterior results.

In the American experience, there have been several Protestant religious revivals, each of which resulted in new forms of social politics. The first, beginning in 1734, began in Northampton, Massachusetts, in the parish of Jonathan Edwards and spread from Massachusetts throughout the colonies, primarily in Presbyterian and Congregationalist churches. When George Whitefield—having preached successful revivals in Bath, Bristol, and Gloucester—arrived in Georgia, he found a ready audience for his message. Conversions and recommitments swept through Georgia and followed the preacher to Philadelphia, where Benjamin Franklin, a close friend of the evangelist, calculated that thirty thousand people heard him preach on the steps of the Philadelphia courthouse. The style of faith that this revival produced was individualistic and reformed, stressing the responsibility of the sinner in accepting salvation by grace. This individualism, when combined with the increasing encroachment of England into the affairs of the colonies, would help feed the revolutionary fervor that resulted in the birth of the United States as a nation.[2]

Interestingly, the Great Awakening also set the tone for a pluralist nation to be formed. For it was not into denominations that Whitefield and the others baptized their new converts, but into Christ. Marshall and Manuel describe the effect of Whitefield's preaching:

> The Lord, through the preaching of this covenanted man, *was* uniting the thirteen colonies—on a level so deep that few people even realized at first what was happening. But wherever Whitefield went, he was preaching the same Gospel. The same Holy Spirit was quickening his message in people's hearts, and Presbyterians, Congregationalists, Episcopalians, Catholics, Quakers, Moravians—all were accepting the same Christ in the same way. In so doing . . . Whitefield was the first man to cut across denominational barriers. He rejected the solution of earlier reformers, who encouraged followers to drop previous loyalties and form a "purer" sect—and thus increase the barriers that divide. (1977: 251)

The parallels between this nondenominational faith and the later, distinctively American, civil religion that would emerge over time are striking. The *E Pluribus Unum* unity in diversity that metaphorically brings all citizens of the United States into the same cultural framework echoes the unity in Christ that Whitefield preached in the mid-1700s. As historian C. C. Goen puts it, "The 'perfection of mechanism' which made Adams's thirteen clocks strike together, in fact, owed a great deal to the pattern of religion brought to the New World by Puritans and pietists, particularly as these groups revived and proliferated through common experiences shared in the evangelical awakenings" (1985: 19).

The Second Great Awakening occurred in various locations from 1787 (at Hampden Sydney College in Virginia) to 1806. The revival spread into the frontier, erupting in Kentucky and parts west, eventually becoming known as the "Camp Meeting Revival." The final event of this revival, the mass-scale conversions that took place at Yale, Andover, Amherst, Dartmouth, and Williams College, resulted in the launching of the American missionary movement. The missionary impulse led to the opening of new frontiers worldwide, with American religious leaders spreading their peculiar blend of religion and culture across the globe.

The impact of the American missionary movement in American history was profound. The notion of Manifest Destiny that drove the pioneer settlers toward the Atlantic Ocean was deeply rooted in the concept of the United States as a divinely ordained entity, fated to control every inch of territory on the North American continent.

> Central to the concept of Manifest Destiny was the belief in American superiority. Like the Founding Fathers, nineteenth-century expansionists lauded the uniqueness of republican governments and extolled the blessings of political liberty. By carrying these institutions across the continent, American expansion would broaden the foundations of liberty, extend the area of freedom, and elevate the benighted peoples who still lived under inferior forms of government. This missionary impulse reinforced a strenuous commitment to the Protestant religion. By transporting the Protestant gospel into the unmapped regions of the West, American evangelicals would protect the virgin lands from the machinations of heathen devils and the serpentine wiles of Spanish Jesuits. Republican government and the Protestant religion thereby promised to preserve the purity of the continent. (Carroll and Noble, 1977: 67)

Moreover, the missionary impulse led to the conquest of the islands of Hawaii, Puerto Rico, and the Philippines, and ultimately to U.S. trading relationships around the world.

Despite the acquisitive and imperial nature many of these ventures took on, the initial motivation for breaking out of the isolationism so comfortable to a nation secure from foreign invaders came from the desire of missionaries (both religious and cultural) to spread "our way of life" into other cultures and other locations.

Not even the heady political theories of the Enlightenment reached so many people and transformed their outlook. For the great mass of ordinary Americans, it was evangelical Christianity that helped to define their experiment in freedom and that shaped their visions of national destiny. The revivals and the multifaceted activities they generated laid the foundation for a religiously based nationalism that transcended sectional differences, tamed the "barbarism" of the frontier, and heightened Americans' sense of fulfilling a special vocation in the purposes of the Almighty. (Goen, 1985: 24)

Before long, the Third Great Awakening took place under the preaching of Charles G. Finney, as the settlers pushed Westward, taking their faith with them. The Awakening of 1830–1842 engendered massive growth in the Baptist, Methodist, and Presbyterian denominations, although it also caused a fracturing of those denominations as the non-renewed sought to resist the efforts of the renewed to take control of the churches. At the same time, revival was occurring in what is today Canada, laying the groundwork for Canadian evangelicalism.

The revivals of this period divided denominations into North and South, Old Light and New Light, and Old School and New School that prefigured the fissures that would occur when the Civil War erupted in 1860. Indeed, Goen hypothesizes that "when Presbyterian, Methodist, and Baptist churches divided along North-South lines, they severed an important bond of national union; that the forebodings of their leaders and of contemporary observers regarding the probability of disastrous political consequences were well founded; and that the denominational schisms, as irreversible steps along the nation's tortuous course to violence, were both portent and catalyst of the imminent national tragedy" (1985: 6). Throughout the history of the United States, religious revival has been responsible for or closely associated with all manner of social and cultural change. Those who act with the expectation of revival, then, should be viewed in the light of the consequences of those expectations.

Taken together, these approaches provide an interesting way for us to look at the abortion abolition enterprise far more extensively than any single focus would allow. While none of the three fully does justice to the complexity of the issues and the individuals involved, each illuminates important pieces of the quilt of social action that is the abolitionist enterprise. Before exploring the history of the abolitionists, however, it is worth remaining briefly in the contemporary arena, to obtain an initial picture of who the modern-day activist is. Then we may return to his roots to see how he arrived where he is today.

THE MODERN-DAY ABORTION ABOLITIONIST

The following discussion introduces the reader to the contemporary abortion abolitionist, his attitudes, opinions, and beliefs. This brief sketch reports the results of a national survey conducted as part of the research for this book. An account of the data and methods involved appears in the Appendix.

This discussion provides the reader with a rough idea of what the "average" abortion abolition activist looks like in terms of demographics, attitudes, and opinions. A more sophisticated portrait will be gleaned through the more careful examination available in the chapters that follow; however, it is felt that a general knowledge of the subjects is useful as a starting point. At the outset, it should be understood that 53.8% of the respondents were male and 46.2% were female. Thus, technically speaking, the average activist is a male.

Who Is the Abortion Abolition Activist?

The average abortion abolition activist is a 34-year-old white male, with an income between $10,000 and $30,000 per year. He has a bachelor's degree and is unmarried. If a woman, she has been pregnant at least once; only 4.8% of the women have had one or more abortions.

The activist is slightly more likely to be Catholic than Protestant, non-denominational Christian, or something else, but considers himself to be accurately described as a "born-again" Christian. Moreover, he believes that "the Bible is God's word, and its teachings are literally true," rejecting the options that it was written by "men inspired by God" and "a good book" written by "wise men." He further rejects both the notion that the Bible is "worth very little today" and the option to disagree with all of the given statements. He prays several times daily, and if we are observing him on a Sunday or a Wednesday night, we stand a good chance of finding him in church, since he attends slightly more than once per week.

On the specific matter of abortion, the activist finds the procedure acceptable *only* to save the life of the mother, and 50% call it "murder." Only 8.7% of activists embrace the oft-mentioned "three exceptions" to opposition—rape, incest, and danger to the mother's life.

When we ask him questions about various social issues, we find that he approves of women working outside the home and believes that women and men are equally adept at politics. On several issues, however, tradition does, indeed, prevail. For example, although he believes that birth control *information* should be made available in public schools, he strongly believes that actual birth control *devices* (condoms) should not be available from the same source. He believes that premarital sex and homosexuality are "always wrong," and that divorce should generally be more difficult to obtain than it is now.

In terms of the information that the activist takes in, he reads a newspaper (more likely to be local than national—not surprisingly, considering the importance of grass-roots activity and community awareness to these activists) a few times a week. He doesn't watch as much television as the typical viewer, and when he listens to the radio it is most likely to a Christian station or a talk program.

Who Does He Like and Dislike?

The activist's feelings about various public figures are interesting, although there are few surprises in the list. Clustering near the top are a predictable group of political conservatives, followed by well-known abortion abolition activists. Ronald Reagan, Dan Quayle, Jack Kemp, and George Bush (in that order) rank among the abolitionist's favorite public personalities. It is interesting to note that the activist generally feels more warmth toward these politicians than toward his own purported leadership.

The next grouping contains Operation Rescue, Pat Buchanan, Clarence Thomas, and Randall Terry. Of these, only Thomas is not directly associated with the abortion issue. Thomas, in fact, claimed in his confirmation hearings to have never discussed *Roe v. Wade* and refused to stake a position on it. However, activist literature has profiled Thomas (a conservative evangelical who credits his survival of the nomination process to the strength of prayer), and he is somewhat idolized—if not idealized—in that literature. This score, then, is no great surprise. In a strange way, our activist seems more attracted to individuals whose primary focus is something other than abortion, but whose position on that issue is compatible with his. This may at first seem counterintuitive but becomes more understandable when we begin to examine the activist's feelings about activism in general. In many ways, the activist views his avocation as something of a duty; generally speaking, he would rather be doing something else.

Moving downward, the House of Representatives and the Senate appear at the next level of the activist's feeling thermometer. There seems to be little difference in the activist's mind between the House and the Senate. The activist seems to harbor a certain ambivalence about politicians and politics in general, though scoring some politicians on the feeling thermometer higher than all nonpolitical figures.

Our activist's feelings about less conservative individuals and groups (or at least those perceived so in activist literature) become apparent as we descend below 50 on the feeling thermometer. First, a grouping appears that contains the three network news anchormen—Peter Jennings,

Tom Brokaw, and Dan Rather. Activist literature indicates a strong belief that the media are part of the enemy camp and that, of the three mentioned here, Rather, in particular, is the most hostile to the cause. These results, then, support the assumptions of that literature.

As we continue to descend into the colder reaches of our activist's feeling thermometer, we find Anita Hill and Albert Gore, with the current president, Bill Clinton, finally appearing at 5.5. It is also worth noting that 90% of respondents score Clinton below 50. In fact, Clinton scores only one point higher than the American Civil Liberties Union— interesting, in light of the fact that this survey was taken before Clinton became president (and therefore before respondents had any knowledge of the scandals that would plague the administration, or of his actual performance as president) and the fact that the ACLU is seen in the activist literature as one of the chief villains in the story of abortion in America. In responding to Clinton and Gore, the subjects are, then, indicating their opinion of the men as men rather than in their roles as elected leaders.

Among the individuals and groups with modal answers of 0, we find (not surprisingly) Planned Parenthood, the National Organization for Women, and "feminist groups," sharing space with the strange pairing of Senator Ted Kennedy and erstwhile Louisiana politician and Klansman David Duke. It would seem, at least from the last two, that our subjects are not reliably ideological in their dislikes, since Kennedy and Duke are about as far apart ideologically as any two politicians could conceivably be.

Finally, there are three individuals for whom our activist seems to feel an intriguing ambivalence. It is worth looking briefly at these separately, for the diversity of their scores makes them difficult to place. This list contains Ross Perot, Pope John Paul II, and Rush Limbaugh.

The scores for Ross Perot range widely. His median score is 28.5, and 90% of respondents score him below 70. The most popular response, however, is 50, indicating that respondents have no feeling about him one way or another. Yet the second most popular response is 0, indicating a strong negative response to him as well. It should be kept in mind that during part of the survey period Perot had dropped out of the presidential race.

The next idiosyncratic scorer is the current pope, John Paul II. The modal score for the Pope is 100 (23.1%). This is not surprising, considering the Catholics' historical dominance of the abolitionist battle and the almost 40% Catholic makeup of the sample. However, it should be borne in mind that 54.8% of the respondents are Protestants and nondenominational Christians. Historically, there is a good deal of distrust between Protestants and Catholics—and particularly between nondenominational Christians and Catholics. In fact, nondenominational Christians are among the most likely to view Catholics as non-Christians. Yet 50% of all respondents score the Pope above 80, indicating that there is some denominational crossover motivated by ideological commonality. Only eight respondents scored the Pope at less than 50.

Finally, the scores for conservative commentator Rush Limbaugh deserve a second glance. Limbaugh is often portrayed in the press (particularly during the survey period) as a major player in the political game, and the Republican freshman class of the House of Representatives elected in 1994 invited him to speak at their celebratory dinner. There is no question that Limbaugh is a beloved figure in the conservative camp. On the issue of abortion, however, Limbaugh generally keeps relatively silent. He is known to be pro-life (as he puts it, "I am pro-choice and the choice is life"), but he prefers not to discuss the issue unless it becomes important in a current political sense, such as when Congress is considering an abortion-related bill.

Limbaugh's scores are interesting in that 50% are above 75. Nine respondents score him at 100, and several attempt to score him beyond the scale. However, the most frequent response (12.5%) is 50, indicating that, while he may be beloved, some activists are still unfamiliar with him. That may seem impossible, given the media exposure Limbaugh has had—with his own top-rated radio show, a television show, two best-selling books, and an enormous amount of media coverage, left and right, positive and negative. Yet, as we shall see, our activist is somewhat disconnected from the wider world in some very significant ways—and media saturation may not always be the best way to get his attention.

Where Is He on the Political Spectrum?

Politically, the activist considers himself Republican but exhibits libertarian tendencies when pressed as to what the role of government should be. In his view, "Government intervention in the economy AND the social sphere should be kept as minimal as possible." The second most popular response on this question was that "Government should use its power to REDUCE ECONOMIC INEQUALITY *AND* TO ENFORCE the SOCIAL ORDER." This response seems to be populist-leaning, perhaps somewhat explaining our activist's feelings for conservative populist Pat Buchanan. The traditional conservative response that "Government should act to PRESERVE the SOCIAL ORDER, but allow the ECONOMY to regulate itself" meets with the approval of only 21.2% of respondents. Only 7.7% chose the liberal response that "Government should PROMOTE ECONOMIC EQUALITY, but allow INDIVIDUALS to regulate their SOCIAL BEHAVIOR." Thus, in his general outlook the activist is better seen as libertarian than conservative, and his populist tendencies may well outweigh his conservatism on general issues of politics.

In his voting behavior, the abortion abolition activist reports that he voted for Gerald Ford in 1976 and Ronald Reagan in 1980. In 1984 he, like the majority of voters, cast his ballot for Reagan again and for George Bush in 1988. In 1992, however, the activist clearly and strongly departed from the majority opinion, voting for Bush again, with only 2.9% in the Clinton camp.

Turning to the 1992 elections, our activist is a relatively well-informed citizen in that 74% of respondents saw all or part of the Democratic convention and 79.8% saw all or part of the Republican convention. Here there is a clear distinction. Two-thirds of activists did not feel that the Democratic convention's speakers represented "people like me," whereas 56.7% felt that the speakers at the GOP convention did. Watching the Democratic convention, the activist responded most negatively to Bill Clinton's speech and least negatively to former president Carter's. Carter's speech was positively received by 10.6% of respondents, compared to only 4.8% reporting a positive reaction to Clinton's. The least positive responses were to the speeches of Ann Richards and Mario Cuomo. This is not difficult to understand, given Richards's strident advocacy of the pro-choice movement and the perception abortion abolitionists have of Cuomo as one who has betrayed his religion in the service of politics. (Cuomo is an outspokenly pro-choice Catholic.) The fact that Carter is known in religious circles as a born-again Christian, coupled with his long silence on the issue of abortion, may be a factor in the activist's esteem for him.

In observing the Republican convention, our activist responded most positively to Ronald Reagan's speech and least positively to Pat Robertson's. Of negative reactions, the strongest reaction was to Pat Buchanan and the weakest to Jack Kemp, who received no negative ratings.

What Does He Want?

When asked what kind of political positions his ideal presidential candidate would take, our activist had some very strong responses. Not surprisingly, 94.2% of respondents want a candidate who is strongly opposed to abortion, 89.4% prefer strong opposition to assisted suicide, and 79.8% look for strong opposition to fetal tissue research.

Our activist's economic concerns are also quite conservative-leaning. He seeks strong support for balancing the federal budget and is a strong supporter of reducing the federal deficit. On the questions concerning the spending of federal money, our activist strongly opposes funding for day care and the National Endowment for the Arts. Surprisingly, however, considering his feelings about those most closely associated with the issue (the Clintons), national health insurance finds a sympathetic audience with our activist. And despite a public image to the contrary, the abortion abolition activist would prefer a candidate who would support increased funding for AIDS prevention and treatment. Finally, it is not surprising, considering the politicians for whom he expresses warmth, that the activist would prefer a candidate who would support a strong national defense.

On less economically driven issues, our activist would like a candidate who would support stricter enforcement of antidrug laws and antipornography statutes, prayer in public schools, and environmental protection. His position on Affirmative Action is negative, though not overwhelmingly so, with 49.4% of respondents opposed, 26% supporting, and 21.2% with no opinion. (As a point of comparison, the reader may wish to keep in mind that California's Proposition 209 to eliminate Affirmative Action programs passed by a wider margin in 1996.)

Finally, it is worth noting that there is no consensus on the issue of capital punishment. Despite the public perception of abortion abolitionists as being death penalty supporters, 45.2% of respondents prefer a candidate who is moderately (25%) or strongly (20.2%) opposed, while 42.3% would choose a candidate moderately (18.3%) or strongly (24%) supportive. This is surprising when one also considers that national polling data consistently demonstrate overwhelming public support for capital punishment.

How Does He Act Out His Convictions?

Our average activist has been active in the movement between six and seven years. More than half of respondents have been involved for less than six years, but 10% have been active for ten or more years. The average activist invests approximately ten hours of his time every week in abolitionist activity; 38.5% devote between one and five hours per week, and 12.5% are involved for more than thirty hours each week. When not directly involved with abortion abolition activity, our activist is volunteering his time to a church group, miscellaneous charity, political party, or education-related charity. Only 17.3% of respondents volunteer time to a political action group of some kind.

What Has He Done, and What Is He Likely to Do?

The single most popular activity among our respondents is signing petitions. Close behind is voting for a pro-life candidate, indicating that the abortion abolitionist is highly dependable as a political resource. His dependability and willingness to do the menial tasks and take the low-echelon positions in politics have been a key part of the growth in the ranks of abortion abolitionists in the Republican party in recent years.

Our activist is likely to have interceded in prayer on the issue of abortion; this is not surprising considering the amount of time he spends in prayer and at church. He has probably participated in an economic boycott on more than one occasion. He is also highly likely to have attended an abortion abolition rally, distributed literature, and given money to an individual more than once.

Our activist is likely to have performed menial chores for a pro-life meeting or to have written a letter to the editor, or to a senator or a member of the House of Representatives. He is likely to have made telephone calls for the cause more than once (50%) or only once and would be willing to do so again.

Moving slightly downward, 39.4% of respondents have given money to an anti-abortion political candidate more than once, making the abortion abolitionist a fairly reliable political resource. Contrary to the often-heard criticism of the pro-life movement that pro-lifers don't care about women, 38.5% of respondents have personally assisted a woman undergoing a crisis pregnancy.

With regard to activities, 36.5% of respondents have given more than one abolitionist speech in a secular setting, 30.8% have picketed, and 31.7% have spoken to the media on the issue on more than one occasion. Also, 33.7% have attended more than one Concert of Prayer; this is an interesting result, since the Concert of Prayer is a relatively recent invention in which large groups of people gather in a particular locality for corporate and small-group prayer. Generally attended by Protestants rather than Catholics, such gatherings are ostensibly aimed at praying for cultural change in the areas in which they take place. It is believed that the participants' prayers will bring about significant social and cultural change, particularly a return to what are popularly called "traditional family values."

Although he is likely to have written letters to his senator or representative, our activist is somewhat less likely to have written one to the president (29.8%). In addition, 26.9% have engaged in the more prosaic activity of canvassing door-to-door for a pro-life issue.

Turning to some of the more obscure (though highly publicized) activities of the abortion abolition effort, only one-fifth of respondents have attended a Rescue. Although it will be discussed in greater detail later in the text, for now it is enough to recall that a Rescue is an event pioneered by Randall Terry and Operation Rescue, aimed at stopping the business of a particular abortion-providing site for a given period of time. Activists meet early in the morning to sing, say the rosary, and pray, then physically blockade the site to prevent anyone from entering it. During a Rescue, "prayer warriors" provide spiritual backup, praying for the protection and success of "rescuers," who go limp and refuse to move from the site, eventually being arrested and carried off. It should be something of a relief to pro-choice activists that, when asked about attending Rescues, nearly one-third replied that they never had *and would never consider* doing so. In all, 20.2% of respondents have been to more than one.

Although 20.2% have been to a Rescue, only 17.3% have actually participated in one, and all of those have been arrested; 69.2% have never participated in a Rescue, and 36.5% have never done so and would never consider it. Thus, it seems clear that the media image of the abolitionist as the protester outside the clinic is somewhat exaggerated. Even within the activist community, actual Rescue is still a somewhat marginalized activity, which a large faction of activists feel quite uncomfortable about. Only slightly more popular is the practice of "sidewalk counseling," in which a female abortion abolition activist approaches women as they enter an abortion-providing site and attempt to talk to them and offer literature, generally on fetal development. Sidewalk counselors are almost always women, and they usually work with a man who remains at the sidelines praying for the woman and protecting her if it should become necessary. Only 18.3% of respondents have engaged in this practice; 71.3% of respondents have never done so, and 25% report that they would never consider doing so. The rest chose not to answer the question.

Finally, lending some support to the accusation that pro-lifers are more concerned with preserving the children in the womb than providing for them after they are born, only 4.8% of respondents have helped someone to put a child up for adoption more than once. However, 50% of them would consider doing so, and 7.7% have done so once and would be willing to again. Yet none of the respondents has actually adopted more than one child; one has adopted one and would be willing to do so again. With regard to adoption, 78.8% report that, though they have not done so, they would be willing to consider it; 14.4%, however, would not consider it.

To What Kind of Group Does the Activist Belong?

The membership of the groups studied here varies widely, ranging from a dozen members to an estimated 350,000. However, in nearly half of all cases, the respondent either did not know or would not reveal the size of his group, so the accuracy of these numbers can fairly be questioned. The median number of members is 120, with the most common estimate being 100.

Also, 40% of respondents did not report how often the group meets. Of those who did, the most common frequency appears to be once a month (33%), with four meeting more than one time a week and one meeting less frequently than once a year. Within the group, the bare majority of respondents (52.9%) have held an office. This is not unusual with solidary groups or with groups that are either small or broken into multiple committees for specific tasks.

Where Does He Come From?

The following chapters will provide a history of the abortion abolition enterprise, exploring the phases through which the entity has gone and providing something of the background out of which the abortion abolitionist perceives himself to have come. In order to understand the activist, it is necessary to go beyond the cold descriptive statistics and explore the culture in which he lives. The next chapters are designed to do just that. Finally, the last chapter provides a suggested framework within which to understand the full complexity of the abortion abolition enterprise as an aspect of American politics and a cultural reality. It is hoped that this will allow us all to more realistically confront abortion and its discontents.

NOTES

1. Whatever the intent of the move, the bill passed easily but was vetoed by President Clinton. The House overrode the veto, but the Senate fell eight votes short of doing so.

In March of 1997, the same bill was reintroduced as HR 1122, amid admissions by Ron Fitzsimmons, head of the National Coalition of Abortion Providers, that he had been "lying through [his] teeth" in claiming that the procedure was rare and done only in cases of danger to the mother's life or severe fetal abnormality. Instead, he admitted, the majority of partial-birth abortions (also called intact dilation and evacuations, or dilation and extractions) were done from twenty to twenty-six weeks of gestation on healthy mothers with healthy fetuses. The House passed HR 1122 with a veto-proof majority of 295. As of this writing, the Senate version (Senate 6) was out of committee but not yet scheduled for a vote.

The "partial-birth abortion" ban is aimed at criminalizing a type of abortion in which the abortionist artificially dilates the woman's cervix, rotates the living fetus to the breech position, delivers the fetus feet first except for the head, punctures the back of the skull with a pair of Metzenbaum scissors, evacuates the brain with a suction device, and then removes the now-dead fetus. From start to finish, the procedure can take up to three days, due to the time needed to dilate the cervix.

2. John Adams credited the first Great Awakening with inspiring the colonial population with the spiritual fever needed to fight and win the American Revolution. In addition, Marty reports that in some circles, the Revolution was known in England as the "Presbyterian Rebellion" (1984: 138).

CHAPTER 2

In the Beginning: The Abortion Abolition Enterprise as a Catholic Moral Crusade

In 1973, Supreme Court Justice Harry Blackmun wrote an opinion that would become a fundamental flashpoint of American history. Throughout the rest of his life, he would be known as the man behind the *Roe* decision. In the same moment that the decision was handed down, a new moral crusade was instantaneously brought into being. Though at first only a sinking feeling in the hearts of abortion opponents, the reaction to the ruling would eventually become a nationwide, fully networked, sophisticated political and cultural enterprise that would outlast both Blackmun and the loyalty of "Roe" herself.[1]

In the beginning, however, there was only a vast, untapped sea of abortion opponents, wondering what to do in a nation in which the highest court could declare that "We need not resolve the difficult issue of when life begins." To those who were opposed to abortion as a matter of course, who saw reverence for the sanctity of life as an unquestioned and unquestionable bedrock value, there are few sentences more incomprehensible than that. For the judiciary of the United States to deny what once seemed a fundamental truth hardly seemed possible.

Immediately, a largely disorganized nationwide effort to repeal the decision sprang up. Kristin Luker documented the beginnings of the abolition enterprise, stating that "More of the people we interviewed joined the pro-life movement in 1973 than any other year, before or since; and almost without exception, they reported that they became mobilized to the cause on the very day the decision was handed down" (1984: 137).

As Luker noted, the abolitionist enterprise as it first materialized was overwhelmingly (80%) made up of practicing Catholics. Many of Luker's conclusions concerning the worldviews of abolitionist activists are more a function of that theological dominance than of the abolitionist effort per se. However, that dominance defined the crusade and the issue itself for the first seven years of its existence. The reasons for this are complex and are best seen as we explore the moral crusade aspects of the abortion abolition effort during this period. Since many of the most vocal abolitionists in the current climate are Protestants, it is worth asking why the abortion issue was so long identified almost exclusively with Catholic traditionalists and the Church. Moreover, we must not only explore why the Catholics were active, but attempt as well to discover why Protestants were not. This chapter will explore that theological split, with the following chapter focusing on more broad-ranging aspects of the moral crusade.

THE STATUS COMMUNITIES

As a community, the Catholic Church at the time *Roe* was handed down was uniquely prone to engage in a moral crusade, particularly on the issue of abortion. Unlike their Protestant brothers and sisters, Catholic believers in 1973 were part of an institution whose boundaries logically demanded loyalty to an abolitionist position. That institution carried with it a deeply embedded image of the role of motherhood and womanhood that did not appear on the surface to allow for a pro-choice position. In addition, the cultural position of American Catholics, both historically and at the time, made an anti-abortion position not merely a matter of faith but of practical survival as well. As the following discussion will show, the traditions, institutions, beliefs, and social needs of the Catholic Church predisposed it to abolitionist activism in ways that those of the Protestant faithful did not. The directives and culture of the Church—and those of the Protestant community— are instructive in explaining why the moral crusade against abortion evolved as it did.

Following the Faith

The community of the Catholic Church operates within very rigidly defined boundaries of acceptable behavior and attitude, even if polls indicate that its members often choose to ignore those directives. Especially during the early years of the abolition movement, the Church's uncompromising position on obedience to her directives was quite clear: Catholics are required to obey the Church and her hierarchical representatives. *The New Catechism*, coincidentally published in 1973, states plainly:

> Are you obliged to honor and obey the authorities of the Catholic church? You are obliged to honor and obey the Pope, the bishop, and your pastor. "Let everyone be subject to the higher authorities, for there exists no authority except from God." (Romans 13:1)

The hierarchical authority of the Church is a matter of certainty, not choice. The spiritual leadership of the Church, the Pope, the cardinals, the bishops, and the parish priests is established through Church teachings and tradition. Stravinskas clarifies:

> From the Greek *hierarchia* (holy rule), this word has been used since the early centuries of the Church to describe the ordered body of clergy which gives spiritual care to the faithful, governs the Church, and guides the Church's mission in the world. *The hierarchy of order* consists of the Pope, bishops, priests, and deacons. Through the sacrament of Holy Orders, their purpose is to carry out the sacramental, teaching, and pastoral ministry of the Church. *The hierarchy of jurisdiction* consists of the Pope and the bishops by the divine institution of Our Lord Himself, for the pastoral governance of the faithful. (Stravinskas, 1991: 470, emphasis in original)

Thus, the doctrines promulgated by the Church are, ecclesiastically speaking, of a sacred nature. No Catholic believer can disobey the Church without understanding the serious nature of that disobedience.

Protestant Christians, on the other hand, answer to no single human authority comparable to the Pope. There is no hierarchy of authority adhered to by all Protestant believers. Each individual denomination has its own structure, and the democratic nature of American Protestantism in general tends to discourage interdenominational unity on theological issues. While Catholics and Protestants share certain Christian beliefs, Protestants generally view the traditions of their denominations as something more akin to habits than doctrine, and the variety of Protestant expressions permits a freedom to roam that Catholics lack.

The Specific Teachings on Abortion

In the case of abortion, disobedience to the Vatican position carries the most serious spiritual consequences. Despite the reluctance of some American Catholics to conform to the teachings of their Church, the Church has never changed her position. Since 1398, procuring an abortion has been held by canon law to be an offense that automatically excommunicates the offender from the moment it takes place. Others who in some way facilitate abortion stand in perpetual danger of formal excommunication, should an interfering cleric choose to take such a drastic step.

The Catholic teaching on abortion justifies the Church's position in several different ways. The act of abortion undermines the Church's ethical and moral codes in a number of areas. First, and most obviously to the abolitionist, abortion violates the Fifth Commandment in that terminating a fetus is an act of murder. Moreover, where Protestants and other Christians seek to follow the Ten Commandments, the Catholic faith defines certain violations as a special kind of offense—a "mortal sin":

> What is a mortal sin?
>> A mortal sin is a serious violation of the law of God.
>>> To be guilty of mortal sin, the action, word, desire, thought or neglect must be seriously wrong; you must know it is seriously wrong; you must deliberately and freely choose to do it.
>
> What happens to your soul if you commit mortal sin?
>> You lose all of the grace you have ever obtained.
>
> What happens if you die in the state of mortal sin?
>> You will go to hell.
>>> "Out of my sight, you cursed ones. Off into everlasting fire prepared for the devil and his ministers" (Matthew 25:41–42). . . .
>
> What is the greatest evil in the world?
>> Mortal sin. (Scholl, 1973: 86)

In the catechismal teaching on the Fifth Commandment, the Church asks and answers:

> What does God forbid in the Fifth Commandment?
>> Murder—the unjust killing of a person.
>>> Euthanasia, abortion, suicide are sins of murder. (Scholl, 1973: 98)

Thus, abortion in the terms of Catholicism is not merely any sin; it is the mortal sin of murder, which removes all grace from the one who commits it and results (if not repented of prior to death) in an eternity in Hell.

For Protestants, there are no particular divisions of sin. While most individuals rank sin in some sense (i.e., murder is worse than, say, cheating on one's taxes), Protestants have never adopted the position that some types of sins are more eternally grievous than others. Even those Protestant denominations that do view abortion as a serious sin or a violation of the Fifth Commandment do not select it out theologically for special treatment as the Vatican does.

A secondary offense to the Catholic faith of the act of abortion is in its perceived role in undermining the family. For Catholic believers, the Church is the "family of God," consisting in the spiritual realm of God the Father, Jesus the Son and brother of believers, the Blessed Virgin Mother Mary, and a holy family of saints throughout time that intercede continually for those still on earth. For the faithful Catholic, this extended family in the spiritual realm is an ideal toward which flesh-and-blood families in the material realm should be striving at all times.

While family is an important aspect of Protestant doctrine, at the time of the *Roe* decision, the notion of "family values" was not yet fully formed, and Protestants generally did not feel driven to move beyond their own families or church communities to defend those values. However, the Vatican and a significant number of Catholic believers made the linkage between abortion and family while Protestants remained silent. To understand why there was such a divide, we must examine the functional role of Mary in the Catholic faith and her relevance to the issue of abortion.

Motherhood and Mary

The role of Mary in the Catholic faith is complex and often not well understood by non-Catholics. However, it is vital to understand her centrality in arriving at a more complete understanding of the Catholic position leading to abortion abolitionism. The following discussion is intended to illuminate the motivations that helped to bring forth the abortion abolition effort as a moral crusade.

There are four essential Marian doctrines, three of which distinguish the Catholic position from the Protestant. All help us to understand why the issue of abortion so disturbs loyal Catholics. First, in A.D. 431 the Council of Ephesus declared the doctrine of the Motherhood of God (*Theotokos*): "the Holy Virgin is the Mother of God since according to the flesh she brought forth the Word of God made flesh." This long-standing doctrine is shared by Catholics and most Protestants alike, and renders

Mary the ideal mother figure. Thus, all mothers and mothers-to-be are in some sense measured by the degree to which they emulate the Virgin Mother.

The second Marian doctrine, declared in 649 by the Lateran Council, is not generally shared by Protestants. This is the doctrine of the "Perpetual Virginity" of Mary, which declares that "she was a virgin before, through, and after the conception and birth of Christ." Moreover, "her maternity extends to encompass all those who are born again in Christ, the 'first-born among many brethren' [Romans 8:29]" (Stravinskas, 1991: 960). Thus, not only are all mothers and mothers-to-be expected to strive to match the image of Mary, but all Christians are children of that image. Therefore, a Catholic woman aborting is not only killing her own child; she is grieving the immaculate heart of Mary by causing the death of one of Mary's family. Abortion, then, compounds the sin of murder itself with an additional offense against Mary. Protestants, on the other hand, reject the notion that Mary is the mother of all Christians. Protestants, since the Reformation, have maintained that Mary, though used by God in a very special way, was as ordinary and human as any other person and deserves no greater veneration for herself (only for her acts) than any other.

The third Marian doctrine is also generally rejected by Protestants. The doctrine of Immaculate Conception (stated *ex cathedra* by Pope Pius IX in 1854) holds that "The Most Holy Virgin Mary was, in the first moment of her conception, by a unique gift of grace and privilege of Almighty God, in view of the merits of Jesus Christ, the Redeemer of mankind, preserved free from all stain of original sin" (Miravelle, 1993: xiv). Thus, there is no question of the perfection of Mary as a model for women. While one could use the excuse that such perfection is unattainable to explain why one *could not* follow her lead, her sinless nature makes it clear that the Catholic has no rational excuse for actively choosing not to try. Protestants, on the other hand, rejecting Immaculate Conception, have no model for sinless femininity, only perfect obedience.

Finally, the fourth Marian doctrine (also rejected by Protestants)—the Assumption of Mary—was declared by Pope Pius XII in 1950. As a doctrine of the Faith, it holds that "Mary, the immaculate perpetually Virgin Mother of God, after the completion of her earthly life, was assumed body and soul into the glory of Heaven" (Miravelle, citing Pope Pius XII, *Munificentissimus Deus*, 1993: xiv). In 1965, the Second Vatican Council added that "Taken up in Heaven she did not lay aside this saving office, but by her manifold intercession continues to bring us the gifts of eternal salvation." Thus, Mary, the perfect mother, is not merely an icon, not simply an image to look up to and strive for—but an active observer of and participant in the activities of Catholic believers. An offense against Mary, then, is essentially less a slur against the perfect image of motherhood than it is an insult to Mary herself, who remains accessible and sees such things—and grieves appropriately. For Protestants, however, there is no need to consider the wishes of Mary in living out one's daily life and walk with God. Mary, though a great person, is, like other ordinary humans, dead and inaccessible.

Thus, in the fourfold Marian doctrine, we find three distinctly Catholic beliefs that make abortion not merely an offense against the law, but an emotional offense against the mother figure Catholics are taught to love as intensely and with as much passion as they love their own mothers. The psychological cost of grieving Mary is difficult to measure for a traditional Catholic believer. It is clear, however, that the sacred reverence such believers hold for Mary extends to their perceptions about motherhood in general. In the absence of Marian spirituality, Protestant views on the family tend to be vastly more democratic, and each denomination is different in its teachings on biblical motherhood. Without either a dynamic spiritual figure like Mary to cling to as a living model or a definite sense that cultural motherhood had somehow gone astray, Protestants in general, even those calling themselves "conservative," remain without a unifying image of the meaning of motherhood.

In his sweeping encyclical, *Evangelium Vitae (The Gospel of Life)*, Pope John Paul II concludes with an explication of the symbology of the Book of Revelation, concentrating on Mary. The opening of this short chapter helps to demonstrate Mary's relevance to the abortion issue within the Church. According to the Pope, Mary is inextricably associated with the gospel of life due to her consent at the Annunciation[2] and the fact that her motherhood permitted Christ's entry into the mortal world. Through that opening, eternal life is made possible. Mary's obedience to God and her acceptance of and love for her unborn child were instrumental in making God's grace available to all humankind. In Mary, the Church has its clearest example of "how life should be welcomed and cared for" (John Paul II, 1995: 182).

Pro-choice activists sometimes accuse their opponents of associating them with Eve—and thereby imputing to them a transcendental guilt beyond the effects of abortion. In part, they are correct. However, it is not the sin of Eve but the rejection of the obedience of Mary in correcting Eve's rebellion that so profoundly offends the abolitionist mindset. Eve's sin had nothing to do with sex, as some infer. Rather, her sin was in rejecting and defying the will of God. In this sense, the pregnant woman who aborts is associated with Eve in that she rejects the gift of pregnancy and defies God's will by terminating it. However, more significantly, the pregnant woman in a crisis situation is being offered the opportunity to emulate the obedience of Mary. To abort is not only to reject life but to fail to emulate the obedience of Mary. To abort is not only to reject life but to fail to return God's grace.

As the papal encyclical states, Mary is the model for how life should be "welcomed and lived," and her example gives no quarter for Catholic believers to find a pro-choice position. Mary, pregnant out of wedlock through circumstances none but the faithful could possibly believe, accepted the new life within her despite her circumstances. She bore her child, watched him suffer and die unjustly, and eventually was rewarded by being taken into Heaven to continue her intercession for those who remain behind. Every woman who conceives is given the opportunity to follow her obedience and fulfill her mission as a woman: "Mary is truly the Mother of God, the *Theotakos*, in whose motherhood *the vocation to motherhood bestowed by God on every woman* is raised to its highest level. Thus Mary becomes the model of the Church, called to be the 'new Eve,' the mother of the 'living' [cf. Gen 3:20]" (John Paul II, 1995: 184, emphasis added).

According to doctrine, motherhood is not merely a matter of choice or desire, not a happy accident, not a simple blessing; instead, it is the "vocation" of "every woman." The refusal of that vocation, by deliberate rejection of the life within by means of abortion, is thus more than mere disobedience to doctrine. Indeed, it is more than just murder or an offense against the Mother of God. It is rejection of God's will for women, tantamount to a rejection of God Himself.

While Protestants do not share the Marian doctrines that so effectively clarify the abolitionist position on abortion, several Protestant churches have taken positions supporting the abortion reform movement, prior to and immediately following *Roe*. As Luker observes:

> [L]iberal clergy—who had already been active in the civil rights movement, the "war on poverty," and anti-war activities—now gave their stamp of approval to the pursuit of abortion rights as a moral enterprise. Interviews and documentary evidence show that well over a hundred clergymen (and women) of various denominations . . . were willing to be publicly identified with the abortion counseling group. Furthermore, many churches passed resolutions in support of women's right to abortion. The Episcopalians, the United Church of Christ, the United Methodist church, and the United Presbyterian church, among others, voted to take a public stand in favor of the right of the woman to have an abortion. Thus, the moral right of a woman to have an abortion was officially sanctioned in some denominations. (Luker, 1984: 123)

Thus, while Catholics had a clear directive leading them to an abolitionist position, Protestants were faced with a variety of positions on the issue, no certain biblical doctrine from which to derive a position, and conflicting and strong statements by Protestant clergy. Mainstream denominations, as with birth control, more or less accepted the cultural norm. At the same time, fundamentalists and evangelicals were in political hibernation, having withdrawn from public life into an anti-intellectual isolationism that followed the Scopes trial (Bloom, 1992: 218–233).

As Marty puts it: "Evangelical leaders protested all through the sixties against mainline and liberal denominations, the National Council of Churches, and the World Council of Churches, for 'meddling' in politics, particularly on the subjects of racial change and protest against the Vietnam War. Religion was to be a private affair, a matter of soul-saving and not world-changing" (Marty, 1984: 471–472). Moreover, this social isolation practiced by religious conservatives had so far protected them from the effects of the dominant culture, and they had no reason to assume it would be otherwise in the case of abortion. Hence, when the *Roe* decision came down, conservative Protestants had effectively abandoned public life, and liberal denominations essentially accepted the status quo, leaving only the Catholics to provide an officially abolitionist voice on the issue of abortion.

CLASS REPRODUCTION

The above discussion addressed the Vatican's theological motivations for embarking on a moral crusade to abolish abortion. However, there are other, more pragmatic, concerns to be taken into account. As Beisel noted, status politics is often observed as a function of class reproduction. The following section examines why the Catholic Church apparently saw abortion reform as a threat to its existence as a status community, while Protestants did not.

Crisis in the Faith

The national legalization of abortion as a right occurred at a sensitive moment in Catholic history. While traditionalists maintained their unwavering respect for Marian doctrine, the teachings on birth control and abortion, and other factors reinforcing the abolitionist position, other long-standing traditions were falling by the wayside. Younger Catholics were beginning to find many of the old ways an uncomfortable fit in the modern world, and the modern world was beginning to intrude into Catholicism.

Encouraged by the liberalizing reforms of Vatican II, young Catholics and those less connected to the traditions and conservatism of the Church found a variety of ways to explore the world beyond. Pope John

XXIII's endorsement of ecumenism gave young Catholics an excuse to breach the walls of the Church and form friendships with non-Catholic Christians. Where before a young Catholic girl might be unlikely to associate (and, especially, date) outside the faith, ecumenism and the new "openness to the totality of Christian and human history" made it acceptable to explore other possibilities (Bokenkotter, 1977: 366). As Marty observes:

> The Council [Vatican II] helped shatter the old image of Catholic unity. Gone was the Latin Mass, one old bond; gone also were many rules that commanded uniform participation. Now Catholics were free to eat meat on Friday; they were not necessarily expected to use the rosary as before for prayer, or to make pilgrimages or attend specified devotions. Priests and nuns often changed from religious garb to street clothes. For an American to be told that someone was a Roman Catholic did little to certify his or her membership in a group; there were fewer distinguishing badges than before. (Marty, 1984: 465)

Finke and Stark state that "[a]lthough there were many within the church who did not greet these changes with open arms, the reactions from non-Catholics were almost universally enthusiastic" (1992: 258). This ecumenism, however, was not welcomed by all.

The evidence indicates that the changes in the Church caused some simply to leave. Vatican II was immediately followed by a precipitous drop in seminary enrollments and in the number of practicing Catholic clergy and "a substantial decline in the proportion of Catholics attending mass during any given week" (Finke and Stark, 1992: 261). As Bokenkotter says, "Having been taught to think of the Mass as a mysterious unchangeable set of ceremonies originating with Christ himself, the average Catholic was not intellectually, spiritually, or emotionally prepared for" the changes in procedure encouraged by Vatican II (Bokenkotter, 1977: 368). The Church, as *Roe* came down, was in a crisis of authority, leadership, and respect. The youth were leaving, the clergy were in rebellion, and few things seemed secure in the Catholic world. The aftermath of Vatican II "amounted to a major revolution or, as some have called it, a Copernican shift in consciousness. Thanks to the Second Vatican Council, Catholics have been forced to re-examine many of their most cherished practices and traditions. Such a process was bound to be disruptive, but the sheer magnitude of the crisis it provoked astonished everyone" (Bokenkotter, 1977: 386).

In the midst of this upheaval, traditional Catholics found comfort in the solidity of their Church's positions on contraception and abortion.

Although many of the ritualistic expressions of Catholicism were relaxed in Vatican II and believers no longer felt pressured to participate in such traditions, the abortion abolition enterprise encouraged symbolic behavior. Prayer cards, novenas, Marian devotions, candle lighting, and the like were familiar and comfortable to Catholic abolitionists, and the enterprise offered an environment in which the most traditional Catholic behaviors were welcomed and nurtured. In the post–Vatican II world, the abortion abolition enterprise offered believers an arena in which they could practice their traditional devotions in a spiritually fulfilling effort with papal support against a hostile outside culture. Remaining strongly pro-life in the post–Vatican II atmosphere allowed believers at least one more of Marty's "distinguishing badges" of Catholicism.

Within the Protestant community, things were also changing but in a different way. Whereas the Catholics were having difficulty obtaining and retaining adherents, Protestants were finding their mainstream denominations losing the faithful to more theologically strict and culturally conservative ones. Whatever the cause of the loss,[3] at the time of *Roe*, mainline Protestants did not voice much of an objection, and conservative denominations, though anti-abortion, remained isolated from the wider culture.

Evangelical growth during the 1970s did not escape the attention of the wider culture, however. At first largely youth-oriented, the new wave of conservative Protestantism found expression in groups like Young Life, Campus Crusade, Navigators, and Inter-Varsity Christian Fellowship, which offered nondenominational, explicitly Christian messages to middle-class youth. At the same time, what Marty calls a "fresh flowering" blossomed in the middle class within the Pentecostal movement.

While the Catholic Church was struggling to retain its membership and standing unapologetically behind its centuries-old tradition of opposing abortion, conservative Protestants, evangelicals, and Pentecostals were reveling in new membership and, to put it in pop theological terms, "majoring on the spiritual." While these citizens did vote, they did not tend to involve themselves in other aspects of politics, as it was a worldly concern. Instead, conservative evangelicals, Pentecostals, and charismatics continued to build their parallel culture, all but ignoring the nation around them.[4]

The new Pentecostalism, at first seen only in isolated instances during the 1950s, initially attained organized public expression through the activities of the Full Gospel Businessmen's Fellowship International (FGBMFI) and David du Plessis. FGBMFI is an organization of businessmen and professionals who share a charismatic Christian outlook on life. Initially founded by Demos Shakarian (a wealthy California dairyman) and Oral Roberts, FGBMFI attracted both Pentecostals and those who were merely interested. At the same time, du Plessis began his life-long work of bringing together the ecumenical movement, the Pentecostals, and the charismatics. By the late 1970s, conservative Christians had their own forms of music, media, and the beginnings of an educational establishment. While the press briefly wondered what effect born-again Christian Jimmy Carter's faith might have on his politics and his presidency, evangelicals did not appear interested in reentering the political arena as a force for most of the decade.

Thus, while Catholicism in America was focused on retaining the membership and keeping them faithful, conservative Protestants were unconcerned with such matters. For conservative Protestants, survival was not an issue; they were too busy anticipating spiritual renewal and revival.

Abortion, Birth Control, and Sexual Morality

For the Catholic Church, a culturewide acceptance of abortion also represented a direct threat to her existence, in its potential both to destroy unborn life and to lure young Catholics into immoral behavior. The Vatican's positions on birth control and nonmarital sex make her especially vulnerable to what pro-choice activists would call a "need" for the availability of abortion.

The association of abortion with what the Church calls artificial birth control and what the pro-choice movement calls family planning adds to its offensiveness to faithful Catholics. The position of the Church, consistently held through her history, is that "deliberately and directly interfering with the marital act in order to prevent conception or birth is a gravely evil action" (Stravinskas, 1991: 139). In 1967, after a three-year period of study, the Pope rejected the recommendations of his commission on contraception and strengthened the Church's position against birth control.

Cunningham helps us to understand the teaching:

> What is interesting about this issue is its complexity. It is a moral position which cannot be deduced from either Scripture or the early teaching of the Church. The ban on artificial birth control is deduced from the Catholic reflection on love, marriage, and the finality of sexuality. On the positive side, the Church teaches that all sexual acts in marriage must be "open" to the possibility of procreation; otherwise the act of marriage is somehow defective and imperfect. When married partners have sex, according to this teaching, they must do nothing to impede the *telos* of the act. Without this "openness," the Church argues, there is no way to discriminate mar-

ried sexuality from, say, homosexuality which is, by nature, not procreative. (Cunningham, 1987: 151)

Thus, the Vatican teaches that all forms of artificial birth control are forbidden, as they usurp the privilege of God in determining when conception takes place.

Protestants, on the other hand, have been conflicted on the issue of birth control since the early beginnings of the contraceptive movement. As Margaret Sanger began her efforts to reform birth control laws, Protestants and Catholics at first stood united. However, in 1930 (after rejecting birth control in 1908, 1914, and 1920), Anglican bishops meeting in Lambeth, England, recommended that the practice be accepted "by married persons under very limited circumstances" (Donovan and Marshall, 1991: 136). This provoked an encyclical from Pope Pius XI condemning both birth control and abortion.

Ironically, by the 1930s, the fundamental Protestants who might have been the greatest allies of the Catholic Church in the fight against artificial birth control had left the political arena, to remain virtually silent until the 1980s. In 1925, John Scopes, a high-school biology teacher in Tennessee, became the focus of national attention as he stood trial for violating Tennessee law by teaching evolution. The trial pitted celebrated defense attorney Clarence Darrow against fundamentalist William Jennings Bryan in what became a microcosm of the fundamentalist battle against creeping modernity. H. L. Mencken, reporting from the trial, succeeded in portraying Bryan and the fundamentalists as little more intelligent than the apes they rejected as their ancestors. Although Scopes was convicted (the decision was later reversed on a technicality), it was a Pyrrhic victory, for the damage to the credibility of fundamentalism had been done. With the failure of Prohibition, fundamentalist politics came, more or less, to an end for the next fifty years.

As the fundamentalists faded from view, mainstream Protestant churches began to join the Sanger crusade, putting Catholics in the position of being the only group known to publicly and consistently oppose the practice of contraception. As Donovan and Marshall observe, "by 1946 the 900-member PPFA [Planned Parenthood Federation of America] Clergyman's Council had grown to 3,200" (1991: 149). By 1973, following the invention of the pill, the advent of the "sexual revolution," and decades of higher biblical criticism, Protestant Christians did not generally share the Church's aversion to birth control.

In the modern era, for Protestants—even conservative ones—the issue of birth control is not so clear-cut. While in general agreement with their Catholic brethren that the *physical* purpose of sex is procreation, most also accept the position of Grunlan and Mayers:

Although sex serves a reproductive function in all of the an-
imal kingdom, it serves a second function among humans. It
reinforces the relationship between a man and a woman (Gen.
2:24; Prov. 5:18–19; Eph. 5:22–31). Sex is a sharing of each
other, a physical intimacy between two people. Sex is God-
ordained. It is not just for reproduction but also for the expression of love between a husband and a wife. (1979: 152)

In addition, the Church finds abortion anathema in that it is often a
murder compounding another sin. Whether it is the failed use of contraception or the uncontrolled use of nonmarital sex, for the Vatican there
is no excuse to use abortion (an act of murder) to correct or to hide the
circumstances of the pregnancy (though these circumstances are also
mortal sins). The social acceptance of abortion as an escape mechanism,
according to the Vatican, increases the incidence of immoral sexual behavior. As long as one can abort an unwanted fetus, there is no real need
to exercise the self-control taught by the Bible and the Church in matters
of personal sexual morality. The Pope states: "the negative values inherent in the 'contraceptive mentality'—which is very different from responsible parenthood, lived in respect for the full truth of the conjugal
act—are such that they in fact strengthen this temptation when an
unwanted life is conceived" (John Paul II, 1995: 23).

These positions, however, effectively require that the Church minimize
the availability of abortion if at all possible. Unless the Church is con-
vincing in her case that abortion is murder, a Catholic woman may well
see it as a way of preventing anyone from finding out that she has committed the sin of premarital sex or adultery. And, even in the case of
married people, in reality, as Noonan recognized as early as 1965, many
American Catholics practice birth control regardless of the teaching. Contraception badly practiced often leads to pregnancy, and once one has
committed one serious sin, there would seem to be little left to argue
against another that has the potential to "fix" the first. In order to prevent Catholics from having abortions, the Church must either convince
her members that abortion is an especially serious sin with mortal consequences, or depend on the surrounding culture to carry the message—
ideally, both. When the surrounding culture, by accepting the *Roe* decision without apparent objection, made it clear that it would no longer
provide that assistance, the Vatican could not help but harden her position.

Remembering the Past

Another consideration that is often overlooked in examining the Catholic position on abortion is that both abortion and birth control, in their

twentieth-century incarnations, are rooted in eugenics. Margaret Sanger's advocacy of birth control was steeped in a cultural elitism that defined certain populations as requiring more control than others: "Birth Control is thus the entering wedge for the Eugenic educator . . . the unbalance between the birth rate of the 'unfit' and the 'fit' admittedly the greatest present menace to civilization. . . . The most urgent problem today is how to limit and discourage the overfertility of the mentally and physically defective" (Sanger, 1921: 5, cited in Donovan and Marshall, 1991: 9).

The Vatican, with its centuries-old adherence to a theology that values sanctity over quality-of-life issues, views such arguments as a violation of the New Testament command to love thy neighbor and resists them accordingly. Pope John Paul II protests the societal tendency to declare war against the weak: "A person who, because of illness, handicap or, more simply, just by existing, compromises the well-being or life-style of those who are more favoured tends to be looked upon as an enemy to be resisted or eliminated. In this way a kind of *conspiracy against life* is unleashed" (John Paul II, 1995: 22; emphasis in original).

We can observe this concern for "unfit" life in the comments of one survey respondent, a 70-year-old Catholic from Alabama who has been in the enterprise since its early days: "As the father of 8 children I have always had a deep concern for life and the welfare of children. For almost 35 years, I worked for a religious organization that operated a handicapped children's center. [I] have been involved with programs and services for the poor, elderly, and handicapped for some 36 years. [I] became actively involved in the pro-life movement in 1975 following the *Roe v. Wade* court decision in 1973."

Moreover, resistance of population control arguments is a form of defensive wisdom in the Church, since a population that leaves its fertility to God is likely to have more children than the population control experts would consider appropriate. Being historically a persecuted minority in the United States, it is not surprising that Catholics would consider a decision countenancing eugenic practices to be an attack on the Church and her people.

Although French Jesuits were among the earliest explorers of what would later become the United States, American culture has usually been interpreted through the Protestant tradition. Scattered periods of U.S. history have seen anti-Catholicism rise and fall, never quite fading away. As Sidney Ahlstrom notes, "colonial history is full of overt and explicit anti-Catholicism" (1972: 558). The Nativist movement built a strong political following until the Civil War interrupted it, but the impulse did not die afterward. The Ku Klux Klan was founded to, among other things, combat the Catholic "menace." Historically a numerical minority, Catholics' fertility and resistance to assimilation have traditionally been sensitive issues. In the birth control crusade of the 1930s, the opposition pulled no punches: "Are Catholic stocks in the United States, taken as a whole, genetically inferior to such non-Catholic libertarian stocks as Unitarians and Universal . . . Freethinkers? Inferior to non-Catholic stocks in general? . . . . My guess is that the answer will someday be made in the affirmative . . . and if the supposed differentials in net productivity are also genuine, the situation is anti-social, perhaps gravely so" (Himes, cited in Donovan and Marshall, 1991: 133).

For Protestants, these considerations were not applicable. Throughout American history, Protestant believers have been in the vast majority, and although one faction may lose adherents to another, Protestants in general have never felt persecuted in the many ways that Catholics have endured. By 1973, the Vatican was well used to being both alone and unpopular in her positions. Despite Vatican II's open-handed offer of ecumenism, the traditional anti-Catholic theological stance of conservative Protestants made them seem unlikely political bedfellows in 1973, and the Church found no obvious allies within mainstream Protestantism.

In essence, the availability of abortion not only offended traditional Catholic believers from a theological standpoint, but also undermined their positions on other issues and represented a direct threat to Catholicism itself. While not made explicit, population control in general seemed, to the Vatican, to be aimed at persecuted minority populations, of which Catholics were one. Moreover, Protestants, having always been in the mainstream of American culture, did not react to the eugenic assumptions that underlay *Roe* in the same way that traditional Catholics did.

SYMBOLIC GOALS AND RITUAL

One characteristic of a moral crusade is its use of symbolic goals and ritual. The history and tradition of the Catholic Church provide a particularly comfortable setting into which to set a moral crusade, in that symbolic and ritualistic behavior is reinforced on a daily basis within the institution. In ways that Protestants are only dimly aware of, Catholicism is deeply bound to centuries-old rituals, all of which have symbolic meaning and many of which have symbolic goals.

The Mass itself, to begin with the most obvious feature, is a daily re-dedication to the faith, in which believers enact ritualistic behaviors (genuflection, the crossing of one's self with holy water, the ingestion of the Host and the wine, etc.) aimed at uniting the believers to one another and all to God. The blessing of the Host and the expectation of transubstantiation[5] are ideal expressions of symbolic goals. Although the participant believes fervently in the "reality" (or what might more accurately be thought of as the "hyper-reality") of the transformations, they are not expressible in the mundane world and are not meant to have immediate visible effects.

Rosaries, novenas, specialized prayers for particular occasions, blessings, the lighting of candles for the sick and the dead, contemplative prayer and meditation—all contribute to the ritualized nature of the Catholic faith. Moreover, many of the rituals of the faith are themselves well-suited to a moral crusade, having as they do the goal of spiritual change, rather than concrete material results. Catholics, particularly traditional Catholics—and particularly those holding fast to tradition following Vatican II at the time of *Roe*—are extremely comfortable with symbolic goals. Unlike political lobbying, where results—positive or negative—are relatively direct in coming, spiritual work is expected to take a great deal of time for results to become evident.

Drawing on ancient texts, the *Catechism* reminds the faithful:

> Do not be troubled if you do not immediately receive from God what you ask him; for he desires to do something even greater for you, while you cling to him in prayer.
>
> God wills that our desire should be exercised in prayer, that we may be able to receive what he is prepared to give. (*Catechism*, 1994: 656)

Thus, for the believer, prayer itself—whether engaged in at home, at church, or at the right-to-life annual meeting—is efficacious. Whereas the reward for working for a political cause is expected to be the victory of the activist, the reward for praying for the unborn is the act of prayer itself. At some point in the future, the cause of the unborn is expected to triumph, but the important goal in symbolic action is simply to do the action faithfully.

In the case of abortion, American Catholics have not only a vast library of ritualized prayers on which to draw that can be applied to the issue, but they also have an army of saints to enlist the aid of in those prayers.[6] Moreover, because Catholics believe in retroactive salvation, a believer can devote himself or herself to praying specifically for the children being aborted. Thus, in many ways, the symbolic nature of the faith allows members to participate in the spirit of the moral crusade without any requirement of what secular observers would consider to be political activity.

Protestants, on the other hand, have not traditionally engaged in such symbolic and ritualistic behaviors. With the exceptions of Anglicans, Episcopalians, and other "high church" traditionalists, American worshippers tend to be less rigid in their worship, preferring spontaneous prayers to pre-written ones and leaning more toward order than liturgy. Although Protestants certainly prayed, it would not be until the 1980s that the "prayer warrior" movement took hold, and at the time of *Roe* Protestants were not well-versed in doing battle in the spiritual realm.

Thus, while the enterprise itself did not appear to be having much political or social effect for the first seven years of its existence, it was sustained and nurtured by the ability of the faithful core that began the backlash in 1973 to focus on higher goals than mere political efficacy. The Catholics, by gathering membership of the like-minded into small statewide groups, producing educational material, and maintaining a solid and publicly known position on the issue, effectively prevented *Roe* from fading quietly into the tapestry of American law.

Despite the appearance of judicial and political failure, and in stubborn opposition to the hostile culture against which they squared off, the Catholic faithful of the abolition effort during the 1970s were able to persevere, due to the symbolic nature of their goals. The moral crusaders have not disappeared from the rank and file, but their centrality in the issue has been overshadowed by the political action of non-Catholics. However, their influence and their emphasis remain vital to the enterprise. One of our survey respondents, a 55-year-old female Catholic with sixteen years' tenure in the enterprise, describes her mission as "To stop abortion by helping change the hearts and minds of the public through education on the realities of this life issue and through the courts and legislation."

Although the "hearts and minds" focus would fade for a time during the 1980s, it would return in a new form. In the meantime, although they had the bulk of the press, the Catholics were not the only people concerned about abortion during the 1970s. Although, as we have seen, some aspects of the Catholic Church particularly suit it to birthing and nurturing a moral crusade, not all aspects of the crusade are necessarily part and parcel of Catholicism. Many features of a moral crusade—particularly this one—are applicable to many faiths or no faith, and it is the persistence of those factors over time that has helped bring the enterprise to its present state. The next chapter will explore less theologically exclusive aspects of the moral crusade and examine its development during the 1970s.

NOTES

1. In July of 1995, in Dallas, Texas, Norma McCorvey (the original "Jane Roe") became a born-again Christian after becoming friends with Operation Rescue's national director, Flip Benham. Benham had moved OR's headquarters into the building housing the abortion clinic in which McCorvey was working. In July, a 7-year-old invited her to church, and in August she was baptized by Benham. Reportedly, her "shock and horror" at seeing a second-trimester abortion caused her to rethink her position on abortion as well. Immediately following the an-

nouncement of her change of heart, she withdrew from the public eye, citing a need for "time to come to terms with her support of first-trimester abortions and with her relationship with her lesbian lover" (*Charisma*, 1995: 18). In addition, the original plaintiff of *Doe v. Bolton*, *Roe*'s companion case, has similarly rejected the pro-choice movement and has produced her anti-abortion testimony for Christian journalists.

2. This refers to the moment in which an angel appeared to Mary and told her what was to come, to which her reply was "Behold the handmaid of the Lord; be it unto me according to thy word" (Luke 2:38).

3. Explanations for the shift have been wide-ranging within the literature. Kelley asserts that mainline religions fail to offer credible religious experience in that they are so accommodated to the culture around them that congregants feel driven to seek membership in churches that more distinguish themselves from "the world." Others, however, take issue with Kelley's explanations, claiming that mainline churches gain adherents during periods of cultural stability and lose them during periods of instability. However, most agree that substantial losses of mainstream congregants seem to coincide during this period with concomitant gains in conservative denominations.

4. The distinctions between these groups are not always clearly made, particularly within the academic world. However, the theological distinctions can be vital, and historically the groups have not always seen eye-to-eye, either theologically or on social matters.

"Evangelical" is a term used to designate that stream of Christian thought that focuses on the "born-again" experience referred to in John 3:3–15 (Jesus' dialogue with Nicodemus) as the fundamental basis for Christian conversion. Although there is no necessary theological connection, "evangelical" has often been used in the media to designate politically conservative Christians.

"Pentecostal" designates those denominations that arose out of the American revival that began on January 1, 1901 in Topeka, Kansas. That event, and the ensuing multiracial three-year revival on Azusa Street presided over by black Holiness preacher William J. Seymour in Los Angeles, marks the restoration of the first-century gift of tongues (technically, "glossolalia") to the modern church. Unlike other streams of conservative Protestantism, Pentecostals believe that the "gifts of the Spirit" function in the modern world. Arising culturally from the transplanted Celtic peoples of West Virginia and Kentucky and Southern black slave society, Pentecostal services are far more focused on celebration and worship than are other theologically conservative Protestant forms. Among those "classic Pentecostal" churches are: Pentecostal Holiness, Church of God (Cleveland, Tennessee), and Church of God in Christ, which were Holiness denominations prior to the revival; and the Assemblies of God, Pentecostal Church of God, International Church of the Foursquare Gospel, and Open Bible Standard churches.

"Charismatic" refers to individual believers who have experienced the "gifts of the Spirit," including (but not limited to) glossolalia, but not necessarily within a Pentecostal denomination. This phenomenon began occurring during the late 1950s, and "by the early 1960s people in virtually every major Protestant tradition were receiving BHS [Baptism in the Holy Spirit] (Baptists, Lutherans, Mennonites, Methodists, and Presbyterians)" (Burgess et al., 1988: 132–133).

Finally, the oft-slung "fundamentalist" theologically refers to one who accepts the five "fundamentals" of the faith: (1) the verbal inerrancy of the Scriptures; (2) the deity and virgin birth of Christ; (3) the substitutionary atonement of Christ; (4) the physical resurrection; and (5) Christ's bodily return to earth. However, fundamentalists, being mostly dispensationalists, part company with Pentecostals and charismatics on the issue of miracles, believing that they ceased with the death of the last apostle.

5. The mystical conversion of bread and wine into Christ's body and blood, by which Christ becomes present in the sacrament of the Eucharist; in the Catholic faith, this transformation is believed to be an actual transformation of the substance of the elements:

In the most blessed sacrament of the Eucharist, the body and blood, together with the soul and divinity, of our Lord Jesus Christ and, therefore, *the whole Christ is truly, really, and substantially* contained. This presence is called "real"—by which is not intended to exclude the other types of presence as if they could not be "real," too, but because it is presence in the fullest sense: that is to say, it is a *substantial* presence by which Christ, God and man, makes himself wholly and entirely present. (*Catechism*, 1994: 346, emphasis in original)

6. A Catholic could reasonably choose a number of patron saints to pray to concerning the issue of abortion, among them Nicholas and Aloysius (the patron saints of boys); Elizabeth of Hungary and Vincent de Paul (charitable societies); Jude and Rita of Cascia (desperate cases); Luke, Cosmas, and Damian (doctors); Agnes, Catherine, and Ursula (girls); Camillus and John of God (hospitals); the Blessed Virgin Mary, Giles, and Monica (mothers); and, perhaps most obviously, Margaret of Antioch (patron saint of pregnant women).

CHAPTER 3

One Body: Building Ecumenism in the Moral Crusade

The previous chapter explored the moral crusade against abortion as a particularly Catholic pursuit. This chapter will demonstrate that the abolitionist message itself had the potential for broad appeal. The psychology and theology of the moral crusade attracts various strands of participants, and the continuing efforts of that initial core of activists kept the issue in play in the public arena. As we shall see, the persuasive polarizing rhetoric used in the crusade, the defensive nature of the enterprise, the goal of moral reform, and the absolutist nature of the underlying assumptions all drew new adherents over time, in the process building toward the social movement into which the enterprise would blossom in the 1980s.

RHETORIC AND THE CHARACTER OF THE OPPOSITION

A moral crusade relies on and carries with it certain assumptions about the nature of the opposition. In the case of abortion abolition, these assumptions are made explicit in the literature circulating within the enterprise. The following discussion is not exhaustive but is meant to give the reader a sense of the kind of picture abolitionists have of aborting women, doctors who perform abortions, and the surrounding culture that remains silent on what abolitionists consider an issue of conscience.

The Woman

Despite the gruesome and accusatory nature of many abolitionist pictures and pamphlets, the aborting woman is nearly always portrayed as an ignorant victim of the wiles of the abortionist and the eugenicist aims of the abortion industry. It is assumed that the woman seeking an abortion is *unaware* that her voluntary submission to an abortion will take the innocent life of an unborn human child. Much is made in the literature of the notion that abortionists and clinics never use the term "baby" to speak of the unborn, preferring instead terms like "fetus," "mass of tissue," or even more abstract and seemingly deceptive language.

Ellen, an activist who heads a crisis pregnancy center, recounts a phone call she made to an abortion clinic. After the receptionist established that the caller's friend's menstrual period was "a few weeks" late and informed her of the fee for the abortion, the activist initiated the following exchange:

> *Ellen*: . . . I need some information first. What about the risks?
>
> *Clinic*: Risks? There are no risks. It's no big deal. It's less risky than going to the dentist. In fact, some people come in for three or four abortions a year. It's just an expensive means of birth control.
>
> *Ellen*: What's the procedure? What happens?
>
> *Clinic*: It's just a menstrual extraction of two periods—a little cramping, and she can go to work afterward.
>
> *Ellen*: What about the baby inside?
>
> *Clinic*: Baby inside? There's no baby inside. Tissue doesn't start forming until the twelfth week. It's just liquid until twelve weeks. Abortion just means stopping a pregnancy. Honey, it's been legal for fifteen years. If there was a baby inside it wouldn't be legal. (Curro, 1990: 50–51)

The literature of abortion abolition is saturated with similar reports. The implication is clear: women abort in ignorance, and the people charged with protecting them are simply lying about the facts to obtain them as clients for abortion. The information on fetal development given in the preceding conversation is demonstrably false, as is evident from sources ranging from biology textbooks to the perennial best-seller *What to Expect When You're Expecting.* The fetus is not "liquid" until twelve weeks. By that stage of development, the fetus has recognizable human features, limbs, independent brain waves, and a detectable heartbeat. The abolitionist maintains that abortionists deliberately keep such information from the pregnant woman, believing that she would not have an abortion if she knew it.

The idea that a woman could or would knowingly cause the death of her own living child is anathema to the abolitionist mindset. It is simply impossible for them to believe that one human being could deliberately take the innocent life of another with a clear conscience—particularly when the victim is the offspring of the murderer. Thus, activists interpret the epithets thrown on the picket lines not as insults but as warnings. For them, the aborting woman is the prey of the avaricious abortionist, and to allow her to enter the clinic or hospital without a chance to discover the real nature of abortion is to act in complicity with the abortionist himself. Both the unborn child and the woman who carries it are members of the human family—members who deserve whatever protection the activist is able to extend.

There is an interesting paradox in the abolitionist view of the woman, which stems from the abolitionist tendency toward political conservatism. In pro-choice writings, the woman impregnated does not significantly change—only her circumstances do. However, for the abolitionist, the woman herself is cast in a different light once conception takes place. For example, conservative rhetoric commonly refers to sexually active unmarried women as "promiscuous," endangering their lives and their futures with their foolish behavior. In this discourse, they are cast as independent actors making bad choices, who are to be held responsible for their behaviors—and, if need be, punished to elicit better ones. Married women in poverty having children on welfare are also portrayed as irresponsible, and the discussion tends to focus on them as being expensive for taxpayers to maintain. Public shame is encouraged to persuade unmarried women or those who are not ready for the financial burden of initial or additional children to be sexually abstinent.

The abolitionist reverence for the sanctity of life—undisturbed by such discussions when focused on public monies and sexual morality—cannot permit the potentially aborting woman to be seen in the same light. Once the specter of abortion has appeared, the woman—whatever the circumstances in which she conceived—is cast in the role of victim. Yet even in the cases of rape and incest, her victimization is not connected to the unborn child—only to the society that shames it, the abortionist who seeks to terminate it, and the father who sired it. The mother-to-be is associatively invested with the innocence the abolitionist holds primarily for the child. Neither mother nor child is "blamed" for the circumstances they find themselves in, and both are to be protected from abortion, whatever the cost in time, money, or convenience.

The concerns expressed by abolitionists for the life and health of the woman are focused on such matters as physical complications, psychological sequelae, long-term clinical depression, and crippling remorse. The woman is portrayed not only as a victim of the single act of abortion, but as one who is unwittingly surrendering herself to a veritable lifetime of misery. This image would be reinforced during the 1980s, when groups sprang up for women who regretted having had abortions, spawning the term "post-abortion syndrome." The most notable of these groups would be Women Exploited by Abortion and Victims of Choice, but before they were founded the abortion abolition enterprise was spreading the word about the dangers of abortion to the women themselves.

As early as 1971, Father Paul Marx reported from a UCLA abortion symposium that, while pro-abortionists insisted that there were no damaging psychological effects from abortion, some psychologists and psychiatrists said otherwise. Marx reports that Freudian psychiatrist-obstetrician Julius Fogel, who had performed hundreds of abortions, still found that the act of seeking one was likely to have severe emotional and psychological effects on the woman. Fogel referred to the abortion as a "trauma," saying that "A level of humanness is touched. This is a part of her own life. She destroys a pregnancy, she is destroying herself. There is no way it can be innocuous" (Marx, 1971: 28). Moreover, Fogel said that it didn't matter whether or not one believed that the fetus constituted "life" because "You cannot deny that something is being created and that this creation is physically happening" (p. 28). The effect, according to Fogel, may not be immediately apparent but could be something as immeasurable as "a pushing away from human warmth, perhaps a hardening of the maternal instinct." Whatever the effect, Fogel insisted, "Something happens on the deeper levels of a woman's consciousness when she destroys a pregnancy" (p. 29).

Feminists for Life (FFL), founded by two women asked to leave the National Organization for Women for their refusal to advocate abortion, saw the woman as a victim not only of the abortionist, but also of the patriarchal system that undervalues women and seeks to find a way to relieve men of responsibility for their own actions. One of the earliest writings of FFL, assumed to be circa 1973, states:

> The strange compulsion for abortion is in reality the ultimate exploitation of women by immature men: technocrats, generally imbued with a myopic sense of social awareness and unable to interpret or control their own sexuality.
>
> The playboys of the Western world and the authoritarian

"adolescents" of the Socialist world sacrifice their women in order to preserve their dream of libidinal freedom. It is the woman who must go to surgery over and over again to insure this dream. The whimpering male refused to take responsibility for his sexual behavior.

It is no surprise that Playboy Foundation money is now competing with Rockefeller Foundation money to promote the concept of permissive abortion. The rich man's solution has become the puerile male's solution and the last vestige of responsibility and commitment has disappeared.

It is the woman who has been deliberately misled by the male-dominated medical profession into thinking that abortion is merely contraception slightly postponed. The serious physical and psychological consequences of this self-serving deception are muted, despite a wealth of medical literature from the United States and foreign countries. (Heffernan, undated pamphlet)

It cannot be denied, however, that, while activists believe themselves to focus on the woman *and* the child, they refuse to relinquish the rhetorical field by considering the woman *without* the child. For abolitionists, a woman who is pregnant has become a new sort of tandem being, one that can no longer be regarded as alone or autonomous. Whereas pro-choice literature often treats the fetus almost as an invader in the woman's body, abolitionist literature invariably treats the fetus as an extension of that body—one that has become so intertwined with the woman as to be unremovable.

While pro-choice activists find this image of woman-as-incubator distasteful, abolitionists find it attractive and reverential. The abolitionist reverence for the sanctity of life imbues the woman with an ethereal, almost supernatural quality. To carry life within is a special privilege, making the rejection of that privilege all the more distasteful and bewildering to the abolitionist. It is significant that Jane Martin's recent play *Keely and Du* focuses on the relationship between an abolitionist and a young woman seeking abortion whom she kidnaps. The character of Du, like the abolitionist movement, is certain of the humanity of her charge, convinced that if she only knew the truth about the life within her, she would refuse to abort and join Du in welcoming unborn life.

When thinking about the image of the woman in abolitionist writings, it is perhaps as important to examine what is absent as it is to note what is there. In discussing the woman seeking an abortion, there is rarely, if ever, any mention made of her political rights or social position. Whereas pro-choice literature focuses on the right of the woman to self-determination and the dangers of past illegal abortion, abolitionist literature is generally silent on both of these matters. As Condit has observed, while the rhetorical strategies of the abolition enterprise in this era focused on constructing the humanity of the fetus, pro-choice strategies were more concerned with establishing the primacy of autonomy (1990: 79–95). In Condit's analysis of images, she concludes that abolitionist documents, being more direct and requiring less interpretation, were more successful in their goal of persuasion than the symbols associated with the pro-choice side of the argument (p. 94).

While the legal arguments of the pro-choice movement proved to be critical during the early phases of the abolition enterprise, the images of the abolitionist effort—perhaps because they directly confronted abortion per se—remained in the public psyche and provided strong support for activists seeking new converts. Moreover, the images developed in the 1970s and disseminated in untitled and undated brochures on street corners and in church basements would find their way into major book-length writings of the enterprise during the 1980s and provide a persuasive backdrop for the least malleable aspects of abolitionist rhetoric. To some degree, abolitionist rhetoric and imagery has succeeded at all phases of the enterprise without any alteration in the image of the aborting woman.

Thus, the abolitionist image of the woman seeking an abortion is largely sympathetic, if patronizing. The mother-to-be is seen as vulnerable to the wiles of the abortionist and the pressures of her partner, her family, her society—all of whom conspire to hide the truth about abortion from her. She is the "second" victim, but her social and political interests are clearly seen as secondary to the vital need to preserve the life of the fetus. The woman should, in the abolitionist view, be the most abolitionist of all individuals and will be once she is confronted with "the truth." Once the societal brainwashing can be overcome, once the woman can be educated, once the details of human development prior to birth can be known and accepted, abolitionists have no doubt that any open-minded pregnant woman will choose not to abort. Thus, their mission for the woman is to provide education, support, and a way to bring the baby to term—as their Yellow Pages listing states, an "Abortion Alternative."

The Abortionist

Although the abortionist is also portrayed as a target for pity and prayer, the grace extended to the aborting woman and the fetus is not as readily applied to the abortionist. Because abortion is defined in abolitionist literature as a greed-driven business, the abortionist is viewed as something akin to a hired killer. Yet the difference between the abortionist and the Mafia hit man is perceived to be one of honesty. The abortionist is portrayed as manipulative and deceptive; the woman (and her family), desperate and unable to perceive the dangers to herself and her child, is the "second victim" of the abortionist.

While few abolitionists would go so far as to claim that such doctors are not "human," they view them in much the same way as the majority of Americans view criminals. Essentially, they are human beings who have misused their liberty to the point that it should be taken from them, if necessary. Stopping their activities is not a violation of their rights but an essential measure to prevent them from committing further crimes. Randy Alcorn, articulating in 1990 the underlying message of countless abolitionist pamphlets and handouts, explains:

> Does the "physician" (baby-killer) really have a right to "earn a living" by killing the innocent? The judge says abortion is a sin, but he still believes that the doctor has the "right" to do that sin simply because it is legal. If it is the Creator who grants rights, however, then the doctor has no right whatsoever to earn a living killing babies. (In any case, the rescuers' goal is not to punish the man for choosing a sinful enterprise, but to save the innocent baby from death.) (Alcorn, 1990: 203–204)

The abortionist has never been portrayed with any of the compassion, good intentions, or human qualities one finds in pro-choice depictions of the doctors who perform the procedure. Father Marx, reporting from the symposium, details the many wiles of the abortionist. First, this speaker demonstrates that the abortionist is dishonest about what "family planning" really means:

> [N]o matter how thin you slice it, ladies and gentlemen, family planning is a euphemism. We don't intend or desire to prevent conception for conception's sake; we want to prevent conception because of what follows conception. Family planning is the prevention of births, and as birth is the end of a sequence which begins with the sexual urge, then family planning is anti-conception, anti-nidation, and the termination of the conceptus if implanted. This is the social role of abortion in the future. (Marx, quoting professor Irvin Cushner, Johns Hopkins School of Medicine, 1971: 122)

Another speaker at the symposium suggests a creative way of obtaining consent for abortion from women entering the clinics: "Why don't we bring on menstrual periods in women who are several days late? . . . Why don't we select women in their reproductive years who had intercourse two weeks ago, who didn't use contraception, or who have a high potential degree of failure in the method they used, let them become five days late—not do a pregnancy test—and ask them if they want a menstrual period?" (Marx, 1971: 124). The same speaker makes it clear that his deceptiveness is not a figment of Father Marx's imagination, as he suggests that women who can't supply the needs of the child should be aborted in the earliest stages of pregnancy, "without even mentioning abortion" (Marx, 1971: 127).

Overall, Father Marx's report from the symposium has served as a valuable tool for the abolition enterprise in its drive to portray abortionists as cold, venal, and unconcerned with either the woman or her unborn child. Moreover, much of its value lies in the fact that the most damning statements (in the view of the abolitionist) concerning abortionists come from the mouths of the abortionists themselves.

In the beginning, former abortionists were rarely available as friendly witnesses (though that has certainly changed in recent years). One vital exception to this rule came in the form of Dr. Bernard Nathanson, whose persuasive value was twofold: he was a repentant abortionist, so he had the "inside story," and he was an atheist, and therefore could not be merely dismissed as a robot of the faith.

Nathanson, moreover, had a sort of I-told-you-so cachet for the abortion abolitionists, as he had been a co-founder of the National Abortion Rights Action League. NARAL (originally the National Association for Repeal of Abortion Laws) was one of the abolitionists' most ardent opponents. Pro-choice physician Don Sloan remembers Dr. Nathanson as a fellow activist:

> Before *Roe* and *Doe*, before the change in the New York State statutes, even before I got involved in abortion politics, Bernie Nathanson was in there fighting for reform. Like a lot of doctors of his generation and mine, he had dealt with the results of back-alley butchery and had both seen and felt the wrenching guilt and emotional upheaval that followed illegal abortions in the fifties and sixties. He wasn't someone who could sit passively by and watch things happen. Not Bernie. He was in at the beginning. (Sloan and Hartz, 1992: 183)

Yet, by 1975, Nathanson had resigned his position. By 1976, he had determined never to perform another abortion. By the end of the 1970s, the doctor was, as Sloan calls him, "a medical jewel in the crown of the antichoice movement" (Sloan and Hartz, 1992: 190). He produced two key tools of the abolitionist movement, the films *Silent Scream* and *Eclipse of Reason*, which are ultrasound films of abortion. Sloan asks his old friend what changed his position: "The change had come after his days

at the Women's Center, when he came into contact with new technologies that, he said, brought him new awareness. 'I saw and realized—the
techniques that showed me the fetus . . . it was a whole other world.' He
became convinced that he was on the wrong track about when life began.
With the aid of high-resolution sonograms and sophisticated fetal-
monitoring equipment, he heard 'the silent scream' " (Sloan and Hartz,
1992: 190–191).

The abolitionist conversion of Dr. Nathanson was a defining moment
for the enterprise, for now there was a real medical authority echoing
what the faithful had been saying all along. No longer need there be any
doubt about the humanity of the bloody corpses in the brochures. Using
the best medical technologies, an author of the abortion reform movement himself had declared that there was life before birth. If Nathanson
could be converted, anyone could. Moreover, Nathanson's depiction of
himself was of a man ignorant of the truth he held in his own hands on
a daily basis, fulfilling part of the abolitionist picture of the abortionist.

The Culture

There is no question in the literature that society itself must bear a
large part of the responsibility for the high incidence of abortion. From
the earliest days of the enterprise, it was recognized that this struggle
was one for America's soul and babies' lives. Abolitionist literature uses
militaristic metaphors to paint a picture of a culture that is hedonistic
and destructive, pursuing abortion out of convenience and ignorance.
Moreover, the rhetoric of the abolitionists presents pro-choice forces with
difficult accusations that cannot easily be dismissed, for they are based
on unsettling and undeniable historical situations in which the majority
was, simply, wrong.

The metaphor of war is at the core of the abolitionist view of abortion.
To activists, the United States has declared a heartless war against her
own children, who are defenseless to stop the invasion. Indeed, the very
act of abortion is portrayed at times as an "invasion" of the fetal
"home."[1] The children killed by abortion are civilians; to kill them is not
only an act of war but one that violates every notion of humane treatment of indigenous people.

But there is more. The metaphor is not only of generalized war, but
evokes the imagery of one particular war of our own recent history. The
35 million children aborted since 1973 have been the "victims" of a "holocaust." The metaphor of the holocaust is compelling, evoking the pa-
thos of defenseless people declared nonexistent, tortured, experimented
on, starved, and killed—while an uncaring world looked away. Activists
see themselves as defenders of the undefended, champions of a persecuted people whose only crime is inconvenient existence.

The linguistic comparisons in service of this metaphor are scattered throughout abolitionist literature. Clinics are "death chambers," "mills," and "killing centers." Doctors are "murderers" and "butchers"—echoing the many Nazi death camp doctors known only as the "butcher of (fill in the camp or town)." Pro-choice activists who transport women into clinics (and who, tellingly, refer to themselves as clinic "defenders," acceding to the metaphor of war) are known within the Rescue camp as "Deathscorts," evoking images of the German death camp guards whose insignia struck terror in the hearts of Jews during World War II. Even today, although the camps are closed and the guards mostly long dead, the very phrase "death camp" sends a shiver through the body politic.

The literature of the enterprise is saturated with the horrors of this metaphor. Like the tortuous and detailed tales of Auschwitz and Dachau that littered the educational experience of the mid-boomer generation, abolitionist documents describe in horrific detail the procedures used in abortion. If pro-choice activists object, abolitionists simply nod their heads knowingly; the Nazis, too, did not believe the blood on their hands deserved a second glance. In relation to the war metaphor, the literature generated within the enterprise functions as wartime propaganda. As an example, let us briefly examine one of the prime tools of abolitionist evangelism—the film *Eclipse of Reason*.

Eclipse of Reason is the follow-up to *Silent Scream*, Bernard Nathanson's cinematic magnum opus of the abolitionist enterprise. *Silent Scream* depicted the fetus in the womb, through an ultrasound film, during an abortion. It suffered from the drawbacks of the technology available at the time of its filming, and because of that was the target of much ridicule from pro-choice critics. Particularly offensive to many was the title; at one point in the film, Nathanson indicates a point on the ultrasound which he claims is the fetal mouth and directs the viewers' attention to the fact that it is open in a "silent scream." The film was attacked as a fraud; accusations were made that the ultrasound photography was edited in such a way as to distort fetal movement to make it appear more frantic than it really was. In addition, many viewers failed to perceive the "mouth," the "scream," or even the outlines of the fetus itself, due to the fuzziness of the ultrasound technique (Condit, 1990: 86–87).

Eclipse of Reason suffers from none of these drawbacks. It bests its predecessor with the use of real-time ultrasonography and an unblinking external view of abortion; the photography, within the womb and without, is sharper and clearer than in the previous film. The fetus and its movements are unmistakably visible.

To watch this film is in itself a near-traumatic experience. After describing and displaying the instruments that will be in use in the filmed abortion, Dr. Nathanson explains the process of abortion in clinical terms. Nathanson describes the instruments as "cold" and "sharp." With the ultrasound, the audience is shown the beating heart and moving limbs of the unborn child. As the instruments are introduced, the movements take on a desperate character. From outside the womb, we watch as tiny bloody limbs are pulled from the fetal body and deposited on a white-sheeted table. There is blood. There is tissue. There are unmistakable hands and feet. Although the film is not long, it is by no means easy to sit through. While it is tempting to find fault with the film, the direct visual evidence is difficult to answer.

Abolitionists often refer to such visual evidence, expressing utter bafflement that others cannot see what they see. For them, the humanity of the unborn is obvious, and the only explanation for permitting abortion is ignorance of its particulars. Psychologically, the "argument of invisibility" evokes disturbing reminders of Pastor Martin Niemoller's famous quotation about the consequences of ignoring the oppression of those whose characteristics one does not share:

> They came for the communists, but I wasn't a communist—so I didn't object;
>
> They came for the socialists, but I wasn't a socialist—so I didn't object;
>
> They came for the trade union leaders, but I wasn't a trade union leader—so I didn't object;
>
> They came for the Jews, but I wasn't a Jew—so I didn't object;
>
> Then they came for me—and there was no one left to object.

If we do not protest when the communists or the socialists or the unionists or the Jews—or the unborn—are taken because we are not yet in the sights of the unnamed "they," who then will be left to protest when they come for us? For the abolitionist, the connection between the "us" and the victim in abortion is yet more urgent: if we do not protest when the lives of the unborn are taken by abortion (because we have been born), who will be there to protest for us when we are old and vulnerable? The logic of the position leads to the conclusion that, by standing silent, those already born not only demonstrate their inhumanity but also risk losing their own lives when the logic of "choice" makes *them* inconvenient and disposable.

The accusation against the German people will forever be "How could you not know?" The defense can only be that the machinations of the National Socialist hierarchy were invisible to the vast majority of German citizens. During the war, some groups attempted to make known the horrors of the camps. To the everlasting shame of the people of the world, the evidence was largely ignored. Despite attempts by the Allied powers to "demonize" the Axis forces, pictures of the camps were not used for such a purpose. Rumors were quieted by permitting the Red Cross to tour a "show camp" at which all seemed well. And, yet, after the war, when the camps were finally opened, the defense of ignorance seemed wholly inadequate to explain what had happened. Even today, fifty years hence, the stark photographic evidence of what happened behind the walls of the Nazi death camps evokes not only disgust in those who view them, but a profound sense of shared guilt. How could they have done this? And could I have done the same?

Abolitionists argue that the unborn are being "exterminated" at the rate of four thousand every day. To them, the only way to lessen or eliminate this "mass murder of the innocent" is to show the world the pictures. For the abortion procedure, whether or not it makes us uncomfortable to admit it, is indeed a bloody business. In talking to abortion abolition activists, one is struck by the pervasive, almost overwhelming belief that the vast majority of Americans are ignorant of the details of abortion, and that if they can be made to see those details, they will understand the damage activists believe is being done by the perpetuation of legal abortion.

It should be noted that the argument against the culture during the moral crusade phase of the enterprise was, despite the horrors of the visual aids, somewhat hopeful. Underlying its harshness was the assumption that individual Americans could eventually, by examining their consciences and reasoning out the issue, understand the wrongness of abortion. There was a redemptive optimism in the abolitionist attitude, one that viewed moral decline as a temporary, albeit agonizing, phase that would pass in time. This vision would not last long into the eighties, when the darker vision of the Protestant activists began to dominate the discourse.

For those disturbed by what came to be known as "abortion-on-demand," the cultural accusation enhances the ambiguity of the pro-choice position. If one is not *certain* that there is no baby, no murder, no guilt, then the example of the Jews evokes unsettling reminders of what has been done in seeming ignorance. Whether or not this argument is effective in its initial appearance, its unsettling echoes last long after the abortion debaters have left the stage. During the next two decades, the abolition enterprise would develop several such historical parallels that trade on the opposition's inability to deny that there are truths that must transcend historical and political situations. However, in building the abolitionist case, the psychological guilt aroused by the holocaust argument has remained an effective aspect of activist rhetoric.

RE-ESTABLISHING PRIOR SOCIAL SUPPORT

Moral crusaders maintain that their aim is to reestablish prior conditions, which they claim formerly enjoyed universal social support. In the case of abortion, the archivists of the enterprise, rejecting the mainstream and academic treatments of the history of abortion, retold the "heritage tale" of abortion abolition. As Condit observes, the abolitionist history depicted the authentic American heritage as one that viewed abortion as a regressive development rather than a progressive one. In this way, the abolitionists sought to usurp the preservationist ground the pro-choice heritage tale had begun to occupy in the immediate post-*Roe* period.

Condit examines the heritage tale:

> [T]he narration, by many advocates, of a selective and coherent account portraying a specific strand of white, Western, Christian history as the authoritative and legitimate American heritage. The pro-Life advocates described how, throughout the Western tradition, abortion had been written and spoken against by important institutional and moral authorities. Although disagreements had occurred in the past, they indicated that there had been a clear path of "moral improvement" through history—prohibitions against abortion had become more and more restrictive through time, as humankind became increasingly aware of the fact that abortion represented the killing of a human being. (1990: 44)

Condit notes that Noonan, the chief historian of this tale, described

> not only a "Western" history but also predominantly a Catholic heritage. Quite simply and visibly the authorities and witnesses he cited favorably were overwhelmingly Catholic (not to mention white, male, and often celibate). Others were dismissed as naive, evil, or at least cautious for an "early" period. At best, this tradition could be stretched to being a "Christian" one, but that Christianity clearly leaned on a narrow set of doctrines and was fundamentally influenced by a vision of Catholicism as the historical center-post of Western Christianity. (1990: 48)

Interestingly, when the Protestant activists began to enter the abolition enterprise in significant numbers, Protestant archivists did not apparently find any need to alter this heritage tale. The "Catholic" slant that Condit finds so important is accepted by Protestant abolitionist historians, such as Marvin Olasky and George Grant, without controversy. It

appears that the cultural minority status of Catholics is of no consequence to their Protestant brethren in the enterprise.

In the later years of the enterprise, the heritage tale was again retold,
this time by Protestants, though without notable change in the general
gist of the material. Perhaps the best-pedigreed and most well-known of
these historians is Marvin Olasky. Though writing in a later period,
Olasky gives voice to the history abolitionists carried in their hearts and
by word of mouth for over two decades. Moreover, his work provides
historical detail, especially in the American case, that activists have often
been accused of lacking.

A professor of journalism at the University of Texas at Austin, Olasky
has emerged as a significant figure in the small fraternity of abolitionist
academics. Although minister George Grant preceded him as a popular-
izer of abolitionist history, it was Olasky who brought the heritage tale
into the respectable world of the academy. In his book, *Abortion Rites: A
Social History of Abortion in America*, Olasky surveys abortion history in
the United States from the colonial period to the Finkbine case.

He finds that during the colonial period, moral and legal pressures
combined to convince the men responsible for illegitimate pregnancies
to take responsibility for their actions and their children. As a result, he
reports that "few pregnant women were abandoned" and that "abandoned unwed mothers were not shunned, and court records show them
marrying other men of the community" (Olasky, 1992: 30, 33).

As urbanization increased, however, the tightly knit community, in
which both family members and indentured servants could depend on
a wider public to defend them against cruelty and exploitation, began to
fade. Paradoxically, in cities and towns, individuals became more isolated, though often living in closer quarters. Without an extended family
to enforce marriage, young women could more easily be abandoned,
once seduced and impregnated. Olasky's investigation leads him to con-
clude that "at no time was abortion considered legitimate and legal, but
the practice did occur when some women fell through the cracks, taking
their unborn children with them" (Olasky, 1992: 40–41).

In examining post–Civil War America, Olasky finds abortion to have
been largely an unintended consequence of prostitution—a practice not
so much desired by women as demanded by men. Moreover, the issue
itself was treated as part of the same degenerate moral code that fostered
prostitution.

These conclusions are important because they conflict with those of
James Mohr, whose *Abortion in America* has been a cornerstone of abortion historiography since its publication in 1978. According to Mohr's
interpretation, abortion was exercised within the mainstream of U.S. life
during this period, and it was relatively common. In addition, Mohr's
contention that "the chief problems associated with abortion were med-

ical rather than moral" has been highly influential in the direction of abortion-related social science research for decades (p. 75). Olasky's differences with Mohr are not, however, limited to the question of morality.

In discussing the sudden explosion of anti-abortion legislation during the last three decades of the nineteenth century, Olasky attempts to dismantle Mohr's thesis on the development of the American Medical Association. In so doing, he sets himself squarely in opposition to the accepted paradigm concerning this period of history. Mohr's thesis that anti-abortion legislation was an outgrowth of the AMA's attempt to legitimize itself against the less professional class of physicians is condemned by Olasky in no uncertain terms. He states: "This book stands in opposition to the oversimplified history that both sides in the abortion wars often prefer. That oversimplification is nowhere more evident than in myths concerning the role of the American Medical Association that have been a staple of speeches and Supreme Court briefs" (Olasky, 1992: 109).

Olasky credits the success of anti-abortion legislation more to a postwar re-examination of questions of life and death and to a general public pressure for "campaigns that tried to preserve family structure" (Olasky, 1992: 128). He observes that many of those active in the abolition movement before the Civil War turned their attention to anti-prostitution and anti-abortion crusades, once that conflict was settled. Furthermore, he argues that newly professionalizing physicians were incapable of influencing law or policy on their own. As he bluntly puts it, "[d]octors were in no position to take unpopular stands because they had to remain popular if they were to have any hope of getting paid" (Olasky, 1992: 124).

In his earlier works, Olasky examines the role of the press in the abortion debate. In American history, the media has proved itself capable of being a powerful political ally—or a devastating enemy. For those who oppose abortion, it has at various times served as both. Olasky shows that, while post-quickening abortion was a criminal activity, the press treated it as one of the most heinous crimes imaginable, tantamount to child murder. Most of its coverage focused on those cases in which the abortionist actually murdered the woman being aborted. As politics and pressure groups changed, however, so did the media.

Olasky traces the slow development of post-quickening abortion remedies as a source of advertising revenue.[2] Whatever one assumes the status of pre-quickening abortion to have been, in the early and mid-nineteenth century, advertisements began appearing that sought to disguise the criminal intent of abortionists through a system of code words that Olasky contends were clearly intended to signify the advertiser's willingness to perform abortions. The ads trumpeted the usefulness of various practitioners and their medications in "regulating" the female monthly cycle.

Using contemporaneous news accounts, Olasky traces the steady slide of abortion solicitors into other, blatantly criminal behaviors, including murder. Contrary to the Mohr thesis that newly professionalizing doctors pressed for abortion legislation to legitimize their craft, Olasky contends that public pressure to criminalize pre- and post-quickening abortion in the nineteenth century stemmed from sensational criminal events. After abortionists had time and again been discovered to have killed their patients to cover their mistakes, public outrage could not be contained.

In 1871, one particular case, and its timing, brought matters to a head. First, reporter Augustus St. Clair wrote a three-column article in the *New York Times* exposing the venality and brutality of the abortion industry. Focusing on the immense wealth of "abortuary" owners and the powerlessness of those who patronized them, the article called the practice "The Evil of the Age." St. Clair described the spacious homes and offices of the abortionists, as well as the gruesome realities of the products of their practice. The article was emotional and hard-hitting. The writing, as was common for the era, was sensationalistic and stark. The article itself, however, held little real power until four days later, when the nude body of a young woman was discovered stuffed into a trunk in a railway station. The autopsy revealed that her death had been caused by an abortion.

When the perpetrator was caught, the *Times* continued its anti-abortion crusade, which was then picked up by the fledgling American Medical Association (AMA). The AMA described abortionists as "modern-day Herods," presenting "as hideous a view of moral deformity as the evil spirit could present" and thundering that "We shall discover an enemy in the camp. . . . It is false brethren we have to fear; men who are false to their professions, false to principle, false to honor, false to humanity, false to God" (Olasky, 1988a: 29). The *New York Tribune* followed suit in exposing and denouncing the practice of abortion. By the end of the nineteenth century, most states had outlawed abortion.

While Olasky finds the press to have been an ally to abolitionists in the nineteenth century, he finds it was equally cozy with abortion reformers in the twentieth century. Stopping short of a theory of media conspiracy, Olasky musters what he believes to be evidence that the press gradually became more and more open to the decriminalization of abortion, finally embracing the pro-choice cause by the time *Roe* became a reality.

Olasky explores the subtle shift in public opinion that he believes was initiated by pro-abortion groups and accelerated by the media. Beginning in 1942, the *New York Times* and other large papers began to report on various conferences being held to discuss family planning and "the public relations problems that a pro-abortion position presented" (1988a: 78). It was at this point, too, that the pro-abortion cause discovered a man who would become perhaps its most important figure, Dr. Alan Guttmacher, then an associate professor at Johns Hopkins. Guttmacher would later become the head of Planned Parenthood and the founder of the Guttmacher Institute, the research and publication arm of Planned Parenthood. The *Times* gave Guttmacher considerable coverage, particularly of his abortion legalization argument that decriminalization would be a way to cheat the criminal abortionist. In addition, the increasing acceptance of the birth control issue as a matter of public debate muddied the waters of the abortion issue.

Olasky demonstrates that, in the 1950s, a distinction was made in the media between the unscrupulous abortionist and those private physicians whose concern for their patients led them to advocate the decriminalization of the procedure. The newspapers covered every conference held by Planned Parenthood, yet continued to occasionally report the abortion-related murders that occurred, especially in New York City. However, even the stories of criminal abortionists convicted of murdering their patients increasingly omitted mention of the unborn child, focusing exclusively on the young girls who were the most frequent victims of abortion-related murder. In addition, the dichotomy between "good" and "bad" abortionists grew more rigid, with papers profiling doctors of impeccable reputation who occasionally performed abortions.

Olasky finds that, as the fifties drew to a close, newspapers began reprinting Planned Parenthood-generated statistics without question. The media picked up on the back-alley abortion image that Guttmacher and others were promoting. Olasky states:

> Newspapers began generalizing, often incorrectly, about patterns of abortion. The New York *Journal-American* stated that in "a typical case" abortions are performed by a woman "totally without any medical training," in a "dirty, smelly apartment," and "on the bed, as a rule, under totally non-sterile conditions." This was not true; even the pro-abortion Kinsey Institute acknowledged that at least 85% of abortions were done by regular doctors under clean conditions—but the press accounts gave a very different impression. (Olasky, 1988a: 90)

As one might expect, during the 1960s, television became more important in the story of abortion in America. For Olasky, the media saturation of the Finkbine case marks the turning point in public attitudes toward abortion. The treatment of the case and its outcome opened the door to abortion reform. Olasky contends that the tone of the press was universally sympathetic to the couple's desire to abort. In addition, most major papers took the opportunity to interview Guttmacher and use his statements that this case exemplified the "idiocy" of American abortion law. Olasky credits the neutrality of the new term "fetus" with alleviating some of the tension between the sympathetic image of the Finkbines and the public impression of abortion that had been built over the years. In addition, he argues, for the first time, abortion itself was portrayed unapologetically as a positive moral act. The Finkbines were reported to be seeking the abortion for the good of the child, to prevent its having to live a miserable life. According to Olasky, no major newspaper or television network questioned the necessity of abortion in this case.

During the 1960s, press articles began to focus on "justifiable" cases of abortion. Particularly during and after the German measles epidemic of 1963–1965, the media ran numerous articles on the necessity of abortion in cases of fetal deformity. Yet the public still resisted the idea of abortion in " 'convenience' situations—where the mother is unmarried, unwilling to marry, poor, or simply did not want any more children" (Olasky, 1988a: 98). However, the 1965 Supreme Court decision on birth control freed the public relations and legal experts of Planned Parenthood and the fledgling National Association for Repeal of Abortion Laws (NARAL, later changed to the National Abortion Rights Action League) to begin work on the issue of abortion. In addition, the invention of the birth control pill and the beginning new resurgence of feminism popularized the notion of the woman's right to full control over her own body, including her right to choose an abortion.

Olasky's interpretation of history is widely accepted within the abolitionist community. Though written during a later period of the enterprise, Olasky's works echo the sentiment that abolition activists had been expressing with frustration since *Roe*. The panoramic history that Noonan presents to justify the abolitionist position as the product of enlightened Western Christian civilization convinces abolitionists that they have God on their side. The specifically Americanized history that Olasky articulates proves (from their perspective) that they are on the side of the Constitution and history as well.

The light and dark conflict noted before in the abolitionist's confrontation of the abortionist is writ large by the drive to reestablish social support. In fighting the deceptiveness of the abortionist, the abolitionist exposes the truth about abortion as a procedure. In reasserting the normative nature of abolitionism, the activist unburies forgotten truths that have been hidden from the nation and reclaims forgotten glory that has been denied the abolitionists themselves. Largely traditional in their faith, their private life, and their habits, activists are secure in the knowledge that tradition is on their side. They have not failed to progress; it is the culture that has lamentably reversed its course. The modern age has not made abortion more necessary, only more readily available. The right to privacy in the Constitution did not evolve gradually and elegantly into a recognition of the woman's right to choose; it was, rather, invented by an activist Court breaking loose from the moorings of centuries of tradition, legislating "abortion on demand" for "the entire nine months of pregnancy."[3]

The desire to reassert traditional values against an allegedly hostile culture has an innate attraction for those to whom law and order is a vital component of community life. Particularly following the turmoil of the 1960s, American traditionalists felt under attack. Old and long-standing beliefs—about parents and children, law and order, government, the family, and individual freedom—were tested in the 1960s, and the youth that emerged out of that turbulent era often replaced them with new ones. For traditionalists whose mainstream churches were sliding leftward, the abolition enterprise offered an explanation and ground on which to fight back. For Catholics longing for the familiarity of the pre-Vatican II days, it provided reassurance that the Church could still be depended on to defend its position. For individuals struggling with their own ambiguities about abortion, the abolitionists offered moral certainty, historical roots, and unwavering loyalty to those who would stand with them. In short, the lure of the moral crusade asserting its normative status is the certainty with which it does so. The historical grounding of the heritage tale presents the opportunity to exercise another attractive aspect of the moral crusade: its single-mindedness in pursuing what is alleged to be a universal truth.

MORAL REFORM AND ABSOLUTISM

In a moral crusade, the aims of the participants are not necessarily wide-ranging. Generally, a moral crusade focuses on one particular question that is invested with far-reaching consequences for both individuals and the society at large. In the case of abortion abolition, during the early formative years of the enterprise, the abortion issue was rarely linked with any other political concern. It was not until the enterprise grew into a social movement that abortion began to be seen as part of a web of other controversial social issues. At the same time, the tunnel-vision with which the original activists pursued their aims permitted them to clearly articulate the moral case without being distracted by other issues.

In making the single-issue case, the moral crusade carries with it a dogmatic assumption that the issue at hand is not a matter of opinion, but a question of universal truth. On this issue, as on almost no other in American life and history, practical material concerns are secondary. In speaking of the pro-life women she interviewed, Luker describes her subjects as "housewives," whose "values and life circumstances made it unlikely that they themselves would need [*sic*] abortions . . . surrounded by people who shared these values (1984: 138).

Luker speculates that what motivated these women—women who "had never been actively concerned with political issues" (Luker, 1984: 138)—were three key aspects of the Court's decision: First, they were offended by the Court's relegation of embryonic life to mere "potential." Second, they were disturbed by the Court's willingness to give equal weight to the arguments of both sides. Lastly, they were horrified by the Court's abandonment of what they felt was its duty to protect the unborn.

While Luker makes a persuasive case for her speculations, she misses the true offense and the ingredient that leads the abolitionist into this moral crusade. Throughout her work, Luker refers to the position of the activist as an "opinion," despite the fact that her own subjects never identify it in such a fashion. Luker maintains that part of what so greatly disturbed the first activists about the *Roe* decision was that it rendered their position on when life begins as just another opinion. Moreover, the offense was compounded by that opinion being treated as a personal and private one, "more like a religious preference than a deeply held social belief, such as belief in the right to free speech" (Luker, 1984: 141).

While Luker hints at the degree to which the activists recoiled at the decision, her comparison here demonstrates that she does not fully understand the way in which they view their position. Luker implies that a "deeply held social belief, such as . . . the right to free speech" is a self-evident value. This, however, fails to accurately convey the abortion opponent's evaluation of the sanctity of life. It would be more accurate to compare the abortion opponent's position to a fact than to a deeply held social belief. For the abolitionist, the wrongness of abortion is as obvious and as certain as the wetness of water—and as much a part of the natural order of things. It is the unshakable nature of the abolitionist conviction that leads to activism within the moral crusade.

When confronted about their "opinions" on abortion, activists tend to argue, as Sproul does, that there are objective truths in life, but they fall into two kinds: those we can know with certainty, and those we cannot. For abolitionists, an action is either "right" or "wrong," and that "rightness" or "wrongness" does not depend on the ability of any living human being to discern it. While this absolute notion of morality is central to the Christian worldview (both Catholic and Protestant—and derivable from traditional Judaism, as well), it appears to be shared by others in the enterprise, both religious and nonreligious. There is nothing quite so maddening for an abolitionist as to be drawn into a debate on this issue. For this is an unbridgeable gap. If one does not believe that there is such a thing as "right" or "wrong" (or, in more theological terms, "good" or "evil"), it becomes difficult to make a moral argument persuasive.

Both the war metaphor and the slavery metaphor that will be explored later in this book fail if the debaters cannot at least agree on some form of binary morality. In summarizing the relativist nature of the pro-choice position, Luker states that it is pluralist, secularist, and ethical rather than moral. When faced with pro-choice relativists, abolitionists often find themselves asking what they consider to be hopelessly stupid questions—questions like "Is slavery wrong?" and "Is murder wrong?" If the answers to those questions are equivocal—"wrong for whom? In what circumstances?"—the discussion is at an impasse. For abolitionists, this denial that an action can, in itself, be absolutely wrong is incomprehensible. It does not fit into the worldview; there are no sensible words to express it. Relativists will sometimes make the claim that something can be "wrong for me, but not for you" or reply to accusations of moral retardation with "that's *your* morality."

Without exception, in abolitionist literature, morality is morality, regardless of the person perceiving it. It is a matter decided by God (or, for the nonreligious, by the human conscience). It is not subject to democratic decision or related to situational context. That which is wrong is wrong—no matter who the actor is or what the motivations may be. Moreover, since human knowledge is by nature imperfect, questions of right and wrong are decided conservatively; if an action is of unknown or ambiguous moral content, it is assumed to be wrong.

As certain as abolitionists are that a definitive morality exists, they are just as certain that modern American society increasingly disagrees with them. As Peter Kreeft puts it, "We have lost objective moral law for the first time in history. The philosophies of moral positivism (that morality is posited or made by man), moral relativism, and subjectivism have become for the first time not a heresy for rebels but the reigning orthodoxy of the intellectual establishment. University faculty and media personnel overwhelmingly reject belief in the notion of any universal and objective morality" (1992: 25).

Again we find the activist self-cast in the position of the underdog, under siege by almost insurmountable forces. To be an abolitionist is to resign one's self to societal martyrdom. Coincidentally or not, the role of the persecuted innocent is strategically interesting, allowing the abolitionist—at least among his fellows—to usurp the victim status that pro-choice forces assign to the woman seeking an abortion. While she is portrayed as the victim of the harassment of the abolitionist, the abolitionists see themselves as standard-bearers of truth and life, pitted against a society bent on silencing *them*. Whether the persecution is real or imagined, the role of victim is attractive, both for its inherent sympathy and for the implication it carries of empathy with the woman in crisis and the unborn child in mortal danger.

MORAL ENTREPRENEURS

Most moral crusades are led by recognizable figures who serve as channels for participation by new converts. But, oddly, the abolitionist enterprise during the 1970s developed no recognizable individuals to fill this position. Because of its tight connection to Catholicism, each successive Pope was seen as a major leader; however, the scope of papal duties did not permit him to be in constant action on the cause itself. Phyllis Schlafly, initially activated to oppose the Equal Rights Amendment, was a leading speaker on abolitionist issues but did not function as a national leader. While the enterprise generated "stars" of a sort—including Judie Brown, Henry Hyde, Joe Scheidler, Father Paul Marx, Mother Teresa, and Joan Bell—no single voice emerged to speak for abolitionists at large.

While the absence of leadership may have prevented the enterprise from becoming a unified political force or attaining legislative success, it also gave the opposition no one figure to target as an enemy. "Catholics," though occasionally attacked in the abortion debate by pro-choice forces, maintained sufficient social deference that a blanket statement condemning them as a group would have been unacceptable. The Pope, particularly following Vatican II, was too highly esteemed a figure to be useful as a surrogate for the perceived evils of the abolition enterprise as a whole. Ironically, when someone did emerge to fill this role, he would not only serve as the lightning-rod for the ire of the opposition, but he would also propel the enterprise out of the status of a moral crusade and into the heady world of social movements.

THE RESULTS

And so, it seems fair to ask, what did the enterprise do during this phase of its existence? What effect did it have on the public, the culture, and its own activists? The quick answer, judging from the public documents, must be "not much." During this period, the issue of abortion was not considered wildly controversial in American culture. American media, though wary of broaching the subject in any concrete way, presented a generally pro-choice perspective as the norm and tended to depict the anti-abortion stance as a rather quaint and archaic attitude at best and a virulently dangerous ignorance at worst.

By the end of the 1970s, the abortion abolitionists had been fighting the dragon for seven years and had seen very little return on their investment. The number of abortions had not been reduced, the general public did not appear to be coming around, and the activists—still primarily Catholic—were becoming marginalized within their own faith tradition. As the gulf between traditionalists and "Americanized" Catholics widened, there seemed little hope of a strong enough shift in public opinion to justify a reversal of *Roe*. Even the election of a devoutly and publicly Christian president had not made any discernible impact in their favor.

Though the abortions did not stop, and the public did not join the crusade in any great numbers, the activists of this period set up a skeletal infrastructure that would become vital in the ensuing years of the enterprise. During this period, Nellie Gray began the March for Life, a yearly abolitionist march and rally in the nation's capital that gradually began to attract important Washington insiders. The National Right-to-Life Committee became a reality at this time, although it did not manage to reach much beyond its initial Catholic base for most of the decade. The American Catholic bishops stood firm in their opposition to abortion, despite increasing calls for the Church to soften her position and despite the bishops' own leftward movement on issues of welfare and warfare.

The first phase of the modern abolitionist enterprise, then, provided a strong, reliable core of true-believer activists undaunted by perceived failure and willing to wait a significant period of time for results. This core attracted like-minded individuals as they became aware of its existence, but failed in the first phase to break much beyond the initial denominational exclusivity with which it began. However, the activists were both willing to wait for new adherents to come to them and able to remain loyal to the cause. In the meantime, their future allies outside the Church were getting their own houses in order, while circumstances and events built toward an eventual partnership between the original activists and socially concerned Protestants who would breathe new life into the enterprise.

NOTES

1. A short film, shown on "The 700 Club" after it won an award for Christian filmmaking, carried this metaphor to its logical extreme. It was essentially a horror film, showing a young girl in a small room, being apparently stalked by an unknown menace, finally pulled screaming through a window to an unidentified fate.

2. "Quickening" is a somewhat archaic term used to designate the point at which the mother-to-be first feels the child move. Although all healthy fetuses are active by the seventh week of gestation, the woman doesn't generally feel that activity until somewhere between the fourteenth and twenty-second weeks (though a number of maternal factors are involved, including her weight and how many children she has previously carried). If movement is not felt by the twenty-second week, many practitioners will order well-being tests to check fetal

progress. This is not a synonym for viability, which is the point at which the baby is believed to be able to survive outside the womb, generally set (and demarcated by *Roe*) at the beginning of the second trimester, or the end of the twenty-fourth week. It should be noted that, under *Roe*, quickening usually falls within the second trimester, during which abortion may be regulated by the state only to protect the mother's life or health.

3. This popular phrase can be found at nearly all stages of the enterprise. Technically correct, it ignores the specifics of *Roe*, which permits states to regulate the procedure at various stages and for various reasons. However, since it is in the hands of the state to regulate or not, activists view the trimester scheme as "permitting" it throughout pregnancy. Less careful activists often follow the phrase with "for any reason," which is less accurate but still derivable from the law, in that the state may not regulate even in the third trimester in ways detrimental to the life or health of the woman. For activists, "health" is interpretable as practically any reason at all, through the Court's findings in *Doe v. Bolton*, *Roe*'s companion case.

CHAPTER 4

Into the Lion's Den: The Abortion Abolition Enterprise Becomes a Social Movement

In *America's Date with Destiny*, Pat Robertson wrote: "April 29, 1980, was the beginning of a spiritual revolution" (Robertson, 1986: 282). He was speaking of an event called the Washington for Jesus rally in Washington, D.C., a day-long prayer meeting attended by (depending on who was counting) anywhere from 250,000 to 500,000 people. The date, significant to conservative activists now for the rally itself, was chosen for its preexisting symbolism:

> The date of April 29 was selected for an important reason. It was April 29, 1607, that the first permanent settlers planted a cross in the sand at Jamestown, Virginia, and prayed that this land might arise and prosper with "His blessing and His glory."
>
> April 29 was the eve of another monumental date in American history. In the anguish of the War Between the States, 256 years after the Jamestown settlers reaffirmed their covenant with God, President Abraham Lincoln proclaimed April 30, 1863 as a day of National Humiliation, Fasting, and Prayer. (Hadden and Shupe, 1988: 21)

Moreover, the event at Jamestown is commemorated every year at the Christian Broadcasting Network, Robertson's Virginia Beach, Virginia, telecommunications complex. Gerry Straub, a former CBN producer, explains that "Pat Robertson viewed CBN as the modern-day fulfillment of the settlers' vision and prayer that 'from these very shores the Gospel shall go forth to not only this new world but to the entire world.' Consequently, every year on that date, CBN televised a prayer service from that location, which today is marked by a large concrete cross" (Straub, 1988: 58–59).

Though not exclusively focused on abortion, the event was a turning point for the abolitionists for several reasons. First, it signaled the willingness of Protestant evangelicals to return to the political arena in large numbers. Until the rally, the evangelical presence had been growing slowly more public throughout the 1970s but had largely been limited to internal communication. The rally, though promoted within the evangelical community as a prayer meeting, was also a deliberate announcement to the wider public that conservative Christians were prepared to take their call for repentance beyond the walls of the electronic church. Robertson's willingness to shift his commemorative attentions from the private realm of his own back yard (or even the limited audience of the Christian Broadcasting Network) to the very public stage of a Mall celebration proclaimed to the wider world that the evangelicals were prepared to bring their faith with them when they emerged from the church into the community.

Second, the overt nature of the perceptibly political stands taken by the speakers at the rally provided those opposed to the abolitionists with identifiable figures on which to focus as "leaders" of the enterprise. When it would become obvious that the "new Christian right" or the "Moral Majority" was a force to be reckoned with, those who chose to do their homework found a Who's Who list of the enemy in the speaker's roster from the rally. Although John Gimenez was the actual mastermind of the rally, it was the co-sponsor, Pat Robertson, who would be best remembered. Those who saw or heard of the event were introduced to some of the rising and risen stars of the electronic church. In addition to Robertson, whose "700 Club" was already growing by leaps and bounds, the rally featured the later infamous Jim and Tammy Faye Bakker, Paul and Jan Crouch of the Trinity Broadcasting Network, Ben Haden, Rex Humbard, D. James Kennedy, James Robison, Lester Sumrall, and Charles Stanley. All were stars of their own television ministries within the electronic church, and each would become more widely known in the political arena in the coming decade.

Finally, the Washington for Jesus rally was instructive to those who participated in it because it gave the newly activated abolitionists their first taste of what the secular media would make of them.

The national media ignored Washington for Jesus, or gave it brief notice. Almost everyone who did cover it noted that the rally failed to produce the million participants forecast by its organizers—supposedly evidence that the meeting was not a success. They also gave nearly as much attention to a hastily organized counter-rally, which attracted only a few hundred. But the media did not mention that it was the largest crowd ever to assemble on the Mall—larger than for any of the civil rights marches on Washington during the 1960s, larger than several antiwar protests during the 1960s and 1970s, larger than the crowd that attended a mass with Pope John Paul II on the same site a few months earlier. The event was telecast over the satellite network of the Christian Broadcasting Network, PTL Network, and Trinity Broadcasting Network, putting several million more faithful in touch with this historic moment. (Hadden and Shupe, 1988: 23)

The politicization of conservative religion, the willingness of individuals to take public responsibility for the cause as a whole, and the love-hate relationship of activists with the media would become vital aspects of the abortion abolition enterprise during the 1980s. If nothing else, the Washington for Jesus rally was a harbinger of the battle between cultural conservatives and liberals that abolitionists would later believe the 1980s became.

Although the rally was the movement abolitionists' first public manifestation, the man whose name would become virtually synonymous with the cause was not present on that fateful April day. Jerry Falwell, who had been increasingly preaching political messages on his "Old Time Gospel Hour" television program, founded the Moral Majority in 1979. He declined to participate in the rally because he felt it was neither politics nor prayer. Moreover, he feared that a small turnout would reduce the credibility of the Religious Right. Not only was the rally seen as a success within the evangelical community, but its fallout fed the streams of frustration that abolitionists and other conservative Christians felt about the condition of the country. When the Moral Majority began extending ecumenical invitations to religious conservatives of all faiths to get involved in the political battles it deemed most urgent, there was a ready audience willing to do so.

Falwell, prompted by Howard Phillips, Robert Billings, Richard Viguerie, Paul Weyrich, and Ed McAteer, set up the Moral Majority, Moral Majority, Inc., and Moral Majority Political Action Committee in 1979. The three subgroups were (respectively) a tax-exempt organization, a political lobby, and a fund-raising Political Action Committee (PAC) for candidates. Falwell's decision to enter the heady world of politics marked a significant shift from his long-standing resistance to public life. In making his decision and in creating the Moral Majority, he shepherded an important shift in both conservative Protestant activity and the abortion abolition enterprise.

In 1965, Falwell declared his distaste for politics and all that it entails. In a sermon entitled "Ministers and Marches," Falwell argued that the proper arena for the minister is not the polling place, but the pulpit, that his charge was not to march the streets, but to minister to the people in them. He stated, "I feel that we need to get off the streets and back into the pulpits and into the prayer rooms. I believe we need to take our Bible and go down into the highways and hedges and bring men to Christ. I believe we need to rededicate ourselves to the great task of turning this world back to God. The preaching of the gospel is the only means by which this can be done" (cited in Young, 1982: 316).

Not two decades later, Falwell would reverse course and preach the need for proclamation in politics. What happened in the intervening years is virtually a textbook study of the birth pangs of a social movement. This chapter will examine how the abortion abolition enterprise became a social movement, and the next will address more personal issues for the individuals involved.

FORMATION AND DYNAMICS

As noted previously, traditional social movement theory is helpful in exploring the process by which issue-oriented, like-minded individuals coalesce into organized entities worthy of the "social movement" label. The abolition enterprise of the 1970s was too narrowly focused, in both its theology and its issue orientation, to be thought of as a social movement. As the 1980s approached, however, a number of cultural and social circumstances changed, expanding the membership and building momentum within the enterprise.

The Condition of the Social Structure

For a social movement to blossom, the social structure that surrounds it must be conducive to its formation. In the case of the abolitionists, there are two social structures to consider: the surrounding culture and the movement culture. During the 1970s, the surrounding culture of mainstream American society seemed at first an unlikely environment for the development of a social movement focused on opposition to abortion. The courts had declared the final word on the subject, the legislatures (federal, state, and local) did not appear inclined to argue about it, and the occupant of the White House was rather preoccupied with the more serious matter of reestablishing the legitimacy of the office for much of the decade. However, as time wore on, a conservative impulse grew in the American voter, and the abolition enterprise would enjoy the fallout from that rightward turn.

After Richard Nixon resigned the presidency, confidence in the government plummeted. The Ford presidency, though clearly a stabilizing force, did little to restore great confidence in the wisdom of elected leaders. Jimmy Carter, whom evangelicals initially hoped would bring their issues to the forefront, proved a disappointment to both the conservatives and the country generally. Unable to check what he himself called the national "malaise," as inflation and unemployment raced each other upward, Carter seemed incapable of making his good intentions into real policy. As the 1980s approached, the public was restive and unhappy with the state of the nation. America, according to the national media, was taking a turn to the right. Since part of that impulse was a desire to return to what would become known in sound-bites as "traditional morality," abolitionists fit smoothly into the conservatizing movement, which, on a variety of issues, fit nicely into the electorate mainstream as the 1980s loomed.

The political culture of the United States is itself far more fertile ground for social movement development than many other nations, due to its democratic tradition. Born in rebellion, tempered in insurrection, the nation has a long and proud tradition of citizen involvement and public dissent. The Bill of Rights preserves the rights of the people to assemble and to petition the government for redress of grievances. While not designed as a total democracy (but instead as a democratic republic), the United States has always been expansive in its extension of the franchise and its development of specific rights. Although change has historically been slow in coming (sometimes glacially so), it has come, time and again, and often as the result of popular restiveness expressed in the social movement form. The extension of the franchise to women and blacks, the abolition of slavery, the existence of labor unions—all owe their triumph, in whole or in part, to social movement activity.

Moreover, the 1950s, '60s, and '70s had been times of massive cultural change, and several social movements were born in those historic decades. The civil rights, free speech, women's liberation, antiwar, and gay rights movements were active in the 1970s and could have been seen as models for activists seeking to create a new movement. The paths to publicity and power had already been established: mass protest strategies, media attention, and agitation for structural change. The moral crusaders of the immediate post-*Roe* period, however, were apparently unwilling to adopt such strategies, perhaps due in part to the politics of those who did, particularly in the antiwar movement of which many liberal clergy were a part.

As Wuthnow observes, however, the developments of those decades sensitized the culture to the importance of morality in public life. Law schools, business schools, and medical societies began formally teaching ethics, while professional societies instituted ethical guidelines. Even the government responded to the impulse:

> Between 1974 and 1978 more than 20 congressmen were investigated for unethical or immoral conduct. . . . The House and Senate adopted codes of ethics and created select committees on ethics. . . . President Carter proposed a comprehensive Ethics in Government Act. . . . While only 63 officials had been indicted by federal grand juries in 1970, this number rose to 255 by 1975 and increased further to 337 in 1976. . . . Articles and editorials dealing with morality and ethics registered more than a 50 percent increase and began to address an increasingly wide range of institutional sectors. . . . By one estimate, the number of articles on abortion in the late 1970s was about four times as high as in the early 1960s, while the number of articles on "sexual ethics" was more than five times as high. (Wuthnow, 1988: 200–201)

Ironically, the new sensitivity to ethics that Wuthnow notes was easily interpretable within the evangelical community as evidence of the drastic moral decline of the culture. Moreover, the culture's willingness to begin discussion on these issues provided an entree for cultural conservatives to voice their concerns, despite the fact that they felt that the issues in question were those on which there could be no compromise.

As the 1970s wore on, new technologies became available that allowed for better, faster, and wider dissemination of information. In addition, direct-mail techniques provided more discreet ways to seek and build membership than visible marches, rallies, or meetings, and membership grew in response to what seemed one outrage from the dominant culture after another. Those who would become principals in the abolition enterprise during the 1980s adopted those technologies, quietly building organizations that would become major players in the politics of that decade. And the surrounding culture not only provided fertile ground for the formation of a social movement, but at times it seemed to practically dare the cultural conservatives to enter the playing field.

In the 1960s, the Federal Communications Commission provided conservative Protestants with telecommunications access that would eventually become vital in building powerhouse organizations for the dissemination of information, gospel and otherwise. In the embryonic years of religious television programming, Brown wrote, "Religious shows are generally . . . cast into TV's Sunday ghetto, those hours when the Nielsen surveys show the least inclination for viewing in the majority of television homes." (1953: 177). By the end of the 1970s, however, television evangelists commanded large blocks of airtime, enviable numbers of viewers, and whole networks of their own. The vast expansion of religious programming was the result of changes in Federal Communications Commission regulations that effectively gave conservative fundamentalists a foothold in a medium formerly dominated by the mainline liberal churches.

According to the FCC regulations in existence when television programming first went on the air, a certain amount of airtime was reserved for material deemed to be in "the public interest." The free time given to religious broadcasting was, with few exceptions, granted by the networks to Catholic and mainstream Protestant clergy, and was generally placed on Sunday mornings and at the beginning or the end of broadcast days. In the early 1950s, the National Council of Churches "pursued an initiative to ensure their exclusive representation with the networks" (Hadden and Shupe, 1988: 47).

In 1960, however, after long years of frustrated lobbying by the evangelical National Religious Broadcasters (NRB), the FCC issued a policy directive that would change the complexion of religious television. That directive ruled that "no important public interest group is served by differentiating between gratis airtime and commercially sponsored programming." In effect, the ruling allowed local stations to *sell* religious airtime and still get credit for "public interest" programming. The conservative evangelicals began to buy airtime, enabling them to capture blocks of television time that had previously been kept from them.

The new FCC policy, coupled with the advent of videotape technology (which made broadcasting generally less expensive than before), made it possible for conservative evangelicals to overtake the mainstream denominations in domination of the religious airwaves. Because the conservative evangelicals were able and willing to pay for airtime, and because local stations could obtain the same public interest credit for commercial airtime, mainstream Protestants found themselves dumped in record numbers by station managers across the country. Between 1959 and 1977, religious broadcasting in the United States that was paid-time programming rose from 59% to 92%.

Pat Robertson was one of those blessed by the FCC changes. On January 11, 1960, he filed the charter of the Christian Broadcasting Network, Inc. During the 1970s, while the Catholic vanguard held the line for the abolitionists, Robertson and the conservative evangelicals built a vast empire of telecommunications technology. Straub describes the commitment of the staff and the heady atmosphere of growth at the ministry during this period: "The late 1970s were a time of great expansion for the ministry. God was blessing us with tremendous growth in both size and scope, and massive amounts of money were being poured into the construction of the new headquarters center and university buildings. It was an exciting time that filled the staff with a sense of pride" (1986: 276).

The growth was no figment of Robertson's imagination. As Reichley reports,

> A study in 1963 showed that only 12 percent of all Protestants regularly watched or listened to religious broadcasts. Gallup polls taken in the late 1970s showed that this figure had more than doubled, and a poll in 1981 found that 27 percent of the national public claimed to have watched more than one religious program in the preceding month. A study in 1984 by Gallup and the Annenberg School of Communications placed the regular audience for religious broadcasts at about 13.3 million. (Reichley, 1985: 315)

During the same period, conservative Christians began to erect a parallel culture within which they could be isolated from the world, without sacrificing the advantages of worldliness. The evangelicals did not just have their own churches; they had their own schools, music, literature, scholarship, clothing, magazines, business networks, gift shops, rock concerts, and theme parks. Moreover, through interaction with such outlets, one could easily find virtually any material object with Scripture or teaching engraved on it, and personalized Bible verse checks. Alongside all this material sat the precious feet pins, right-to-life roses, videos of *Silent Scream* and *Eclipse of Reason*, and whole shelves of the political issues sections of Christian bookstores stocked with books about abortion. When the conservative evangelicals decided to return to the political arena, they had in place a formidable structure with which to disseminate information. And before the election process had gathered steam, they already had a few good reasons to join the fray.

The Appropriate Strain

It could be argued that the *Roe* decision should have provided the strain required for the formation of a social movement, given its suddenness and its shock value for potential participants. However, as we have seen, non-Catholics that might have entered the arena were otherwise occupied. Even those who did enter the moral crusade reflected, to a certain extent, the assumption that abortion could not possibly become a permanent feature of the American landscape. The reactions of the moral crusaders mirrored the initial feelings of those professionals who were positioned to see the decision coming. Luker reports the pre-*Roe* reaction of a college professor who had been disturbed by the first reforms in California but did little about it. Not until 1970, when the Bielson bill was being considered, did he feel moved to take action because he felt that the bill "would knock down all the restrictions to abortion" (Luker, 1984: 135).

The beginnings of the abortion reform movement did not attract the attention of large numbers of potential abolitionists, primarily because they could not believe that Americans could countenance a change in abortion law. In many ways, the Protestant nonreaction to *Roe* is rooted in a similar cognitive process. Unable to believe that the United States would long permit something as obviously and utterly wrong as legal abortion, conservative Protestants focused on preserving their own children from the culture around them. Until movement conservatives began to see abortion as a persistent evil and a long-term threat, the duty to get involved simply did not occur to them. However, the time would come when the culture they had sought to avoid became unavoidable, and when it did, the evangelicals brought *all* the grievances to the table.

In 1962 (*Engle v. Vitale*), the Supreme Court prohibited nondenominational organized prayer in the public schools. The following year, in *Abington School District v. Shempp*, the Court completed the process of (in the language of conservative activists) throwing God out of the public schools, by finding Bible readings in violation of the First Amendment's establishment clause. Already annoyed at the encroachment of secularism into public education in such areas as evolution and values clarification, conservative evangelicals—particularly in the South, in which the 1954 desegregation decision was also a sore subject—began establishing "Christian academies." Wuthnow notes that, "By 1978, almost 6,000 Protestant-supported Christian schools were in existence, employing some 66,000 teachers, and counting pupils in excess of 1 million. In that year, these schools represented about one-third of all nonpublic schools and about one-fifth of all pupils enrolled in nonpublic schools" (1988: 198). These schools allowed Christian parents to impart traditional values to their children without fear of crossing the line of separation of church and state—or so they thought.

When *Roe* arrived, evangelicals decried it, but they did so from within the walls they had erected around themselves. It was another item on the list of things hideously wrong with the dominant culture, but, if one had no need of interaction with the dominant culture, it didn't reach the level of importance required for political involvement. By the end of the 1970s, however, conservative Protestants were fed up with waiting for the culture to come to its senses. Moreover, a new intrusiveness on the part of the government was beginning to encroach on what they considered their educational prerogatives.

After prayer and the Bible were taken out of the public schools, Protestant Christians began to follow the age-old path of their Catholic brethren and opened their own schools, where they could teach the traditional values they themselves had learned in public schools—values now perceived as too restrictive for taxpayer-funded education. In these schools, they could teach values, enforce discipline, and protect their children from the perceived dangers of the New Age movement, values clarification exercises, and other "child abuse in the classroom" (Schlafly, 1984). In 1978, however, Jimmy Carter (who had found some support among evangelicals in his election) added an unacceptable insult to the injury he had already done the evangelicals by his failure to implement their agenda: he tightened the standards for tax exemption for schools. This meant that the Christian academies had to conform to the racial quotas all other schools were bound to.

When the IRS began stepping into what cultural conservatives considered their private educational sphere, the evangelicals reached their breaking point. If the culture wanted to destroy itself in ignorance, that was one thing. To force its heathen values into the homes and hearths of the saved, however—that was a different story. Faced with what they considered to be unreasonable government intrusion, the schools fought back, and Paul Weyrich of the Committee for the Survival of a Free Congress encouraged Robert Billings, an educator and former failed congressional candidate from Indiana, to run a national organization aimed at representing the political interests of the Christian academies.

The 1978 move merely gave focus to a gradual politicizing that had been moving through the evangelical community. Wuthnow notes that, in the early 1970s, polls showed religious conservatives to be among the least likely groups to be politically active, but "[b]y the late 1970s, these patterns were beginning to change. A national study done in 1976 . . . showed that born-again churchgoers were just as likely as other churchgoers to be registered to vote and to say they planned to vote" (1988: 198–199).

By 1976, Jerry Falwell was staging "I Love America" rallies on state capitol steps all over the nation. By 1978, fundamentalists fighting a California proposition expanding legal protection for homosexuals had founded Christian Voice. By 1980, Christian Voice had charted new waters in grass-roots politics with its use of what would become the first of many "moral report cards" (Diamond, 1989: 62). Programs like "The 700 Club" and "The Old Time Gospel Hour" were mixing politics and proclamation, and politically oriented guests became commonplace, especially on "The 700 Club."

In 1979, Falwell founded the Moral Majority, and the movement strategy was in place. The New Right, personified by Weyrich, Howard Phillips of the Conservative Caucus, and Richard Viguerie, the father of direct-mail solicitation, would concentrate on social issues. Reichley says: "The old right, according to *Conservative Digest*, published by Viguerie, had 'stressed almost exclusively economic and foreign policy' issues. The new right, while not abandoning these issues, would emphasize concerns like 'busing, abortion, pornography, education, traditional biblical moral values, and quotas,' which specially motivated 'ethnic and blue-collar Americans, born-again Christians, pro-life Catholics, and Jews' " (1985: 319).

As conservatives became actively involved in politics, they had a pre-existing set of interlocking information networks through which to work. Moreover, when they chose abortion to be the vanguard issue of the movement, they tapped into a well-established moral crusade with a history and literature already available to them. It became clear that control of the culture had not only fallen into intolerable wickedness, but now it would no longer let the conservatives simply be their separate selves. As the varieties of conservatism began to coalesce around the abolition issue, relegating other movement concerns to lesser positions, a generalized belief began to develop as to just what was wrong with the culture and what could be done about it.

A Generalized Belief and an Optimal Solution

Developing a generalized belief among movement conservatives about the causes of the moral malaise was not at all difficult. Both Catholic and Protestant activists subscribed to theologies that maintain that those who are without God are also without wisdom. Quite obviously, the Supreme Court, through the prayer and Bible reading cases and the *Roe* decision, had rejected God as a proper source of wisdom. No agent of government appeared prepared to oppose such declarations. Therefore, the nation had lost its way spiritually and could only be saved through a return to God and traditional values. Jerry Falwell championed a return "back to basics, back to values, back to biblical morality, back to sensibility, and back to patriotism" (Falwell, quoted in Hadden and Shupe, 1988: 163).

The solution of repentance and recommitment to God and to the values allegedly lost within the space of a mere thirty years was believed by cultural conservatives to be workable in all areas of life. Education, public or private, needed to return to its former basics, and prayer should be reinstated in the public schools. For the millions of evangelical conservatives who would charge the public square in 1980, it seemed evident that the rules of individual salvation could be applied to a nation. If only the formerly Christian country would bend its knee, all manner of social, political, and economic judgments could be reversed.

Recalling (or manufacturing, depending on one's historical and ideological perspective) the Christian foundations of the nation, religious conservatives portrayed themselves as the rightful inheritors of a cultural heritage that had been virtually destroyed by secularism, a theory that would become quite popular during the 1980s within the movement. Moreover, conservative Christians were not only called to the polls to change things—they also had to shoulder a fair bit of the blame for the way things were. If conservative evangelicals hadn't yet gotten the message through the television evangelists, *Moody Monthly*, one of the most respected Christian magazines in the country, issued a scathing indictment of and a clear challenge to the silent evangelical majority: "Evangelicalism as a whole has uttered no real outcry. We've organized no protest. Do we need time to think abortion through? Isn't seven years enough? The Catholics have called abortion *the Silent Holocaust*. The deeper horror is the silence of the Evangelical" (quoted in Grant, 1991: 145).

Not only did newly politicized Christians have the motivation to end that silence, but they felt sure that they also had the solution to the core problem. As Wuthnow notes, "If public morality was indeed the mainstay of national strength, evangelicals could hardly stand by, knowing that God had given them both the answers and the opportunity to voice their answers, while the social fabric decayed. In the biblical prophets evangelicals found dramatic examples of persons who had been called to speak out against moral decay, and the new group of conservative spokesman who rose to national prominence consciously adopted these models" (1988: 204).

Social Control

There are two types of social control: preventive and reactive. In the case of abortion abolitionists, the moral crusade had been at work since 1973, more notable for its endurance than its stridency. The spiritual work of the 1970s, while generally disdained by pro-choice activists, had not earned the enterprise a reputation that would require social control. Largely peaceful, the activists of the early period had acclimated the public and the police to their presence, earning a certain respect, at least for the sincerity of their belief. The need for preventive social control had not generally arisen during the moral crusade period. Thus, when new activists began to enter the burgeoning social movement, they did so first as co-workers with the moral crusaders. The preexisting structures served adequately for the social movement activists; they merely expanded the membership and widened the scope of the enterprise. Reactive social control would come later.

Thus, with a social structure in the dominant culture that the movement culture could thrive in, abolitionists found themselves in the midst of the suddenly like-minded. The general public and formerly silent religious conservatives seemed to be willing to put their shoulders to the wheel and bring the issue back to the forefront of national political debate. Abolitionists at heart who had long been maddeningly silent were led out of their churches, by ministers and television evangelists, who also had a state-of-the-art information distribution network with which to bring out the faithful. The perceived evils of the surrounding culture had become too offensive to bear, and too close for comfort. The abortion abolitionists knew what the problem was and what to do about it, and were ready to put their considerable talents to work in an all-out effort to solve not just the abortion problem, but the whole panoply of related spiritual, social, and economic ills. As the 1980 elections appeared on the horizon, the culture was prepared for the advent of a social movement, and the new activists were well positioned for the move, willing and eager to make it. And make it they did.

LIFE CYCLE OF THE SOCIAL MOVEMENT

Traditional social movement theory provides a picture of the expected life cycle of such an organization. Once the Protestants had come into the activist community, the abolitionists began to turn their attention not only to abortion, but to ancillary issues as well. Moreover, the enterprise itself began to behave in ways one would expect of a social movement, pursuing more political and pragmatic goals, and fewer symbolic ones. The following section explores the phases of the abortion abolition enterprise as it expanded and prospered during the 1980s.

Preliminary Stage of Social Unrest

As noted previously, the period from the *Roe* decision to the 1980 election season could be seen as a preliminary stage of social unrest. During the moral crusade period, abolitionists were unable to bridge the gap between socially oriented Catholics and heavenly minded Protestants. However, after the disillusionment of Watergate and the disappointment of Carter, evangelicals were ready to take politics into their own hands. Although they were still insistent on the spiritual, they no longer felt that it was the sole arena fitting for their participation. After a few years of preparation, they were ready to come out swinging by the time of the 1980 election.

Disseminating the Social Myths

During the 1980s, the abortion abolitionists disseminated a series of social myths about abortion and the pro-choice movement, which served to perpetuate participation in the movement and sustain the commitment of the membership. This discussion will focus on three of the most important myths: the slavery parallel, the story of Planned Parenthood, and the Christian nation narrative. All three developed during the 1980s, served to help activists construct a cognitive structure through which to view their efforts, and endured beyond the decade.

Building on the success of the military metaphors connected with the holocaust parallel, abolitionists began in the mid-1980s to connect abortion to another shameful episode of U.S. history—the era of legalized slavery. In this argument, the denial of humanity to the unborn is directly compared to the denial of the humanity of slaves. Just as white slave owners were able to act with impunity and a clear conscience because of their conviction that slaves were property rather than people, pro-choice activists are portrayed as dehumanizing the unborn in order to steal their right to live.

In addition, the slavery metaphor has important saving elements in the pragmatic politics of abortion, in that the *Dred Scott* decision and the *Roe* decision can be used as parallel cases in which the law (according to abolitionists) is wrong and should be reversed. Slaveholding was considered to be a right of slaveholders, just as abortion is legally and culturally portrayed not as an outrage against the humanity of the unborn but as a technical right of privacy and personal autonomy. The Courts, the Congress, even the President may well be on the side of pro-choice, activists contend, but they all agreed on the inhumanity of slaves at one time, too. They were wrong then, and they are wrong now.

In *Judgment Without Justice: The Dred Scott and Roe Vs. Wade Decisions*, published by Jerry Falwell's Old Time Gospel Hour, the evangelist provides a brief introduction in which he addresses abortion. A six-page "Commentary" follows, which superficially summarizes the two legal cases. In a short comparison of pro-slavery and pro-choice arguments, Dr. Patrick Derr of Clark University identifies fourteen points on which the two positions converge. The points cover the gamut of economic, religious, and cultural arguments. Perhaps the most surprising facet of the book is that 141 of its 166 pages are simply the texts of the two Supreme Court decisions. This could be seen as a key indicator of the importance of the metaphor. Evangelical literature in general does not often delve into the density of language or the technicality of argument found in a Supreme Court decision. This is not a tract, a work of popular nonfiction, or anything similar to the standard literary fare one expects to receive from a television evangelist; it is a resource book for those unfamiliar with the cases.

Like the war metaphor, the slavery metaphor evokes strong references of personal and national guilt. While the activists see themselves as dutiful soldiers when using the metaphors of war, they contend as abolitionists when employing the metaphors of slavery. The abolition movement existed long before the nation as a whole determined that slavery was an issue that deserved the attention of every American. Smaller battles over the rights of slaves were won and lost long before the first shots were fired in the War Between the States. The Underground Railroad is thought in retrospect to be a valiant means of bringing justice in a nation where oppression was officially sanctioned, but at the time it was a dangerous and illegal enterprise. This is the light in which abortion abolitionists see themselves when comparing abortion to slavery.

The use of the slavery metaphor provides a "moral high ground" from which activists can debate. War may, in itself, be seen as a problematic moral dilemma, but to resist an unjust and oppressive society by peaceful means is portrayed, in hindsight, as a heroic effort. Americans may disagree as to whether the nation should have gone to war in any of its prior efforts. They may debate the wisdom of the secession of the Southern states and the use of the military to bring them into line. However, only the most blatantly racist Americans are willing, in the twentieth century, to advocate the enslavement of other Americans or to contend that efforts to free the slaves were anything less than necessary and righteous.

The factual division on the matter prior to the Civil War, however, offers evidence that U.S. citizens and their government are not always capable of discerning right from wrong. This concession is an important component of the abolitionist argument, because its force is largely moral: abortion is wrong. Opponents are often put in the position of being unable to address the question of whether it is "wrong," falling back on the argument that it may or may not be wrong, but it remains a legal right. It is at this moment of semantic vulnerability that the slavery metaphor is generally invoked, with the "holocaust" argument coming soon after, to extend the logic of assuming an equivalence between morality and law.

In addition, the failure of so many Americans to perceive the moral repugnance of slavery remains an open wound in the American psyche. Abortion abolitionists remind us of the insecurity of relying on legal judgments and political policies to bring about a more just society. The slavery metaphor in the abortion argument is accusative of those who either believe the status quo is morally wrong and do nothing to stop it or do not see it as wrong, but cannot articulate how it is not. For there is no denying that multitudes of Americans in the pre-Civil War period held the same positions with regard to slavery; and there is no denying in the twentieth century that those well-meaning Americans were simply wrong. Thus, the metaphor of slavery serves to point back once more to the metaphor of war. Abortion is both an act of war and an act over which the nation is *at* war.

Comparing slavery to abortion is psychologically deft and argumentatively shrewd. It is difficult indeed to deny the similarity of the arguments, and once that accession in the debate is made, the pro-choice argument finds itself on the defensive. It is a shameful truth of U.S. history that slaves were once not considered to be people; such a case cannot credibly be made in the closing days of the twentieth century. With the benefit of hindsight, the pro-choice discussant finds herself forced to admit that the declarations of the Supreme Court and the government do not carry with them a moral high ground. The abolitionist response asks how we can be sure that, a century from now, people won't find abortion every bit as barbaric as we find slavery now. Since there is no way to know such a thing, the argument must inevitably be reduced once more to "personhood," a concept almost universally rejected by abolitionists as unnecessarily abstract. For abolitionists, a "person" is simply a "human being." For pro-choice activists, it is something both more complex and more subjectively identified by the one doing the naming. The question of personhood will be further explored in the next chapter as part of the examination of issues of framing.

Another vital part of the myth structure of the movement abolitionists is the perception they have of the pro-choice movement in general and Planned Parenthood in particular. By combing Margaret Sanger's documents for their now rather distasteful Malthusian thrust and eugenicist enthusiasms, abolitionists have been able to ascribe cynical and even sinister motives to pro-choice forces. One of the most important authors in this genre has been George Grant.

After authoring several books on homelessness and poverty, George Grant set his sights squarely on Planned Parenthood. *Grand Illusions* explores the history of Planned Parenthood, setting out his thesis at the outset: "Just as Planned Parenthood's wealth and prestige has been built on death, defilement, and destruction, its reputation has been built on deception, disinformation, and distortion. It is a reputation built on illusions. Planned Parenthood is not all that it is cracked up to be. In fact, it is not *anything* that it is cracked up to be. It is not even close" (Grant, 1988: 24; emphasis in original). Using both abolitionist and pro-choice sources, Grant sets out to demonstrate that Planned Parenthood's foundations lie not in individual rights but in eugenics, the pet project of its founder, Margaret Sanger. He contends that Planned Parenthood is concerned not with individual family planning, but with preventing certain types of individuals from having families at all.

The interpretations found in *Grand Illusions* have important ramifications for the abolition enterprise. Because Grant's assumptions and conclusions are universally accepted in the activist community, it is important to be aware of them; however, in the interest of brevity, I will merely summarize and note them here. Some of the most significant contentions of the work are as follows.

- Planned Parenthood has systematically buried the facts surrounding its foundation, including the shadowy biography of Margaret Sanger and her racist theories about global population control.

- The physical and psychological complications of legal abortion have been underemphasized, in large part as a result of efforts by Planned Parenthood and other pro-abortion organizations to convince the public of the safety and necessity of abortion.

- Abortion is the only surgical procedure in the United States that is legally protected from any sort of government regulation.

- The sexual education programs advocated by Planned Parenthood are antibiblical, psychologically damaging to children—and they don't reduce teen pregnancy rates.

- Planned Parenthood staffers are trained salespersons for abortion services.

- Planned Parenthood's real interest in establishing school-based clinics is to create further clientele for its birth control and abortion programs.

- U.S. taxpayers unknowingly contribute billions of dollars annually to Planned Parenthood, due to a complicated set of program sharing networks and regulations for the allocation of federal funds.

- Television and print media commentators, for the most part, misrepresent abortion, are hostile to pro-life concerns, and favor pro-abortion interests. (The single exception Grant found is *Village Voice* commentator Nat Hentoff, a pro-life civil libertarian. However, after announcing his pro-life sentiments, Hentoff was removed from the governing board of the American Civil Liberties Union.)

- The mainline Christian denominations bear much of the guilt for the continuing existence of legal abortion in the United States.

- The church in America (by which is meant the "invisible church," the corporate body of believers in Christ, individuals of common spirit who are linked through Jesus, though holding membership in a diversity of denominations) must confront abortion and offer alternatives.

Finally, the abolitionists developed a narrative interpretation of United States history that presupposed abortion to have been a modern deviation from the normal civilizing trend of the nation. Using quotations from the Founding Fathers, Marshall and Manuel, Tim LaHaye, and others presented the case for a "Christian nation." Their interpretation would become the accepted version of American history within the abolitionist movement and for conservative Christians in general, particularly those in Academy schools, or, later, among home-schooling Christians.

The abolitionists' American heritage tale argues that the first settlers sought to come to the New World for religious reasons, dedicating both their efforts and the land they settled to Jesus. Whether Catholic or Protestant, colonists are depicted as being religious in the evangelical sense of the word, and the sources provided support such an interpretation. It is difficult to deny that the original settlers of the New World were vastly more conservatively faithful than their modern progeny. Documents from the Mayflower Compact to the Declaration of Independence, in language and form, undeniably feature a distinctly religious flavor.

LaHaye goes through seven influential Founding Fathers, citing their prayers, their statements about the Bible, and the prevalence of ministers among them. He finds them to be thoroughly Christian men, and he declares, as a chapter heading, "Help! We've Been Robbed!" Generally speaking, the abolitionist archivists seize on any mention of God as evidence for the Christian nature of the cultural heritage. It is not my purpose to evaluate the truth of these claims. It is necessary, however, to realize that the abolitionists believe them to be true and are baffled by the distance the United States appears to have come from its initial destiny as a Christian nation ordained by God to spread the gospel to the entire world.

The Agitators, Prophets, and Reformers

The process of displacement (as the movement progresses, prophets are replaced by agitators, who are, in turn, superseded by reformers with concrete proposals) occurred within the abortion abolition enterprise with astonishing rapidity. The speed with which the abolitionists abandoned the central emphasis of moral reform and embraced the political goals and means of a social movement indicates the power that the abortion issue has to transform and motivate individual activists. Abortion is such an intensely personal and powerfully symbolic issue that one does not so much change one's mind to accept the abolitionist viewpoint as "convert" to the cause. Thus, movement from one mode of active involvement to another can be quite swift, given the right opportunity and circumstances.

Luker's respondents reported their decision to get involved in aboli-

tion activity as one that was very deeply personal and generally motivated by a particular event. For the moral crusaders, the *Roe* decision
helped convert their preexisting abolitionist sentiments into activism. For
many of those who would enter the social movement phase, abolitionism
was part of a general conversion to Christianity; for others, the awareness of movement activity, coupled with a realization that the issue was
part and parcel of their faith, enabled them to jump out of the silent
majority. Throughout the enterprise, however, there does not appear to
be a tendency to wade slowly into the cause. Whether coming out of a
pro-choice worldview, or moving from passive to active abolitionism,
activists in the enterprise seem to share the experience of quick movement into intense commitment and active participation.

When we consider the speed with which abortion becomes a galva-
nizing issue for abolitionists, it is not difficult to understand that abolitionism moved from the churches to the polls virtually overnight (and,
later, from the polls to the streets in a similarly short period of time).
Television evangelists in the role of prophets stirred up the faithful with
sermons and accusations, jeremiads that demand action. Adding to the
voices of the priests of the moral crusade, Protestant clergy and laypeople began to call attention to the evils of American society, encouraging
religious conservatives to search themselves and the culture to divine
where the fault had opened.

Stewart, Smith, and Denton identify three types of movements that are
generated by prophet figures: revivalistic, innovative, and resistance. The
prophets of the abolitionist social movement presented arguments for all
three. According to these authors, revivalistic movements "address a
venerable, idealized past to which society must return" (1989: 22). The
prophets of the abolitionist social movement drew deeply from the heritage tale developed by the moral crusaders, to argue that the United
States had once been a nation that was virtually abortion-free. Innovative
movements "address an intolerable present and prescribe a means to
reach a glorious future" (Stewart et al., 1989: 22). The abolitionists produced copious amounts of literature on the gruesomeness of abortion,
the vast number of procedures performed each day, and the terrible societal consequences that were resulting from legalized abortion. The glorious future to which abolitionists looked forward was the same ideal
past that revivalist literature remembered with fondness. Finally, resistance movements "address a terrible future that is certain to result if
current trends or movements are not stifled" (Stewart et al., 1989: 22).
The abolitionist prophets warned darkly of the loss of humanity that
would necessarily result once America began the slide down the slippery
slope of abortion (infanticide, euthanasia, assisted suicide, and the like).

Although it would seem that these three movement types ought to be
separable, it is in the nature of the abortion issue that they cannot be
made so. To attempt to disentangle the several streams of abortion ad-

vocacy and opposition essentially denies the fundamental complexity of the issue itself. The emotional conflicts that attend an individual's journey to form an abortion position are not simple, and abortion cannot be fairly restricted to any one category of study. Abortion is an issue that demands all three types of movement rhetoric, because it presents complex questions about the past, the present, and the future.

The literature generated during the moral crusade period provided the prophets with a platform from which to launch movement arguments that spoke powerfully to the complexities of abortion. Using the heritage tale that provided a moral high ground for abolitionists, activists were able to evoke powerful nationalistic impulses and arouse uncertainty about the future of the nation so revered in that tale. When the prophets became displaced by the agitators, the thoroughness with which the abortion issue had been examined would provide a rich populist tradition, both written and oral, from which to draw fuel for agitation.

Jerry Falwell began organizing his "I Love America" rallies in 1976, and the keynote issue of every speech on the steps of the state capitols was abortion. The nation was swimming in an ocean of blood of our own creation. Moreover, the outrage of abortion led to a series of related failures of compassion and righteousness. A nation that can kill her children is capable of anything. A nation that can kill her children should not be surprised when those children who do survive are ungovernable. A nation that can kill her children is not "pro-choice"; rather, it "permits" "abortion-on-demand." The message of the rallies was that America and Americans must turn back to their God and their moral roots. Only then could the country be saved from the perceived plethora of economic, social, and cultural evils that had arisen since the 1950s.

Falwell, Robertson, Swaggart, and others in the electronic church disseminated the abolitionist message skillfully, issuing a call to arms to the faithful. The Christian publishing industry spread the gospel of the sanctity of life through its magazines, books, and recordings. The political restiveness of Christians and non-Christians alike provided an open door for abolitionists to enter into a public dialogue on the subject. Moreover, within the ranks of the newly politicized were the newest cultural conservatives on the block—the charismatics.

The charismatics, like the classic Pentecostals, strongly emphasize experiential Christianity. Charismatics and Pentecostals believe in the singular personal revelation of being "born again," and they also believe in and expect manifestations of the miraculous and the prophetic to be part of one's normal Christian life. Unlike classical Pentecostalism, the charismatic renewal that began in 1959 and grew throughout the 1960s and 1970s did not generate new denominations. Instead, charismatic believers remained in the churches in which they found themselves when they became charismatic. As Quebedeaux observes, "new participants in charismatic renewal are urged by the movement's leaders not only to remain in their churches, but also to become *better* church members as a result of their experience" (1976: 144). Thus, during the 1970s a powerful new strain of Christian believer—one who emphasized prophecy, duty, and action—arose within the Protestant church, adding to the ranks of potential social movement participants.

In 1967, beginning at Duquesne University in Pittsburgh, another important theological move took place that would eventually ease the transition of the abolition enterprise from a predominantly Catholic moral crusade to a multidenominational social movement. In that year, a wave of charismatic renewal began in the Catholic Church. The renewal spread quickly across the nation, and by October of 1970, there were charismatic prayer groups among Catholics throughout the country, as well as in Canada, England, New Zealand, Australia, Latin America, and Africa.

By the time the abolitionist enterprise was ready to cross denominational boundaries, linking Catholic, Protestant, Jew, and Mormon, spiritual bonds had been forged between Protestants and Catholics in that part of the movement most likely to consider active political involvement a divine right. That conservative Protestants entered the enterprise in large numbers during this decade is supported by responses to the survey. In our sample, 66.7% of those who became active during this phase of the enterprise describe themselves as "born-again Christians." In addition, 27% describe themselves as "Protestant," while 36.5% self-identify as "nondenominational Protestant." Once the fundamentalists had come to the conclusion that politics could be preached, others in the spiritual fold were waiting for them. Essentially, it was not until the late 1970s that the groups that would make up the abolitionist enterprise in its movement incarnation could have been brought together. The fundamentalists needed allies, the Catholics needed a way to bridge the gap between Catholic and Protestant after long years of hostility, and the charismatics and Pentecostals needed a few years to develop as a faction.

Once the call had been issued, however, the prophets quickly became agitators.

> The prophets turn into, or join, "agitators"—literally ones who stir things up. Together they begin to organize the disparate elements of the movement and to take it beyond the drawing room and the lecture hall. An initial act is often the calling of a convention or conference of like-minded people for the purpose of framing a manifesto, proclamation, or declaration. The manifesto sets forth the movement's ideology, an "elaboration of rationalizations and stereotypes into a consistent pattern." The manifesto serves three important functions: (1) to describe the problem, (2) to identify the devils,

scapegoats, and faulty principles that have caused and maintained the problem, and (3) to prescribe the solution and the
gods, principles, and procedures that will bring it about.
The ideology tends to identify the movement with "the people" and with established norms and values. (Stewart et al.,
1989: 24)

The Washington for Jesus rally with which this chapter began is a
perfect picture of agitation. The problem was described as (1) a spiritual
malaise; caused by (2) secular humanists, abortionists, homosexuals, and
other heathens; which could only be redressed by (3) a return to God
and the Godly principles on which the nation was founded. The very
act of staging the event in the nation's capital symbolically identified the
participants with the national heritage they claimed in their literature,
and, by implication, with the mainstream of America and her established
norms and values.

Almost instantaneously, however, the agitators took on the role of reformers. Once a candidate had been identified as the proper vehicle to
bring about the change they wanted, the movement abolitionists sprang
into action, activating nationwide networks of church and community
groups, lobbying efforts, and sophisticated political and media strategies
aimed at abolishing abortion by electing a president willing to openly
declare his allegiance to God and the right-to-life movement.

The television evangelists pulled out all the stops in 1980, using their
electronic pulpits to disseminate political advice and direct-mail saturation to raise money for various political action committees. "The 700
Club" began producing a segment of the show called "Perspective," in
which genial host Pat Robertson explained the biblical principles that
were to be applied to political leadership. The television evangelists of
the Moral Majority uniformly endorsed Reagan over Carter, and their
efforts did not go unrewarded. At the 1980 Republican National Convention, primarily at the urging of Jerry Falwell and the conservative
evangelical contingent among the delegates, the party platform included,
for the first time, a plank opposing abortion.

Following the convention, more than fifteen thousand evangelical
Christians gathered in Dallas, Texas, for a National Affairs Briefing sponsored by the Religious Roundtable. Candidate Reagan addressed the
group, stating: "I know you can't endorse me. But . . . I want you to
know that I endorse you" (Reagan, cited in Pierard, 1983: 1184). Reagan,
unlike Carter, did not abandon them upon taking office. In 1984, he
wrote two books published by Christian publishing houses, one of which
was specifically on the issue of abortion (*Abortions and the Conscience of
the Nation*), and he declared 1983 the "Year of the Bible" by presidential
proclamation.

Formal Organization

The formal organization of the abolition enterprise began slowly as a network of churches and affiliated right-to-life groups during the 1970s and then virtually exploded in the 1980s with sophisticated marketing techniques, plastic membership cards, dues-gathering organizations, lobbying groups, and strategies designed to get abolitionists into public office from the precinct to the presidency. The electoral successes of the 1980 elections provided a boost to the enterprise, electing unprecedented numbers of explicitly abolitionist candidates to the House and Senate, and placing abolitionists in some statehouses. As "mandate" became the word of the day, abolitionists dared to believe that the government might finally be in God's hands. It seemed that the electoral victories won by the organizational efforts of abolitionists would pay off in the institutionalization of the abolitionist movement.

The Institutional Stage

Despite the unprecedented access granted to evangelicals during the Reagan and Bush administrations, few of the faithful were appointed to high positions. The number of abortions did not appreciably drop. To abolitionist eyes, there appeared to be little progress where it really counted—babies were still being murdered, *Roe* was still in place, and pro-choice forces seemed to control the media, the educational establishment, and other important socialization tools. By the time Pat Robertson decided to become a candidate for the presidency himself, the abolitionist movement was large enough and dedicated enough for him to believe that he had a chance to win. However, when he moved beyond the faithful and tried to gather followers among the highways and hedgerows, he discovered that, for all their technological savvy and depth of commitment, the abolitionist enterprise had not yet won the hearts and minds of the nation at large.

By the 1980s, the Christian Broadcasting Network had been up and running for twenty years, and every year it claimed there were more Christians on the earth because of it. The salvations and the memberships to the Club boasted of at every telethon event built adherents not only to the cross of Christ but also to the politics of Falwell and Robertson. The kingdom-building done by the television evangelists during the 1970s would pay off in voters during the 1980s and 1990s. The loyalty of those who followed Robertson as a broadcaster helped him make history when he ran for office in 1988, and the political remnant of that campaign would later be turned to the distinct advantage of the GOP.

Following his failed candidacy, Robertson tapped newly minted history Ph.D. Ralph Reed to head the Christian Coalition (CC), the goal of which was to train conservative Christians to run for political office—and win. Beginning at the bottom, CC members entered races such as precinct committeeman, convention delegate, city council, and school board. By 1992, 42% of the delegates to the Republican National Convention would be evangelical Christians. The convention made manifest the vast gulf between the two parties on the issue of abortion (though, despite media predictions to the contrary, the Republican convention did not fracture over it; instead, the platform retained the language of the previous platform). Undaunted by the perceived failures of abolitionist efforts in the 1992 elections, the Christian Coalition and other right-to-life groups held their ground until 1994, when, as noted in the introduction, no explicitly abolitionist candidate was defeated. However, it remains to be seen whether the enterprise will be able to retain its legitimacy in the face of recent developments discussed in the final chapters of this book.

While this chapter has looked at the abolitionist enterprise as a social movement using traditional theories of formation and dynamics, other social movement issues remain to be discussed. The next chapter will examine some of the more recent concerns of social movement theorists, including psychological factors and issues of framing. In the process, it will evaluate the degree to which the enterprise could be said to have run its course as a social movement, and the developments of the 1980s that affected its successes and failures.

CHAPTER 5

The Scorn of Men: Actors, Images, and the Public

In thinking about the abortion abolition enterprise as a social movement, a number of issues arise that were not addressed in the previous chapter. This chapter explores some of those aspects of the social movement phase that address internal concerns, rather than exclusively focusing on collective action. In this discussion, we address the concerns of newer forms of social movement research.

THE RATIONAL ACTOR MODEL AND THE "FREE-RIDER" PROBLEM

Mancur Olson maintained that rational actors will not strive to bring about changes that will accrue to them regardless of their participation. For example, it is not in the interest of any single individual to lobby for an across-the-board increase in wages if he perceives that there are other actors sufficient to bring about the change from which he will benefit. Olson referred to this as the paradox of the "free rider." Essentially, there is no rational reason for anyone to push the wagon if he can get a ride on one that is already in motion.

At first glance, this concern seems out of place when speaking of abortion. If abortion were to be abolished, the primary beneficiary would appear to be the unborn child, not the abolitionist. In this case, Olson's paradox would seem insurmountable. The abolitionists do not benefit directly from the change they are seeking, and no individual abolitionist, given the social costs of the activity, would be likely to engage in movement activity when he or she could simply go along for the ride and enjoy an abortion-free society when it arrives. However, the abortion abolitionist is motivated by more than the simple cost-benefit analysis Olson implies.

Luker theorizes that the activists she studied felt a strong pull toward the abolitionist enterprise because they had made a social investment in the gender roles embedded in the abolitionist viewpoint. Most of Luker's activists were housewives, who had forsaken the world of working outside the home in order to live out their beliefs about motherhood and marriage. In Luker's view, abortion, because it theoretically frees women to break out of traditional stereotypes about women's role and women's work, threatened the social basis on which her activists had founded their own lives.

I argue, however, that the threat to her activists was not merely a matter of personal investment. The moral crusaders recognized that legal abortion sent a societal message to all people, including their own children, which they could no longer control. While abortion was both illegal and widely considered to be immoral, abolitionists had no need to worry about the possible consequences of abortion, unless it became a personal concern. As the *Roe* decision approached and the society appeared to be moving closer to a reform position, potential activists could take comfort in the fact that the laws were still on their side. Had the issue been allowed to evolve gradually, in accordance with public sentiment, the blow to abolitionists might not have been felt so keenly. Instead, those who held what seemed a "traditional" position on abortion found themselves suddenly at the mercy of "the extreme and isolating version of individual liberty the Supreme Court endorsed in 1973, at the instance of small elites" (Glendon, 1987: 62). While, as noted in previous chapters, the Catholic activists immediately understood the long-term threat that abortion represented to them and their progeny, it would take others considerably longer to see the same handwriting on the wall.

As the 1980s approached, however—and the American public became increasingly restive about the failures of the 1970s—a general trend toward conservatism emerged. Abortion, being widely associated with a right-of-center worldview, naturally again became part of the national discussion. Cultural conservatives blamed the falling social barometer on the abandonment of God in public and private life—but especially in the public square. And abortion, for those yearning to return to a more comprehensible moral atmosphere, became the exemplar of the consequences of that foolish abandon.

F. LaGard Smith argues that the "culture war" is only tangentially about abortion. Abortion is merely the most obvious sign of the battle over the amorphous and ill-defined "right to choose" (Smith, 1990: 9). According to Smith's argument, there is no such right, and the desire to invent one is what has led the nation to the condition it is in—and that condition is critical, if not terminal. Smith asserts that "in one generation," America has embraced pro-choice thinking to the point that Americans can no longer tell right from wrong. Personal morality, he states, is given no more serious thought than whether one will eat at McDonald's or Burger King before deciding which of the fourteen movies at the cineplex to see on Friday night.

Smith's paradigm is discernible, though not always explicit, in much of the abolitionist literature concerning the social movement phase of the enterprise. Abortion is blamed for or connected with a wide variety of social ills, many of which are not only clearly evident in society, but also universally thought of as detrimental to it. The abolitionists link abortion with two sets of consequences. On one side, they decry a laundry list of genuinely catastrophic social problems, which few are willing to defend. On the other, they present the staggering array of personal freedoms brought about since the 1950s, condemning them in the same breath because they are part of the fruit of the poisoned tree of pro-choice thinking.

For abolitionists, both sets of consequences are equally bad because they reject the divine right of God to have the last word in personal morality. Thus, teen pregnancy and sex education, child molesting and gay rights, divorce and feminism, juvenile crime and day care centers— all fall under the same column in the good/bad dichotomy of abolitionist thinking. In this way, the social agenda of conservatism becomes something more than mere politics; it takes on the cast of divine mandate.

There is little doubt that, by the 1980s, the United States had a number of severe social problems that were getting worse. In 1980, Russell Chandler wrote an article in the *Wall Street Journal* about the impact (or, rather, the nonimpact) that the 50 million American adults claiming to be born-again Christians were having on the nation as a whole. Reporting his reaction to the article, Bill Bright wrote:

> I hung my head in sorrow as I read that article and thought of how relatively little evangelical Christians were doing, relative to their numbers, to be "salt" and "light" in our society (Matt. 5:13, 14). . . .
>
> The number of innocent unborn children murdered under the aegis of the U.S. Supreme Court's *Roe v. Wade* decision has grown not by thousands or tens of thousands but by millions. Pornography's stench rises from magazine and book racks in

virtually every community in the land, even in thousands of grocery and convenience stores with a heavily "family" clientele, and those who produce and market porn are pushing aggressively into the field of television. Child pornography is an increasing problem.

The classrooms of the nation, at all levels, remain a battleground where concerned parents often find themselves struggling against both the growing influence of secular humanism and the subtle inroads of Eastern religious values touted as perfect for a "New Age" when Judeo-Christian values have supposedly lost their validity. And then there is the insidious poison of sheer late twentieth-century materialism, as great a threat in its own way as the uglier and more obvious forms in which 1980s-style evil confronts us.

These problems are part of the reality of life in the United States of America in the 1980s, and I have, of course, hardly scratched the surface. (Bright, 1986: 7–8)

In *Children at Risk*, Christian radio superstar Dr. James Dobson and former Reagan aide Gary Bauer address the special concerns of parents for the safety and adjustment of their children. Dobson tells of befriending a young boy named Josh and watching him play:

Then a certain sadness came over me. I thought about the 25 million little babies who have been killed through abortion since the Supreme Court legalized their slaughter in 1973. Their numbers would amount to ten percent of today's entire population of Americans.

Each of those tiny infants had the potential to be like Josh— incredibly precious, worth more than the combined wealth of the entire world. If they had been permitted to live, six million of them would now be journeying through the teenage years and pressing toward adulthood. Nearly eleven million would be in elementary school, carrying their Crayolas and Mickey Mouse lunch boxes to class each morning.

Then I looked again at Josh. Incredibly, more than a million of those nameless, faceless aborted babies would now be three years old, like my little friend there in the gym. They would be toddling and giggling and hugging the necks of their parents today. I tried to imagine that sea of humanity—a million little bundles of energy—who were savagely dismembered and poisoned before they could even plead for their lives. Something within me screamed, "No, it can't be!" But, alas, the killing continues to this hour.

Not only do I mourn for those millions of babies who were taken from their places of safety, but I also worry about Josh and his contemporaries who *were* permitted to live. Theirs will not be an easy journey, either. The same twisted philosophy that permits us to kill infants with impunity is now prevalent throughout the Western world. (Dobson and Bauer, 1990: 2–3)

Dobson is not speaking of abortion when he refers to that "twisted philosophy." Rather, the real problem is the cultural relativism that animates the abortion debate itself. By linking the notion of autonomy that is the core of the pro-choice argument with (in their view) the logical consequences of relativism, abolitionists of the social movement phase neatly braided the abortion issue into an already existing set of societal concerns. By doing so, the base of the abolition enterprise was expanded, maximizing the constituency for an argument of cultural conservatism whose centerpiece was opposition to abortion.

The free-rider paradox assumes two things: that the reform or benefit in question is perceived as solvable by others; and that the individual potential activist will act only out of self-interest. In the case of the abortion abolition enterprise, the paradox was overcome first by the historical evidence that nonaction had not solved the problem and had only made the situation more intolerable. Essentially, there was no evident agent for change on the horizon which the enterprise could free-ride on. Even in accepting Ronald Reagan as "their" candidate, the abolitionists did not abandon their own efforts to pursue the movement strategy. Although they hoped that the president would prove to be their champion, they did not reduce their attempts to get explicitly abolitionist candidates and officials into other areas of government and life.

Second, the activists who joined the movement came from various streams of new Protestantism. Charismatics, Pentecostals, and those who became "born-again" during the 1960s under the Jesus People movement and the 1970s under the auspices of the electronic church and the megachurches shared with the Catholics a theology that emphasized spiritual self-sacrifice. The experience of being "born-again" is a singularly humbling one, which demands that the believer submit his will completely to the will of God. The teaching and preaching of these churches stress self-sacrifice over self as well as personal and corporate responsibility. Once the fundamentalist, charismatic and Pentecostal streams of Protestantism had grafted their spiritual single-mindedness to a political agenda, and once they had joined their Catholic brethren in vocalizing their lamentations to the nation as a whole, there would be very little in the way of cost that could discourage them from fulfilling what they felt to be their duty as Christians and as citizens.

In his fifth postconversion book, Charles Colson contends that it is not only the right, but the *duty* of the committed Christian to be involved in the political arena:

> First, as citizens of the nation-state, Christians have the same civic duties all citizens have: to serve on juries, to pay taxes, to vote, to support candidates they think are best qualified. They are commanded to pray for and respect governing authorities. . . .
>
> Second, as citizens of the Kingdom of God they are to bring God's standards of righteousness to bear on the kingdoms of this world. . . .
>
> Third, Christians have an obligation to bring transcendent moral values into the public debate. All law implicitly involves morality; the popular idea that "you can't legislate morality" is a myth. Morality is legislated every day from the vantage point of one value system or another. The question is not whether we will legislate morality, but whose morality we will legislate. . . . The real issue for Christians is not whether they should be involved in politics or contend for laws that affect moral behavior. The question is how. (Colson, 1987: 278–279)

By the time the Moral Majority became an organization, its emotional and intellectual foundation had already solidified. The growth of the conservative church had increased the numbers of potential activists, and those potential activists had begun to discover that their spiritual convictions about the sin of abortion could be channeled into pragmatic political goals that might enable them to reestablish the crime of abortion. The founding of the Moral Majority merely gave a name to the activists and a direction to their political agenda. Falwell's leadership mobilized the discontent of countless millions of evangelical conservatives for whom "free-riding" was barely a consideration.

ISSUES OF RESOURCE MOBILIZATION

The resource mobilization school, which uses Olson's rational choice paradigm, focuses on the ways in which grievance groups mobilize constituencies to act against their interests as rational actors. Resource mobilization is essentially an economic explanation of cognitive behavior, relying on cost-benefit analysis to provide predictive direction. While its core assumptions appear to the layperson to be rather uncontroversial, the theorists' interpretations of them are less so. This brief discussion will provide an elementary grounding in resource mobilization theory and explore its potential relation to an understanding of the abortion abolition enterprise.

The Costs of Acting

Mayer Zald (1992) has provided a particularly useful summary of the core assumptions of the resource mobilization paradigm, on which the following discussion draws. Resource mobilization theory maintains that behavior entails costs. While this might seem intuitively obvious, it is an important consideration when exploring social movement mobilization. Previous paradigms argued that internal processes, such as developing the capacity to take the role of the other in social interaction, were the key to understanding behavior. The relationship between the self and the society was seen as a series of exchanged gestures between social actors. Resource mobilization theorists focus on the rational rather than the reflexive; behavior is judged from the outside, without necessary reference to the individual actor's personal situation or psychological composition.

Under traditional movement theories, it was assumed that internal grievances were motivation enough to mobilize individuals to start or join (or remain in) social movements. However, the resource mobilization approach argued that movement activity—especially that which carries with it a high risk of failure, exposure, or danger—requires that the actor weigh the costs of the activity against the potential benefits and make a rational choice to enter into the movement.

In exploring the degree to which abortion abolitionists consider the cost of their involvement, it is necessary to understand the gravity with which activists view the abortion situation itself. As with any position, high costs become more acceptable as high benefits become more evident—and, as in this case, the high cost of *not* acting becomes clear. The predictions in abolitionist literature are even more dire than their vision of present conditions. While society is generally portrayed as less civil, decent, and reverent than it once was, things could certainly be worse. And, argue the abolitionists, they surely will be if abortion and its attendant mentality are not purged from American society.

John Jefferson Davis reports that Eastern European studies have found a disturbing number of complications of all kinds following abortion. Davis concludes: "Thus far, these somber warnings have gone largely unheeded in the United States. Neither the mass media nor the American medical establishment has properly publicized the documented hazards of abortion. As a result, growing numbers of American women, many of them unmarried teenagers, *may soon awaken to the tragic discovery that they have impaired their health and their childbearing capacities in the process*" (Davis, 1984: 34; emphasis added).

Davis also summarizes the theological position of evangelical scholar Harold O. J. Brown on the issue of abortion, after which he asserts that "To accept the utilitarian conception of the value of human life presupposed by abortion on demand would, in Brown's view, amount to accepting a most tragic erosion of the very basis of Western civilization" (p. 19). In discussing the "population problem," Davis writes: "[T]he severity of the population problem and the need for abortion as its solution were overstated in the 1960s. The facts of recent history have shown that population concerns do not support legalized abortion. If anything, concern in the United States should now focus not on a 'population explosion,' but on plummeting fertility rates, *which will produce serious imbalances in the proportion of elderly people in our population*" (p. 74; emphasis added).

In 1979, Francis A. Schaeffer and C. Everett Koop co-wrote *Whatever Happened to the Human Race*, which discusses abortion, infanticide, and euthanasia. Chapter Four, "The Basis for Human Dignity," opens: "So far in this book we have been considering an evil as great as any practiced in human history. Our society has put to death its own offspring, millions upon millions of them. Our society has justified taking their lives, even claiming it a virtue to do so. It has been said this is a new step in our progress toward a liberated humanity" (Koop and Schaeffer, 1983: 78). In the concluding chapter, they issue a call to action, goading the reader to help avoid the dark future that could lie ahead:

> If, in this last part of the twentieth century, the Christian community does not take a prolonged and vocal stand for the dignity of the individual and each person's right to life—for the right of each individual to be treated as created in the image of God, rather than as a collection of molecules with no unique value—we feel that as Christians we have failed the greatest moral test to be put before us in this century. . . . If we do not take a stand here and now, we certainly cannot lay any claim to being the salt of the earth in our generation. We are neither preserving moral values and the dignity of the individual nor showing compassion for our fellow human beings. (Koop and Schaeffer, 1983: 133)

The stakes are high, according to the abolitionists. The battle lines are drawn, and the call to conscience is clear. The future is bleak, unless something is done. Moreover, for abolitionists, there is no shirking the responsibility to live out the courage of their convictions. Koop and Schaeffer continue:

Will future generations look back and remember that—even if the twentieth century *did* end with a great surge of inhumanity—at least there was one group who stood consistently, whatever the price, for the value of the individual, thus passing on some hope to future generations? Or are we Christians going to be merely swept along with the trends—our own moral values becoming increasingly befuddled, our own apathy reflecting the apathy of the world around us, our own inactivity sharing the inertia of the masses around us, our own leadership becoming soft? (Koop and Schaeffer, 1983: 133; emphasis in original)

Interestingly, the literature says little about the benefits of acting. It seems to be assumed that the reader, once faced with the litany of evils claimed to be associated with abortion, will understand the advantages of its demise. The few rewards associated with the activist appear to be of an eternal nature, along the lines of the biblical commendation of Jesus, "Well done, my good and faithful servant." This impression was reinforced for me by the subjects I spoke to during the abolitionist events in Wichita and Buffalo. Curious about the lack of apparent benefits to the activists, I asked directly.

Everyone of whom I asked the question indicated in one fashion or another that ending abortion *was* the reward. While pro-choice activists find abortion to be a social need for many material reasons (maternal health, financial strain, pregnancies resulting from rape or incest, population control, etc.), abolitionists not only reject those reasons, but they claim to have no personal material investment in the triumph of their own cause. There appears to be no correspondence between the cost-benefit expectations of the rational choice theorists and the motivations and actions of abolitionists.

The Minor Players

The resource mobilization school theorizes that social movement resources come from many sources. Aggrieved groups, particularly those having a scarcity of resources but an abundance of grievance, are likely to make contact with other resource-carrying groups. Staggenborg (1989) has examined social movement organization (SMO) interaction within the pro-choice movement and has found that a number of other grievance groups and support structures exist outside the pro-choice constituency and are often tapped for resource support.

When looking at the enterprise as the primary leader of the cultural conservative movement of the 1980s, we can observe a number of related constituencies that did not specifically address abortion, yet were more

than willing to include it in their agenda as part of the umbrella movement. By linking Catholic concerns about cultural and social problems
with conservative Protestant issues of economic stewardship, the enterprise, as a social movement, opened a vast network of groups and institutions that might not agree on everything—but the singular
agreement on the issue of abortion was sufficient to swell other constituencies.

Abortion is an issue about which those who feel anything feel it very
intensely. Few other matters of American culture have the ability—or
even the potential—to draw such a fiercely loyal constituency. While
abortion was a matter of opinion or religious doctrine, as it was treated
during the 1970s, its political impact was largely cosmetic. Once those
who held the opinion or adhered to the doctrine began to see it as a fit
matter for community and national politics, however, it became something of a "cash cow" for the conservative cause.

In his study of congressional lobbying by religious groups, Alan D.
Hertzke depicts the view from the Hill of the abolitionists and their associates:

> From one unsympathetic Republican senatorial office came
> this response: "They play hard ball. Compared to the whole
> universe of lobbies out there, they are tough. . . . They are
> broad-based, organized, and mechanized. The number of peo-
> ple they can generate is excellent." This theme was echoed by
> another senatorial aide: "Ninety percent [of religious mail] is
> from conservative activists. They are very fervent, they are
> adamant, better organized. They don't have what they want."
> . . . Said one director of a mainline Protestant denomination,
> "They're smart. They are employing the same tactics with
> more vigor, more vitality. They have a narrow perspective.
> We have a thousand issues, and they have five and they go
> for it." (Hertzke, 1988: 54)

Yet, in reality, those five issues tended to be tightly linked to abortion and related "traditional family" concerns. If one examines the lobbying groups that carry abolition as one of their leading issues, it is
clear that the organizations take great care to connect each other issue
to it. The Family Research Council (FRC), for example, opposes abortion, pornography, and tax increases. When Marian Wright Edelman
orchestrated the Stand for Children in May of 1996, the FRC held a
press conference the night before, condemning the march and rally as
partisan and more for "big government" than for children. Ken Wein-
stein of the Heritage Foundation analyzed the list of groups supporting

the event, concluding that it represented the "last gasp" of old-guard liberalism.

Driving home the salient point to the FRC constituency, the Council representative noted that two of the groups represented were Planned Parenthood and Zero Population Growth. This rhetorical strategy did precisely what it was designed to do. In one sentence, it reaffirmed the FRC's abolitionist stand, assuring its core constituency of their importance to the cause, and it freed the news conference to attend to the rest of the issues at hand—most notably the FRC's advocacy of a $500-per-child tax credit.

Direction and Stage Management

Resource mobilization theory also claims that change cannot occur unless resources and individuals are effectively organized. Under the auspices of the Moral Majority, Christian Voice, and other such groups, abolitionists were able to place the abortion issue front and center on the agenda of the nation's millions of evangelical voters. Although the Catholic Church has at its disposal a formidable array of resources, during the moral crusade phase of the enterprise it chose, for whatever reason, not to level them directly against abortion. The groups mobilized out of the Moral Majority and the Christian Voice were concerned primarily with lobbying, and they quickly became a force in Washington.

As the social movement grew into its prime, however, it became evident that the abolitionist viewpoint was missing a voice in government itself. Although Ronald Reagan was the most pro-life president in the history of the controversy, the House and the Senate remained pro-choice. The judiciary, despite the president's best efforts to find conservative judges, stubbornly refused every chance to overturn *Roe*. It was clear—at least to Pat Robertson—that abolitionists were not yet skilled enough at the fine art of grass-roots politics. During his failed campaign for the presidency and after, Robertson determined to fix that problem. Although he did not win the Republican nomination he sought in 1988, Robertson did solidify his stature within the party, speaking at the convention in 1988 and again in 1992. Between those speeches, he helped to construct a nationwide, grass-roots network of community activists—the Christian Coalition.

The Christian Coalition is an excellent example of the impact political organization and training can have. As Ralph Reed tells it, Pat Robertson asked him to head a grass-roots organization aimed at continuing the work he began during the 1988 campaign, after a chance meeting at President Bush's inauguration. Somewhat stunned, Reed replied that he was still writing his dissertation in American History at Emory University. Robertson asked him to write up a memo anyway, "about what the group might look like" (Reed, 1994: 1). After Reed drew up a proposed scenario suggesting that, by 1992, "it would be possible to construct an organization with 'membership of 3 million, chapters operating in at least 350 of the nation's 435 congressional districts, a field staff of fifteen full-time recruiters, at least 5,000 graduates from training schools, and an annual budget of $10 million,' " Robertson invited him to a strategy meeting at which he introduced him as the "first staff member of a group that as yet had no name" (Reed, 1994: 2–3).

From an initial contributor base of $3,000, Reed and Robertson began to build an organization. Reed writes that "The Christian Coalition checking account was opened with a $100 personal check, the phones turned on with a credit card, while Pat loaned the funds to get the first fundraising letter in the mail, which went to 134,325 former supporters of his campaign. . . . By November 1989 we had raised $82,000 and brought on 2,000 members of the organization, many of whom pledged to give ten dollars a month. We were off and running" (Reed, 1994: 4).

The Christian Coalition's initial introduction to the broader public came during the Clarence Thomas confirmation hearings, during which the organization mobilized its constituency to lobby Capitol Hill and bought radio and television time in areas whose senators appeared to be undecided. According to Reed, a Thomas witness even contacted the Coalition before approaching the Judiciary Committee. Although Thomas's confirmation cannot be laid entirely at the feet of the Coalition, it clearly represented an early win for the fledgling organization.

Reed continued to build gradually, training evangelicals to take positions within their parties. (The Coalition does not specify party, although in its present condition the Democratic party is generally hostile to its agenda. One notable exception, often mentioned in Coalition statements as evidence of the "closed" nature of the Democratic party on the abortion issue, is Pennsylvania governor Robert Casey.) By 1992, evangelical Christians comprised 42% of the delegation to the Republican National Convention in Houston. It should be no surprise that our survey subjects reported that the Republican convention, more than the Democratic, represented "people like me."

Although President Bush lost the election, the voting patterns were not lost on the Christian Coalition. The following day on "The 700 Club," Robertson noted what Reed would later confirm in his book, *Politically Incorrect*:

> On election day, exit polls confirmed what we expected: the largest turnout of conservative churchgoing voters in history. A total of 24 million self-identified, born-again evangelicals cast ballots in 1992, representing one out of every four ballots cast (compared to 18 percent in 1988). These voters were the

only core constituency that remained loyal to the Republican party, and their concentration in the South made it the only region that George Bush carried. Although Bush lost the White House, pro-family candidates running for state and local offices won across the country. (Reed, 1994: 199)

The small beginnings of the Coalition and its current ability to turn out voters for abolitionist and pro-family candidates demonstrate the savvy that movement abolitionists developed during the 1980s. Whether they can maintain such gains—and retain their current strengths in the House of Representatives—has yet to be seen. It seems clear, however, that the organizational skill developed during the 1980s is unlikely simply to fade away in the future. (How that savvy will be put to use in the future, however, has yet to be seen; Ralph Reed announced his September 1 resignation as head of the Coalition in April of 1997.)

The Audience and the Critics

The resource mobilization paradigm also addresses the impact of changing authority structures. Costs that an individual actor or a group might be willing to endure for sufficient perceived benefits may become unacceptable when they include various kinds of persecution, public ridicule, prosecution, or peril. Similarly, if the costs of a perceived action are somehow lowered, it is possible that actors who might not have participated before will be more easily persuaded to do so.

As the movement picked up steam in the late 1970s and early 1980s, there was little in the way of authoritative opposition. The Congress, though mostly opposed to the reforms sought by abolitionists, would not address the actions of abolitionists until the next decade, when hearings would be held on violence within the abolition movement, and several laws would be passed making abolitionist protest more difficult and more costly. The popular media, however, which James Davison Hunter calls "the single most important instrument in cultural warfare," continued to portray the abolitionists and their cause as irrational, backward, and cruel (1991: 174). Hunter describes something of the view abolitionists have of their portrayal by the news media:

> We begin by considering a brief vignette of an event that occurred at a pro-life march in Washington, D.C. The day was filled with speeches from politicians, religious leaders, pro-life leaders, and other luminaries. Several hundred thousand people listened attentively, cheered, chanted, prayed, and sang songs. Such are the rituals of modern political rallies. At one point during the rally, however, a number of pro-life advo-

cates spontaneously turned toward a television news crew filming the event from atop a nearby platform and began to chant in unison, "Tell the truth! Tell the truth!" What began as a rumble within a few moments had caught on within the crowd. Soon, tens of thousands of people were chanting "Tell the truth! Tell the truth! Tell the truth!" Of all the aspects of the rally covered in the newscast that evening or in the newspapers the following day, this brief and curious event was not among them. (Hunter, 1991: 226)

There is a distinct feeling among abolitionists that the "mainstream media" have a pro-choice bias, a feeling of persecution they share with other conservative activists. Here is a sampling of our activists' responses as to their feelings about the media:

"The media seem to portray only the womens [sic] choice side. They don't say anything about the child's choice." (35-year-old female, nondenominational)

"Media=80% or 90% or more pro-abortion, so they are almost always harmful. They don't understand pro-life so their articles are negatively biased." (37-year-old male, nondenominational)

"[The media are] harmful. I think they sensationalize. They look for ways to make prolifers look odd. Even the terms used are negative—they say 'anti-abortion'." (36-year-old female)

"Much more time and space devoted to pro-abort events and people and picking the most inflammatory and bizarre depictions of pro-life movement to publicize." (60-year-old Catholic female)

"[The media are] harmful—they want us to be seen as have-no-fun-kooky—and trying to put women down." (36-year-old female Republican union member)

"The media are completely bias [sic] against the pro-life cause. I was at the rally in Wash., D.C. in April of 1990 and even though the projected crowds were well above 700,000 people, the media was downplaying it and giving out unbelievably low head counts (CNN said 5,000?). . . . There are two sides to the pro-life movement. The one side is militaristic, loud, boisterous, and dangerous. Unfortunately, this is the only side that is shown by the media which turns many people against us just because of the way we bring our cause to them. The other side is the quiet undercurrent of Christians who are praying and contributing, finding where there is a need (pregnancy centers) and helping there, bringing the cause to a street level, helping the women who need help and giving them love. I feel the general public wants to see the soft side of the pro-life movement." (31-year-old male, New York)

Though not an official part of the authority structure, the media is considered by abolitionists to be an institutional obstruction to their efforts.

The 1980 election results determined the authority structure under which abolitionists would function for the next eight years. In 1977, Congress had passed the Hyde Amendment, which prohibited the use of federal funds for abortion through Medicaid. The Supreme Court upheld the constitutionality of that legislation in 1980 with *Harris v. McRae*. By the time the abolitionists had the Senate and the White House they had so fervently prayed for (or so they at first thought), it appeared likely that the social movement strategy might be the one that abolished abortion once and for all.

As the Reagan years played out, however, it became clear that the street-level aspects of abortion were not changing. A number of versions of human life amendments were introduced in congressional hearings or on the floor during the decade, but none went very far. Although pro-choice groups lamented the perceived encroachment on the right to choose they saw in Supreme Court decisions, abolitionists took no joy in them either, since the Court consistently upheld the essential ruling in *Roe*. Whereas the abolitionists clearly preferred Bush to Dukakis, they became wary of him as his presidency proceeded. Media reports that Mrs. Bush (and Mrs. Reagan) might be somewhat pro-choice infuriated abolitionists, and the failure of the political system to respond to their concerns began to wear on them as well. However, social movement activists continued their loyal work for the Republican party, despite its seeming failure to follow through.

Actors, Large and Small

There is an old theater adage that "there are no small parts, only small actors." For a social movement to be successful, the activists must believe that their participation is of some consequence, that what an individual actor does—whatever he or she does—has meaning to the organization as a whole. Resource mobilization theorists are concerned with movement outcomes and the difficulty of linking activity to outcome. It appears that no clear correspondence exists between quantitative movement activity and successful movement outcome. In exploring the world of the abolitionist, however, it quickly becomes clear that the social movement theorists, with their cost-benefit analysis and their crassly economic view of human nature, are simply not defining success in the terms of the activists themselves.

The scope and range of activities engaged in by abolitionist activists indicate that even the smallest roles in the activist drama are performed by the bulk of the actors. A total of 52.9% of our survey activists have performed menial chores for a meeting, and 50% have made phone calls, both rather high-effort, low-reward activities. Moreover, abolitionist literature is chock-full of cheerful suggestions as to what one can do to help the cause. One popular book, *52 Simple Things You Can Do to Be Pro-Life*, offers information about getting involved that runs the gamut from "pray for a pro-life ministry" to "consider adopting a 'special needs' child" (Pierson, 1991: 11–12, 75–76). This small book is often sent out free by abolitionist ministries along with requested information, but it is also generally available either in stock or on order from Christian bookstores. The authors exhort the reader to make a contribution to the movement, assuring him or her that any amount of effort is worthwhile:

> Because of this vast scope of human need, the pro-life movement can involve us all. Everyone—especially we who are the body of Christ—can be doing something that is pro-life. Children, grandparents, mothers, and fathers; our churches, businesses, youth groups, classrooms, Bible studies, and prayer groups—all can play a simple but *vital* role in this move of God that is sweeping our country.
>
> Perhaps you have wondered, *what can I do in the pro-life movement that will make a difference? What can I do that will have an impact and make a change?* The ideas presented here are simple, but each one is like a cleansing, preserving touch of salt. Jesus doesn't ask that you be a whole box of salt—only a pinch of it (Matthew 5:13). Will you be salt? (Pierson, 1991: 9, emphasis in original)

The concern of social movement theory with the measurement of success seems, in this context, rather obsessively irrelevant. For the participants, any amount of success is considered to be a triumph. After abolitionist rallies, it is common for participants to note that turnout numbers do not matter; what matters is that there are still soldiers willing to carry the banner of the abolitionist cause.[1] While large-scale successes would be preferred, abolitionists generally insist that if even one baby is saved through their efforts, whatever sacrifice and investment they have made will have been justified.

In attempting to measure success or failure, it is important to note the degree to which the abolitionist enterprise has theologized the issue. As previously demonstrated, the political and legal issues of abortion are tied to the religious by the underlying assumptions of the Christian nation narrative. By framing the sociocultural issues in theological terms, the activists expand the potential definitions of success. Theologically, although miracles are instantaneous, the actual transformation of an individual or a nation is plotted on the timetable of God, not man. Thus, as Noah spent 120 years building the Ark, the circumstances around him increasingly argued against the wisdom of his industry; yet, when the rains came, in God's time, his labors were abundantly rewarded. When Moses led the children of Israel out of Egypt, though their ultimate destination was not far off, God set them to wander for forty years in the desert. Similarly, if and when abortion is indeed abolished—whether it takes twenty years or twenty thousand—no doubt the abolitionists of the time (assuming the issue is not stripped of its theological underpinnings) will assign the victory to God first and then to the earliest activist they can find to honor. In matters of faith, patience is indeed a virtue. In the abolitionist enterprise, it often must also serve as its own reward.

Yet there are, indeed, more pragmatic ways of measuring success if the enterprise is assessed as a political movement. In those terms, although the 1980s were fruitful for the abolitionists, they did not exactly reap the harvest one might have expected from the diligence with which the seeds were sown. After much hard work expended on the part of the abolitionists to get President Reagan elected, the overall outcome of his presidential years was somewhat of a disappointment to the faithful. During most of the Reagan presidency, while liberals complained that conservatives had taken over the country, abolitionist leaders became more and more frustrated at the way Reagan seemed to be ignoring the importance of their constituency. It was not until the later years of Reagan's second term that they were able to gain more than just moral support from the man they believed they had put in office.

Contemporary observers in the evangelical camp attribute Reagan's initial coolness to a wise recognition that the constituency of the Reagan mandate was only partially made up of abolitionists and Christian conservatives. Practical politics dictated that Reagan tailor his administration to the broader coalition of conservatives, not merely reward the evangelical contingent for its votes. As Colonel Doner, a founding member of what would be called the New Christian Right, tells it, "while the Christian Right's leadership had an agenda beyond Ronald Reagan, most of the 'grassroots' did not" (Doner, 1988: 31). The evangelical leadership of the New Christian Right managed to attract a great many conservative followers who shared their Reaganism—but not their idealism. The evangelical nature of the leadership was quickly undermined by the compromises and alliances of simple practical politics. Most voters, conservative or not, simply did not think there was any great necessity to bring prayer back to the public schools or to return to the restrictive moralism of the 1950s; they were just tired of Jimmy Carter.

Thus, while expanding the abolitionist agenda to include other issues enabled the enterprise to grow into a social movement, that growth itself undermined the ability of the abolitionists to be successful on their own core issue. The abolitionists, believing the social agenda of Christian conservatism—indeed, of conservatism in general—would be best served by rolling back the tide of abortion, assumed that the pivotal issue *they* carried was embraced by all who allied with them. Evidence seems to indicate, however, particularly after the defeat of George Bush (who, as mentioned earlier, retained *only* the evangelical vote), that voters who joined the abolitionists did not necessarily accept their core premises. Because the abolitionists were so skillful at mobilizing voters, they inferred that all the voters so mobilized were entirely of like mind. Yet, when unreservedly abolitionist candidates—Pat Robertson in 1988, Pat Buchanan in 1992 and 1995, and Alan Keyes in 1995—offered themselves on the altar of presidential politics, the Reagan coalition rejected them, favoring instead more moderate candidates.

When he ran for president, Pat Robertson's explicitly Christian agenda was too extreme for many, including some of the born-again. Eight years of Ronald Reagan had produced (for white evangelicals, at any rate) greater prosperity, a stronger defense, and a general atmosphere of pride and patriotism; the social agenda was something they were learning to handle themselves. While Bush was not Reagan, he had been his second-in-command. The Republicans opted for the safe bet—Reagan's hand-picked successor. Buchanan and Keyes, though ideologically appropriate, simply could not overcome the perception that they could not win.

The abolitionists, however, are far from prepared for the sackcloth and ashes. There is no mourning in the camp for the pragmatic failures of the 1980s. During that period, the abolitionists also picked up numerous new members of Congress and senators. Moreover, their victories in the House and Senate tended to endure, so that, following the 1994 congressional elections, key committee chairs were firmly in the abolitionist camp. Thanks at least in part to the tireless efforts of abolitionists during the social movement period, the House and Senate leadership were solidly anti-abortion and passed the Partial-Birth Abortion Ban Bill, which President Clinton vetoed. Despite losing the bill in practice, abolitionists saw its passage as a victory in spirit, and looked forward to the time when they could expect an abolitionist president to sign similar legislation.

Even by official estimates, attendance at the annual March for Life grew from six thousand in 1974 to more than ten times that in 1989. During the 1980s, abolitionists produced copious amounts of literature, bumper stickers, buttons, t-shirts, and other merchandise that could be purchased through Christian magazines and in Christian bookstores. Despite the scandalous goings-on with Jim and Tammy Faye Bakker at the PTL Club and the near-destruction of Jimmy Swaggart's ministry empire, televangelists continued to build their worldwide ministries, and Dr. James Dobson and Focus on the Family set up permanent shop in Colorado. There Dobson and his organization made quite a national name for themselves not only as abolitionists, but also as a key part of the front-line resistance against the expansion of legal protections for homosexuals. Thus, while some would consider the 1980s rather devoid of clear wins for the abortion abolitionists, the activists themselves point to the growth of their movement and its endurance as signs that, little by little, they are moving closer to eventual victory.

SOCIAL EXPERIENCE

Myra Marx Ferree (1992) objects to the failure of rational choice theory to situate individual actors in their social experience. The requirement of rationality discounts several important motivational aspects of individual decision making which are empirically observable or can be intuitively derived from the reflexive meditations of activists themselves. Specifically, the rational actor model, with its dogmatic interpretation of rationality, its preoccupation with the free-rider problem, and its reductionist view of the individual, limits the degree to which we can understand the behavior of individuals within the social movement. This discussion will address those concerns in the context of the abortion abolition enterprise.

The Universal Actor

The rational actor model presupposes a specific definition of rationality which is explicitly economic, maximizing self-interest and profit. The problem with this model, as Ferree points out, is that it both ignores noninstrumental motivations and simplifies the complex relation between short- and long-term thinking. For abortion abolitionists, the costs of nonaction are sufficient to overwhelm any concern one might have about the costs of engaging in movement action. That is not to say that *all* behaviors are acceptable; however, the personal cost involved to the activist is rarely a matter deemed grave enough to prevent him or her from attempting to act.

Another problem Ferree identifies with the rational choice model is that it begins with a predetermined vision of the "pseudo-universal human actor: a person for whom race, class, gender, and historical circumstances do not determine perceptions in any systematic or socially significant way. In practice, this means that the values and perspectives attributed to everyone are those of white, middle-class men in Western capitalist societies" (1992: 41). Clearly, the activists of the social movement phase fit easily into that vision demographically but cannot fully be seen as represented in the rational choice model. The faith of the abolitionist activist—whether expressed in Catholicism, Protestantism, or another moral grounding—fundamentally violates the precepts of the rational actor model. Where the rational actor is assumed to maximize self-interest, the Christian is expected to minimize it. Where rational actors measure success as profit-making activity, Christians are told to build up their treasures in Heaven, not on earth. Though charged with stewardship, they are also compelled to charity. Thus, the underlying assumption of the rational actor paradigm is at best an uneasy fit for our activists.

Moreover, the various theological and political streams from which the 1980s activists came had given them a good deal of experience in existing outside the dominant paradigm. Although despairing at the culture's distance from their God, they were undisturbed by their own distinctiveness from the culture. They were not going to maximize their acceptability by watering down their message, for to do so would be false to their beliefs, which are far more important to them than their material condition. The conservatizing impulse in the populace that grew during the 1970s enabled the abolitionists to fade into the mainstream politically, without sacrificing any of their spiritual concerns. In fact, many of their spiritual issues struck a sympathetic chord with nonreligious voters casting about for a way to recover the economic and moral conditions perceived to have prevailed in the past.

The importance of social experience must not be underestimated, although rational choice theory certainly makes the attempt. However, while social experience is and should be a significant concern of all social movement theory, I would argue that, in this case, general demographic characteristics are distantly secondary to the singular social experience that motivates the actor to activism. Whether one is Catholic, Protestant, or otherwise religious, nearly all abolitionist activists share a life-changing experience of commitment to God.

It seems clear from both the survey subjects' reports and the literature in general that those who become abolitionist activists also have a watershed experience on the issue of abortion. For some, that experience is closely linked to the conversion experience or the baptism experience. For others, it comes in the form of an emotional response to an intellectual argument. What seems clear, however, is that the impulse to become an abolitionist activist is more in the nature of a conversion than a simple decision.

Luker found that her pro-life activists differed from their opposition in the way in which they became activists. Whereas pro-choicers were persuaded by consciousness-raising efforts, abolitionists first learned about abortion and then sought out organized groups with which to become involved. This self-recruitment seems to continue throughout all phases of the enterprise.

One of the activists I talked to in Buffalo described for me the circumstances under which he became galvanized to the cause. One day after a church service a fellow parishioner approached him with a black garbage bag he had taken from behind the local abortion clinic. Together, they examined the contents. "You can't imagine how sickening it was. How sad. The place just threw out its dead babies. It made me physically ill. Not just the actual physical disgustingness of it—but that was bad, too. But it was the very idea—the fact that someone—that *anyone* could just throw out human babies like that. After that, I couldn't *not* do anything, it struck me so hard."

Even for those who are solidly anti-abortion, the spur to activism—or to a specific form of it—is often a sudden and unexpected encounter, an emotional lightning bolt that haunts the activist until he or she moves to action. In describing the event that led to his founding of Liberty Godparent Homes, Jerry Falwell tells of a reporter's question that he could not forget:

> "What are you doing for women who want to keep their babies but can't find any way to do it?" she asked again. "They have no money for medical treatment let alone to pay for the delivery of their child. They have no way to support themselves, no place to live while they are pregnant. They are young and poor and powerless," she said. "Is it enough to take a stand against abortion," the woman concluded, "when you aren't doing anything to help the pregnant girls who have no other way?"
>
> "No other way," she said, and the words echoed in my mind as the reporters thanked me for the press conference and a policeman led us through the crowd of onlookers that had gathered.
>
> Out of that confrontation a dream was born. I decided that the reporter was right. It wasn't enough to be against abortion. Millions of babies were being killed, and I would go on fighting to save their lives, but what about the other victims of abortion, the mothers of those babies who desperately need help to save their babies? (Falwell, 1986: 11)

Kay James, former director of Public Affairs of the National Right to Life Committee,[2] describes her entry into the movement:

One Wednesday morning at the young mothers' Bible study, one of the women spoke about her involvement with a crisis pregnancy center called Birthright. She let us know that they needed volunteers. She said to me later (as I was one of a few black mothers in the Bible study) that a number of the women who called in were black and that it would be very nice to have some black counselors who could make these young women feel more comfortable. I came home not knowing for certain how Charles felt about abortion because we had never had a conversation about it. I was very proud of myself for volunteering to work at Birthright, and I hoped that he would be proud of me, too. And he was. He felt even more passionately about the need for black mothers like me to volunteer at crisis pregnancy centers than I did.

So with Charles's blessing, I would pack up Chuck a few days a week and take him with me to the Birthright center to answer phones or stuff envelopes in between calls. That was my first exposure to the issue. I was horrified at what I learned and saw. I knew instinctively that killing an unborn baby was wrong, but I had never studied it as an issue. When I began to read the literature and see the pictures and as I became more educated about the issue, I felt very deeply about it. Something akin to righteous indignation stirred within. (James, 1992: 125–126)

After abortionist Carol Everett (now a leading abolitionist speaker) prayed for salvation with her counselor, she returned to the abortion clinic in which she was a partner. She had not thought of her job as a stumbling block to her new faith, but when she reached the clinic:

I noticed something was different. When I left, it had seemed all the women were dancing in through the door singing, "I'm pregnant. Do my abortion." But when I got back, all the women were coming in the front door crying. I had never noticed that before.

I went up to the receptionist and the counselors on duty and asked, "What happened while I was gone?"

"Nothing that I know of." The answer was unanimous.

For some reason I was not comfortable in my normal working environment. (Everett, 1991: 199)

Her discomfort was so severe that Everett walked out of her clinic, after six years in the abortion business and an estimated "35,001 abortions,[3] one mother's death, and multiple botched abortions" (Everett, 1991: 191).

Like other activists, her conversion to the abolitionist cause was dramatic and enduring.

The failure to take into account the social experience of this "second conversion" that abolitionists share is a distinct disadvantage to the social movement model. At least in this case, Ferree's objections are well taken, for the social experience in which the abolitionist is embedded—not by demographics, nor by choice, but by spiritual and cognitive transformation—is a key factor in understanding the motivations of the activist. While those who are active in other causes may have dramatic issue conversions, these activists in particular need to be situated in their motivational milieu—for it is from their faith that their activism springs. Moreover, the activists who were the architects of the social movement phase of the enterprise shared not only the fact of this experience, but much of its doctrinal content as well. The faith they emerged from into activism was (and is) one that demands much of its people and that—after the linkage was made between proclamation and politics—refused to be confined to the walls of the church.

The Rationality of the Actor

Another problem with resource mobilization theory is its insistence on divorcing reason from emotion. The notion of rationality implied does not adequately address the outward behavior or the apparent internal motivation of the abolitionists. Neither the Catholic moral crusaders nor those brought into the social movement by the growth of the enterprise in the 1980s nor the new activists from the Pentecostal, charismatic, and newly evangelical strand of abolitionism can be fully understood through a model that separates the instrumental from the expressive or reason from emotion. Both sets of activists appear, both from the literature and the survey responses, to be among the most fervent of believers. (Of our survey respondents, 69.2% pray several times daily, and the majority attend church once a week or more.) Moreover, those beliefs demand that one's faith permeate every aspect of one's life. Unlike more modernist and mainline denominations, the evangelical denominations that activated during the 1980s consider "biblically based" to be a bare minimum requirement for acceptable life choices.

The charismatic and Pentecostal literature, while not discounting rationality per se, values emotion and experience over analysis and knowledge. The conversion experience does not separate reason and emotion; rather, it illuminates reason with spiritual enlightenment. The Pentecostal glossolalic experience to which these Christians aspire releases the actor to surrender his or her will and reason to the overwhelming power of the Holy Spirit.

Jaggar's notion of the value of emotion is well displayed in the activities of the social movement activists. Their rhetoric and literature go far beyond the usual pragmatic appeals of politics and directly to the emotional core of the audience. In many ways, this emotionalism may be what attracted activists to the Reagan candidacy—even those who were familiar with his record in California. It is instructive to note that, despite his command of the evangelical vote, Bush was unable to win their hearts with the strength that Reagan did. This is the appeal of Jerry Falwell, Pat Robertson, Pat Buchanan, Alan Keyes, and other abolitionist public figures. They speak politics in tongues of fire, and like the multitudes in the second chapter of Acts, the abolitionists hear their own language and respond.

ISSUES OF FRAMING: BRINGING IN AND RETAINING ADHERENTS

In their discussion of cycles of protest, Snow and Benford theorize that the movements that develop earliest in a cycle of protest will supply the primary worldviews that provide the overall interpretive guidelines for subsequent movements within the cycle. In discussing the abortion abolition enterprise, it is important to note the degree to which activists almost universally accept the core beliefs of the "master frame." I have argued, essentially, that the abolitionist frame in the social movement period depicts *Roe* as the push that sent American society hurtling down the mountain of cultural relativism. The early existence of the Catholic moral argument provided the initial master frame for the social movement activists, on which they built an argument that addressed wider societal concerns.

The work of Snow and Benford focuses on what they refer to as collective action frames, which result from purposeful strategies on the part of movement actors to define meaning. They write that "we see movement organizations and actors as actively engaged in the production and maintenance of meaning for constituents, antagonists, and bystanders or observers. . . . We thus view movements as functioning in part as signifying agents that often are deeply embroiled, along with the media, local governments, and the state, in what has been referred to aptly as the 'politics of signification' " (Snow and Benford, 1992: 136).

As Condit has noted, the abolitionists, through their heritage tale and other rhetorical strategies, have sought to frame the abortion issue not only for their own constituency, but for the wider public as well. One of the ways they have attempted to do so is by trying to delegitimize the pro-choice concept of "personhood."

In addressing the notion of personhood, we once again find ourselves forced to choose between the interpretations of the pro-choice movement and those of the abolitionists. The pro-choice frame of the abortion debate values its notion of personhood over the abolitionist notion of life. For its part, the abolitionist frame portrays the pro-choice concept of personhood as illegitimate, deceptive, and indefinable.

Despite the distaste abolitionists harbor for the concept of "personhood," the notion is widely discussed in their literature. Personhood is portrayed as a smokescreen for pro-abortion sentiment, a way of disguising what is really happening in an abortion. Activist writers and speakers link this naming process to an overall strategy to "dehumanize" the unborn. As D. James Kennedy writes:

> Abortionists use the term *fetus*. Why do they use that term? Do you know what a fetus is? Do you know what *fetus* means? *Fetus* is a perfectly good Latin word. It simply means an unborn baby. Martin Luther knew how important it was for the Latin Scriptures to be translated into the vernacular so people would know what is going on. And the abortionists know how important it is to translate the English words into Latin so that young women won't know what is going on.
>
> We are told that the fetus is not a person. As the abortionist backs away semantically, he says, "Well, yes, it may be a living human being, but it does not really have personhood." . . . It reminds me of Nazi Germany where the Nazis maintained that the Jew was not a person. You see, *these people knew that before you can enslave or exterminate human beings, you have to depersonalize them—dehumanize them*. You have to semantically destroy them before you physically destroy them. You have to make them into something less than human persons. That is exactly what they did then, and that is what is being done now. (Kennedy, 1985: 23; emphasis in original)

F. LaGard Smith cautions that use of the word "personhood" to demarcate where life begins and ends draws us into philosophically dangerous waters:

> Bound by the potentially bizarre implications of what we determine "personhood" to be, how then shall we define it? If, as is often proposed, it is the point when the developing fetus or baby is a "self-conscious or rational being," then a human being, philosophically speaking, may not become a person for months, perhaps years, after birth. Wide latitude indeed! In the hands of secularist philosophers and pop psychologists, "personhood" exists only at the mercy of trendy psychobabble. (Smith, 1990: 117)

The discussion of "personhood," which seems so important to those adversaries in the abortion rights movement, is pure nonsense to those on the other side of the issue. As one young interviewee in Wichita said to me, "When a woman is pregnant, what does she give birth to nine months later? Not a fish, not a Mazda Miata—a *person*." For abolitionists, the observation that fetuses, which we may or may not think of as human persons, *become* individuals that we consider *obviously* persons is enough evidence to grant personhood to the fetus itself. No person since Adam and Eve has existed without being a fetus, it is argued.

When a child is born, it is not completely developed (the nervous system is not completely connected, and the skull remains slightly open for a time), yet there are laws to prevent the murder of a child *after* it is born. Abolitionists are genuinely puzzled by what are, in their view, totally arbitrary distinctions made by pro-choice people concerning when life begins. Indeed, for them, the case is a simple one: "What is a fetus? The question is objective, not subjective. To determine the status of a fetus is not a matter of personal arbitrary caprice. The fetus is either alive or not alive. The fetus is either human, or not human. The fetus is either a person, or not a person. What I think the fetus is does not determine which of these it actually is" (Sproul, 1990: 17).

Moreover, for the abolitionist, there is an important conclusion that follows the clear inability to determine precisely when life begins or when "personhood" inheres. Given that the *actual* personhood (or lack thereof) of the fetus is a matter of fact, which we are unable to determine, we must weigh the various potential consequences of our actions regarding the fetus. Their logic argues that it is a better "choice" to incorrectly assign "personhood" to a fetus and refuse to terminate it than to risk erroneously assuming that it is not a person and unwittingly commit murder.

One of the survey respondents puts it this way: "I would also make one thing perfectly loud and clear to Christians who believe in abortion: since only God knows when life starts, is it better to be conservative and believe it starts at conception, or take a risk, be damned to hell for eternity if you are wrong, and say it starts at birth?" The fact that even pro-choice individuals appear unable to settle on a satisfactory definition of "personhood" that would exclude all members of the category of fetuses and include all members of the category of born people argues against the use of "personhood" as a criterion for protection.

In the view of abolitionists, the "personhood" debate has created a number of societal problems in recent years. Indeed, they feel that the arbitrary demarcations implied by "personhood" have fulfilled the dire predictions that have been made by writers and theorists since *Roe* came down. Not long after the decision, Feminists for Life warned:

At least some current precedent seems to exist relative to pressures for legalized euthanasia following hard upon the legitimation of abortion. Even before the U.S. Supreme Court's legalization of abortion on demand, the London, England, *Observer* of January 14, 1973, found that in Britain, "the main basis for opposition" to any form of legalized euthanasia proposal was the so-called "wedge" argument: the danger that legalizing the taking of human life, however desirable in one case or another, would, if raised to a general line of conduct, encourage moves towards all sorts of other forms of euthanasia, for deformed children, the mentally handicapped of all ages, psychotic criminals—thus opening the way to a terrifying degradation of society. (Braun, assumed 1973: 2)

To abolitionist observers, current headlines continuously prove such predictions tragically true, as evidenced by the Baby Doe decision, efforts to declare anencephalic babies dead at birth, the inability of the state of Michigan to convict Dr. Jack Kervorkian of murder, and the passage in the state of Oregon of a ballot measure to permit physician-assisted suicide. Without absolute knowledge of who truly is and is not a "person," abolitionists argue that it is up to the one doing the naming to assign the attribute of personhood in whatever way serves the interests of the controlling agent. Women's rights activists argue that only the woman can act as the controlling agent; abolitionists insist that no one should.

In addition to dismissing "personhood" and other pro-choice concepts, activists have developed their own terminology in an attempt to resist what is viewed as the pro-choice ownership of the terms of public debate. As in any military operation, "code words" are in widespread use within the enterprise that are known to the participants and are rarely used outside of it. Use of such terminology is not only a vehicle through which activists make known their position to the outside world; like the "passwords" of military service, these words and phrases are also convenient ways for abolitionists to identify the speaker's position and to gauge how deeply his or her sentiments run. Because of their perceived status as a persecuted group within American culture, abolitionists tend to be cautious in providing information to "outsiders," although they are generally ready and willing to articulate their position on the issue. To speak the language of the enterprise is a way of proving one's loyalty to the cause and reliability as a repository of information.

Before moving on to examples of such words, one more observation about the language itself is in order. In her exploration of the linguistic choices made in the world of defense intellectuals, Carol Cohn observes that internally generated language tendencies serve to reinforce the values, assumptions, and expectations of the group.

> I found, however, that the better I got at engaging in [the discourse of defense intellectuals], the more impossible it became for me to express my own ideas, my own values. I could adopt the language and gain a wealth of new concepts and reasoning strategies—but at the same time as the language gave me access to things I had been unable to speak about before, it radically excluded others. I could not use the language to express my own concerns because it was physically impossible.
>
> To pick a bald example: the word "peace" is not a part of this discourse. As close as one can come is "strategic stability," a term that refers to a balance of numbers and types of weapons systems—not the political, social, economic, and psychological conditions implied by the word "peace." Not only is there no word signifying peace in this discourse, but the word "peace" itself cannot be used. To speak it is immediately to brand oneself as a soft-headed activist instead of an expert, a professional to be taken seriously. (Cohn, 1987: 708)

Just as in the world of defense intellectuals, there are certain concepts that simply do not exist for abolitionists. For example, the word "choice" is never used in the sense it is used by pro-choice activists. As with "peace" for Cohn's intellectuals, the application of the word "choice" to the concept of "abortion" links the speaker to the opposition, and betrays him or her as ignorant of facts, uncaring of heart, or bereft of true spirituality.

Abolitionist literature dismisses the pro-choice activist question of "Who will choose?" For them, the "who" must be secondary to the "what." "Choice" per se is a meaningless noun, requiring an object to be chosen, a set of options from which to choose. And, for abolitionists, abortion is never a "choice." Even when exercised to save the mother's life, abortion is seen as an absence of choice—an absolutely last resort. In fact, there is no word used in the literature to signify abortion which does not connote a terrible evil or a deep sadness.

To give the reader a sense of the degree to which abolitionists distinguish themselves from their opponents in the language they use, the following is reproduced from a handout I received at a rally. Its primary concern was that pro-choice forces not be permitted to define the terms of the debate, suggesting the following substitutions for "mainstream" or "pro-choice" words and phrases:

Pro-Choice Term	Abolitionist Term
Fetus/zygote/tissue mass	Baby/child/victim/unborn/ pre-born child

Clinic	Abortuary/killing center/mill/ death chamber
Doctor	Murderer/baby-killer/abortionist/ Herod
Pro-choice	Pro-abortion/pro-abort/pro-death/ anti-life
Abortion	Murder/slaughter/holocaust
Abort/terminate	Murder/kill/dismember/execute/ destroy
Harass/intimidate/oppress (women)	Rescue (the unborn)
Clinic defenders/escorts	Deathscorts
Anti-choice	Pro-life/anti-abortion/pro-child/ pro-family
Harassment (of women going to a clinic)	Sidewalk counseling
Terrorists/protesters	Prayer warriors

Another interesting aspect of the framing question is the way in which the abolitionists reinterpret the frames of the pro-choice movement, denying them legitimacy. For example, the pro-choice concern about the prevalence of illegal abortion that harmed women prior to the *Roe* decision is dismissed in abolitionist literature in several ways. First, it is alleged that the numbers used in the argument were entirely fabricated by early abortion reformers, one of which was Dr. Nathanson, who claimed in his autobiography that he and others in NARAL knew they were false, because they invented them:

> How many deaths were we talking about when abortion was illegal? In NARAL, we generally emphasized the drama of the individual case, not the mass statistics, but when we spoke of the latter it was always "5,000 to 10,000 deaths a year." I confess that I knew the figures were totally false, and I suppose the others did too if they stopped to think of it. But in the "morality" of our revolution, it was a useful figure, widely accepted, so why go out of the way to correct it with honest statistics? The overriding concern was to get the laws eliminated, and anything within reason that had to be done was permissible. (Nathanson, 1979: 193)

Second, abolitionists claim that abortion is never "safe" for the child involved and that its "safety" for the mother is wildly overstated. The dangers of abortion are no different now, they argue, than when the practice was illegal. Moreover, they claim that there is no consumer regulation of abortion clinics, one need not be a doctor or even a licensed practitioner to perform an abortion, and its psychological and emotional consequences are never addressed.[4] At this point, it is appropriate to recall Olasky's historical argument as to the criminalization of abortion, noting that it was the butchery of the *legal* practice that he claims caused it to become banished.

Another pro-choice frame reinterpreted by the abolitionists is the notion of "wanted child." In pro-choice rhetoric, every child should be planned and wanted. The abolitionists, however, argue that every child is "wanted" by someone and that no person has the right to declare another "unwanted." Moreover, abolitionists contend that a child need not be planned at its conception to be wanted by the time it is born. In explaining her opposition to "safe sex" education for teenagers, Kay Cole James recalls her personal experience with family planning:

> I had learned to be meticulous about birth control but I couldn't take birth control pills because I became violently ill. When I was on the pill, I felt pregnant all the time, not a good feeling. So we began to use condoms and spermicide as a method of birth control. Like they say, this is not a one-hundred percent effective method of birth control. We know. As soon as Charles suspected the condom had torn, he got down on his knees and prayed, "Lord, please let this not happen. Please, Lord, don't let Kay be pregnant."
>
> While waiting for the results of the pregnancy test, I went shopping with Sharon, the friend who had introduced me to Charles. We were in the grocery store—the produce section to be exact—when it was time to call the doctor's office. "Congratulations, Mrs. James," the voice said, "you're pregnant." As upset as I had been up until that point, as soon as it became clear that I was going to have another child, I felt a certain peace. Charles and I had done everything possible (except abstinence) to prevent a pregnancy and if despite our best efforts I was still pregnant, then I knew that it was God's will for us to have another child. For my husband and me, the result of a condom breaking was my only daughter—Elizabeth—the sunshine of my life. Three years later, the same thing happened, and I became pregnant with my pride and joy, Robbie, our third child. (James, 1992: 120–121)

James's experience makes the abolitionist point that not all unwanted pregnancies remain unwanted.

ISSUES OF FRAMING: CULTURAL CHANGE

One aim of constructing frames is to produce new understandings among a mass public. Snow et al. (1986) identify four types of frame alignment in collective action frames: bridging, amplification, extension, and transformation. Frame bridging is the process by which two previously unrelated frames are cognitively linked in the context of the movement issue. In the abolitionist enterprise, we find that the frames of the right to life (a traditional American value enshrined in the Declaration of Independence) was linked, albeit not always successfully, to the negative frame of taking innocent life, which also draws on deeply held and nationally agreed-upon values. In making this linkage, the movement activists sought to convince the public that the abolitionist position was one that the public latently held, whether or not it was aware of that sentiment. It is this bridging that activists address when they advance the theory that it is the public's ignorance of the reality of abortion that keeps the procedure legal.

Frame amplification is the process by which an interpretive frame is clarified with reference to the issue. During the 1980s, the social movement activists used the bridged frames referred to above and explored their meaning as one of patriotic and historical concern. The right to life was not solely to be confined to the Declaration of Independence, for (as many abolitionists—most recently, the 1996 GOP presidential candidate Alan Keyes—argue) the Declaration is a precursor to the Constitution and therefore should be invested with constitutional weight. The unborn, then, have a constitutional right to life, and to take away that right is a taking of innocent life. The visual material distributed by the groups within the movement and carried by activists amplified the "innocent life" frame by giving it "persons" that could be used as referents and by making fetal development explicit to the outside observer.

Frame extension is the means by which the movement demonstrates that its aims are the same as those of potential allies. During the social movement period, the linking of abortion with the roll call of social ills that beset the society allowed the enterprise to claim that its motivations, ideology, and solutions were those of the general public. The frame that portrayed autonomy as a fundamentally flawed basis for social policy allowed the abolitionists to bring in adherents of other conservative causes, for whom the master frame of abortion as progenitor of social decay simplified their concerns and provided direction for escaping the societal quagmire in which they felt themselves trapped.

Finally, frame transformation is the process of denying old understandings and replacing them with new ones and reinterpreting frames that the activists believe to have been misframed in the first place. This process can be seen in the discussion above, regarding the manner in which abolitionist frames not only opposed pro-choice frames, but actively recast them in a manner that supported the abolitionist position. Another instance of frame transformation might be the attempt to replace the term "fetus" with "unborn" or "pre-born" child, though it is unclear to what extent that transformative attempt has been successful with the general public.

Condit concludes that "In the contemporary abortion controversy the pro-Life images were more powerfully persuasive than the pro-Choice images" (1990: 94). However, it is difficult to find evidence for such persuasive force in the general public, the media, or the academic world. While the images may have been more persuasive, it seems rather clear that the abortion abolition enterprise has not, as yet, been successful in making its collective action frames part of the political culture. The frames most used in the abolitionist argument are also those most often dismissed by analysts of those arguments, be they in print or on the six-o'clock news. For abolitionists, the failure of their frame alignment to affect significant change in the law or the practice of abortion is evidence enough that theirs is still a culturally minority position (though they continue to argue that, properly explained, it is a position that most Americans hold).

The new social movement concern with issues of framing is an important consideration when observing the abortion abolition enterprise during the 1980s. The Reagan and Bush years were perhaps the most active period in recent memory for abortion-oriented legislation and public discussion. Thus, control of the debate during the 1980s became a key target for both abolitionist and pro-choice forces. Particularly following *Webster*, control of the public debate became crucial. However, as we shall see in succeeding chapters, the ability of the abolitionists to control their own frames was severely damaged when destructive forces sympathetic to the movement used them as well.

Craig and O'Brien observe that "[w]hen abortion was elevated to the national policy agenda in 1973, it had to compete with a number of other pressing policy issues, prime among them inflation, unemployment, and energy" (1993: 132). Yet when the abolitionist enterprise emerged as a social movement, all these considerations had resurged, and more strongly than ever before. Why did the issue of abortion capture public attention in 1979, when it could not do so in any significant way in 1973?

If we consider the framing question, we begin to see that the 1973 activists were unable to skillfully articulate the threat of abortion in ways that reached the general public, or even large parts of their most natural constituencies (those who already held a negative opinion of abortion). The strategy of the movement abolitionists in setting abortion-as-social-disaster at the heart of the cultural conservative master frame enabled them to capture the public's attention at a time when significant social and economic concerns were competing with their focus. Rather than play into that competition by insisting that abortion was the *most* significant issue facing the voters and the nation, abolitionists re-framed the political question to make abortion the *first* significant issue, from which all others followed. By doing so, they linked the abortion frame to a series of other conservative frames, which enabled them to build the movement without demanding total agreement on abortion itself. Those who entered the cause further down the line, with the "pro-family" frame or the "moral decay" frame, did not have to accept the master frame, providing they did not explicitly reject it.

Ronald Reagan, as the only candidate these linked movements could depend on even to attempt to implement their agendas, became their choice. His abolitionism was part of his attraction to the voters, but it was not its totality. However, the abolitionist enterprise, by controlling the master frame and dictating the terms of succeeding linked frames, was able to convincingly claim that abortion was a key issue in the election. Despite that success, abolitionists were unable to maintain the linkages between the master frame and succeeding frames when President Bush downplayed their issue and sought to reframe his presidency in other terms (primarily as the winner of the Gulf War).

CONSENSUS AND CONFLICT

McCarthy and Wolfson identify two types of social movements, conflict and consensus:

> *Conflict movements* have long been the focus of most research and, as a consequence, the source of our major theoretical insights about the emergence, mobilization, and change of social movements in modern societies. Conflict movements—such as the labor movement, poor people's movements, the feminist movements, and the civil rights movement—are typically supported by minorities or slim majorities of populations and confront fundamental, organized opposition in attempting to bring about social change. *Consensus movements*, on the other hand, are those organized movements for change that find widespread support for their goals and little or no organized opposition from the population of a geographic community. (McCarthy and Wolfson, 1992: 273–274)

In exploring the abolitionist enterprise during its movement phase, we can observe an interesting phenomenon at work. When the movement phase began and previously dormant cultural conservatives joined the abolitionist sector of the total movement, the manner in which they linked their master frame to other important frames that attracted other conservative voters enabled them to believe that they were acting in consonance with the will of the people as a whole. The acknowledged shift to the right of the electorate that resulted in the elections of Reagan and Bush provided the opportunity for abolitionists to dominate the debate within conservatism because they were prepared to do so. While other issues were important to conservatives, none had a preexisting constituency and a sufficiently persuasive master frame to lead the pack the way the abolitionist cause did.

The coincidental expansion of their core constituency (true abolitionists, for whom abortion was clearly the predominant issue) and their linkage constituencies (other conservatives, for whom abortion was a concern but only one of many) gave abolitionists the impression that theirs was a consensus movement. Because abolitionists expanded their goals to include generalized cultural change, rather than solely abortion abolition, they were able to find widespread support for their goals. The insularity of movement leaders and their overrepresentation of those for whom abortion genuinely *was* the core issue led them to assume that the movement as a whole would be able to draw enough followers to implement a strongly abolitionist agenda.

Other cultural conservatives, though concerned about abortion, did not necessarily view it as the key issue. Even for those who did, those who did not theologize the concept in the manner that the abolitionists did were more willing to be flexible on it. As the social movement phase approached its second decade, it became clear that the activists for whom abortion was not a matter for compromise had significantly misread the attitudes of many of their allies. Although the movement theorists hedge that "consensus movements . . . are probably rare at the national level" (McCarthy and Wolfson, 1992: 275), in this case, the abortion abolition enterprise broadened its base sufficiently as it came out of the moral crusade phase to become a consensus movement. While it is certainly true that there was clear opposition to the movement, that opposition largely failed to identify and confront the abolitionists until the second campaign against Ronald Reagan.

Essentially, the abolitionist enterprise emerged from the moral crusade phase as a social movement tied to a vast array of other consensus issues. Its opposition, the pro-choice movement, was itself tightly tied to a broad-based constituency that failed to precisely articulate the primacy of the abortion issue within either social movement. Reagan and other conservative candidates, while clearly sympathetic to the abolitionist cause, did not centralize abortion except when speaking to like-minded audiences.[5] Instead, they tended to focus on less controversial issues that were more clearly targeted at the national interest, such as the economy and rebuilding a strong national defense. Since the broad range of conservative issues met with their agreement, and since the spokespersons for those issues were clearly allies in the fight against abortion, abolitionists believed themselves in the mainstream.

As the decade wore on, abolitionists found that practical politics obscured their agenda. Moreover, their desire to preserve abortion as the leading issue for conservatives was publicly creating political difficulties for both the party and conservatism as a whole. To put it bluntly, abolitionists began the decade as the leaders of what they thought was a consensus movement and ended it as the puzzled remnant of what now appeared to be a conflict movement.

NOTES

1. Each year, however, there is some controversy about the media reporting of the crowd sizes, which the activists believe are deliberately underreported. After the Million Man March, when Minister Louis Farrakhan announced his outrage at the official Park Police crowd estimates, charging that there was a conspiracy to hide the success of the event, "The 700 Club" host Pat Robertson commented that Christians had been fighting this problem for decades. In fact, most large events in Washington have resulted in some degree of participant dissatisfaction with the official estimates of their turnout.

2. Kay James has also served as associate director of the Office of National Drug Control Policy, assistant secretary for Public Affairs at the U.S. Department of Health and Human Services, executive vice president of One-to-One Partnership, Inc., and a speechwriter for the secretary of Health and Human Affairs.

3. The odd "one" represents Everett's own abortion.

4. As with so many "facts" promulgated on both sides of this issue, these are not entirely false, but they are not precisely correct either. The regulations concerning abortion clinics vary widely by state, and in those states that have regulations, enforcement is unpredictable. Thus, in some states this is an accurate assessment, while in others it is a wild exaggeration.

5. See, for example, Reagan's 1984 speech to the Annual Convention of National Religious Broadcasters, January 30, 1984, in *Public Papers of the Presidents of the United States, 1984*, Book 1 (Washington, D.C.: Government Printing Office, 1986), p. 119.

CHAPTER 6

The Latter Days: The Abortion Abolition Enterprise and Religious Revival

On November 28, 1987, an event took place that served as the opening bell for what would become a national effort to stop abortions through direct, nonviolent action. At 6:00 A.M., the beginnings of what later swelled to a crowd of three hundred people arrived at the Cherry Hill Women's Center in Cherry Hill, New Jersey. The early morning arrivals were able to block access to the building before the staff arrived. As Operation Rescue founder Randall Terry would later write, the facility was "sitting vulnerable and unprotected" when the abortion abolitionists showed up (1988: 24).

It is instructive to examine Terry's perspective on the event, for it provides several important insights into the segment of abortion abolitionists we will here refer to as "revivalist" activists. He writes:

> [We] sealed off access to the building . . . sang, prayed, read psalms, and basically had a church service on the doorstep of hell for nearly eleven hours! No babies died. It was glorious, peaceful, and prayerful.
>
> When the police arrived . . . [t]hey did not have the manpower to deal with us. From six o'clock to ten thirty, they let us sing and pray without making any arrests. . . .

At ten thirty, the police began carrying people away one at a time. Mothers, fathers, grandmothers, grandfathers, and singles were arrested for saving babies from death. All were charged with trespassing and later released.

Our group left Cherry Hill charged up, full of vision, and bubbling over with excitement. We had successfully closed down an abortion center for an entire day. No children were killed there that day. No women were exploited.

The sidewalk counselors told me three mothers changed their minds and ultimately chose life for their babies because we were there. Lives were saved because people willfully placed their bodies between the victims and the murderers. (Terry, 1988: 24–25).

Cherry Hill marked the first large-scale rescue in the abolitionist movement. Previously, individuals had used blockade techniques here and there, but until Randall Terry arrived with his troops, there had been no sizable direct actions by concerted individuals to specifically shut down an abortion-providing facility. That Thanksgiving weekend opened a new chapter of the abortion abolition enterprise, one that would produce both triumph and tragedy—and earn the abolitionists both admiration and contempt among the general public.

The Cherry Hill rescue and Terry's report of it highlight several important factors that help us to understand the revivalist abolitionists and the attraction they represent to other elements of the enterprise. First, the revivalist efforts have perceptible and quickly apparent effects; a clinic is closed, and planned abortions are postponed or canceled altogether. Second, revivalist direct action is done simultaneously with the prayer, intercession, and rosary-counting that the moral crusaders spent a decade doing inside the church; one can save babies physically and not neglect one's duty to their souls. Finally, rescuers demonstrate a serious commitment to the cause in a way that no amount of praying and voting can convey; they go to jail for what they believe.

Although their focus is spiritual, their actions are direct and physical. Whereas the moral crusaders largely stayed inside the church and the social movement activists marched to the courthouse steps, the revivalist abolitionists simply sit, stand, or kneel where abortion takes place, "on the doorstep of hell," as Terry says above. Rather than asking God to intervene and waiting for Him to do so, or asking the state to intervene and trying to obtain the power to make it so, they determined to do the intervening themselves, convinced that God desires it and the unjust laws of the state require it. In the fight against abortion, they use not only the weapon of intercessory prayer, as the moral crusaders did, not only the power of the ballot, as the social movement activists did, but the only weapon they have that cannot be taken from them: their own bodies. Ironically, while pro-choice activists focus their attention on women's (pregnant) bodies, chanting, "my body, my choice," revivalist abolitionists answer with the grim insistence that they will place their own bodies between the abortionist and his target.

Before moving on to a more thorough exploration of the rise of revivalism within the abortion abolition enterprise, the following discussion will dwell on the three factors above, demonstrating how they distinguish the revivalists from those who came before them. This discussion is also aimed at helping those unfamiliar with or hostile to rescue to begin to understand why some activists deem such direct action an acceptable, even compelling, way in which to witness one's abolitionist convictions. The primary exemplars of revivalist abolitionism are found in Operation Rescue, and within the movement we will examine that group most closely. However, it is important to understand that countless numbers of abolitionists who do not rescue not only support the rescue movement but also share the theology propounded by the revivalists within the enterprise.

THE ATTRACTION OF RESCUE

While the moral crusaders were content to wait upon the Lord for a solution that might come sometime in the future, and the social movement activists could expect their results to come within an election cycle or two, the revivalists (while, as we shall see, believing complete abolition to be a long way off) can see the results of their rescues come that very day—either the clinic is closed, or it is not. Either the abortions are canceled, or they are not. They have the satisfaction of seeing their efforts come to fruition with immediacy. Philip Lawler describes a rescue in which he participated:

> Left by herself, the young woman who came to seek an abortion this morning heads back to her own car. But two other young women approach her. One is dressed in black, with a "Pro-Choice" button on her leather jacket. The other wears a bright red sweater and carries a handful of pro-life pamphlets. At first the troubled young woman waves away the pro-life counselor, bursting into tears on the other woman's shoulder. After several minutes, however, she wipes her eyes, and when the pro-life worker returns, she agrees to look at a pamphlet that describes the development of her unborn child. The black-clad woman protests angrily, snatches the pamphlet and shreds it. But the pro-life counselor offers another copy; the young woman takes it. They strike up a conversation, and

soon the . . . two women leave the scene together, headed for breakfast at a local coffee shop. Before the end of the day the pregnant woman will decide to cancel her scheduled abortion, continue her pregnancy, and keep the baby. Operation Rescue has its first "save" of the day. . . .

[By the end of the day], the police claim victory because the clinic doors were opened. The clinic workers claim victory because they won access to their office. The pro-abortion activists outside claim victory because, by the time eighty Rescuers have been carted off to jail, the pro-abortion crowd outnumbers the remaining pro-lifers.

Operation Rescue claims victory because at this one place, on this one day, no unborn babies died. (Lawler, 1992: 12–13)

In some sense, the revivalist abolitionists can see themselves as being far more successful than either of the preceding groups, because their triumphs are tangible—real human children whose mothers can testify of their change of heart, crediting the work of the rescuers. While the prayers of the righteous availeth much, there is nothing that lifts the spirit like a direct save. And while legislation, regulation, and elections can bring with them the heady feeling of a job well done, those feelings rarely last until the next political challenge comes over the horizon. A child that was born instead of aborted, a newly Christian mother—these are treasures that can be counted not just in heaven but on earth as well. A 35-year-old Baptist female survey respondent speaks of her experiences:

My involvement has been local and national as I've helped lead rescues. It would be very hard to recount the myriad of experiences—they have been so constant and numerous.

My experiences have taken me all over the U.S., to jail, to areas that I would usually never go to minister. We have clothed the cold and fed the hungry through this ministry. I have helped deliver babies that were spared death and had the opportunity to bring others to Christ.

I have had my heart broken as this is the darkest of arenas in our land. Child-killing. There is nothing more sinister. I have had occasion to help people flee this industry and that has brought me great joy.

Rescue offers a sense of direct action and the opportunity to see immediate success.

The second attraction of revivalist abolitionism is that it quite satisfactorily re-marries clearly spiritual work with action. While the social movement activists brought their religious beliefs to the public square, they usually left their religious practices at home. Although Washington for Jesus was a prayer rally, the activity that followed its imprecations during the 1980s was more hard-headedly secular in expression. An opening prayer here and there might be observed, and the participants might pray with each other, at breakfasts or in cloakrooms—but the dedicated saying of the rosary, the importuning of God for His intervention, and the self-abasement of groups kneeling in submission to the Lord were absent from the public activities of that period.

With the revivalists, however, there is no divorcing belief and action, no separation between the sacred and the secular. There is no question that the activities of Operation Rescue are thoroughly religious, despite their potential and actual political impact. The men, women, and children who arrive on the abortionist's doorstep in the very early morning and remain until forcibly carried off in handcuffs clearly believe themselves to be obeying a direct command of God—not merely the vague "values" championed by the social movement activists. In so doing, they refuse for a minute to neglect the spiritual acts they believe God has called them to. Indeed, it is the spiritual acts that fuel the activists' stubborn stamina and provide the fire that warms them to the task.

Lawler describes the preparations for a rescue: "Back on Thursday evening we raised the roof of a nearby church with our foot-stomping hymns. Our prayers were loud and fervent that night. They were fervent earlier this morning, too, when we gathered for four-A.M. worship services: Mass for the Catholics, a prayer service for Protestants. The fervor stays with us still, beneath a layer of quiet anticipation" (Lawler, 1992: 9).

Moreover, it is not just in preparation that the rescuers pray, sing hymns, say rosaries, and worship—and it is not only the rescuers who do so. The rescuers meet their adversaries on the pro-choice side of the barricade with rosaries and Bibles in hand, as well as pamphlets. In the "What Can You Expect" chapter of his book on Operation Rescue, Randall Terry states: "Upon arriving . . . rescuers should position themselves around the door. . . . the group will pray, repent, and sing as . . . leaders intermittently address the rescuers who have assembled" (Terry, 1988: 231–232). Those who do not choose to rescue, but stand with those who will, also sing, pray, and count rosaries before, during, and after the rescue.

The site chosen to be the location of a large and protracted national rescue, as the event continues over a period of days or weeks, takes on something of the character of a public shrine, with abolition activists and their supporters gravitating toward it to perform a wide variety of spiritual ablutions. During the Wichita Hope for the Heartland abolitionist event, large groups of men, women, and children camped out on the lawn of abortionist George Tiller day and night, singing, praying, evangelizing, and talking, when not picketing. In researching this book, I was able to observe both the Wichita and the Buffalo campaigns. In Wichita I witnessed several executives of a major northeastern corporation who had traveled on their vacations to be present at the protest site. While carrying signs, they walked in a circle, quietly praying the rosary. They would not be rescuing that day, but they would be present as witnesses against what they believed to be the moral horror of abortion. Several feet away, nearer the front of the building, sat a lone woman, weeping her prayers aloud and occasionally reading from the large black Bible that sat open on her lap.

Before my arrival, someone had placed a sticker bearing the likeness of the Virgin Mary on the gas pipe that activists claimed led to the incinerator Tiller used to burn the bodies of late-term aborted babies. (One of the reasons Tiller's clinic was chosen for the site of a national rescue event was his willingness to perform late third-trimester abortions and his national advertising of that service.) Later that day, a man arrived alone, took a trumpet from its case, stood on the lawn, played "Taps," and departed without a word. One night, around two in the morning, as I sat interviewing a group from the local high school who had come that night (as they did every night—though not always the same young people—for nearly two weeks) to sit and pray and talk about Jesus, a car drove up and a woman leaned out the passenger's side door. One of the activists approached the car, and the woman handed several boxed pizzas out the window to him. "It's all I can do," she said quietly. "God bless you." (It was not until half the pizza had been eaten and a car drove by, out of which flew a half-empty beer bottle that smashed to the sidewalk, that it occurred to anyone present not to accept the food as a gift from God.)

Thus, rescue provides a place for those moral crusaders who are uncomfortable with the worldliness of the political scene, who believe that God's higher law is best served within the community of believers, not through political or regulatory means. In addition, it offers a more active role in the direct cessation of abortion itself for the fervent believer dissatisfied with the apparent failure of the political system to address abortion. Moreover, it offers a camaraderie and a sense of community that is difficult to sustain through the use of short-term political events, such as rallies, or long-term ones, such as elections. By acting on their spiritual impulses, rescuers believe that they fulfill the command that the moral crusaders responded to, and by placing themselves physically in harm's way they believe that they provide a severe rebuke to the nation's conscience that will eventually result in social, political, legal, and cultural reform.

Finally, the attraction of physically obstructing what one believes to be tangibly evil while risking the very real possibility of going to jail cannot be underestimated. As noted in previous chapters, the characterization of abortion and the abortionist in the abolitionist literature is a study in darkness and deception. There is no place in the abolitionist literature for the good doctor seeking to preserve a woman's constitutional right to choose. The abolitionist enterprise not only so paints the abortionist, but it has also plucked a number of traitors from the enemy camp to testify to the truth of the abolitionists' claims about abortion providers.[1] The revivalists believe, even more fervently than others in the enterprise, that they have a moral obligation to stop abortion, even if the law says otherwise. While the moral crusaders were content to pray against the law, and the social movement activists strive to change it, the revivalists eschew man's law to respond to what they believe is a higher law. Randy Alcorn explains:

> In twenty-seven cases, including Proverbs 24:11, *nasal* (the Hebrew word interpreted as "rescue") is used as an imperative or command. It is a plea of desperation to rescue those about to be physically killed (Gen. 32:11; Judg. 10:15; Ps. 59:1–2; 142: 6–7). In one of those cases, God says it is evil not to try to rescue the innocent person (Jer. 21:12).
>
> Most usages of *nasal* refer to a physical situation in which an innocent person is faced with imminent harm, often death. There is frequently a strong sense of desperation and immediacy. While some cases are figurative or "spiritual" rescues (Ps. 34:4; 54:7; 56:13), the type of rescue required depends entirely on the nature of the situation. That is, if people are being "spiritually" oppressed, then they need to be spiritually rescued. But if they are in physical danger, then they need to be physically rescued. (Alcorn, 1990: 155–156)

Paul deParrie describes the decision of an abolitionist activist to begin rescuing:

> But in October of 1984, while she was sidewalk counseling, there was another rescue. She watched as rescuers were manhandled like sides of beef. Carelessly, police bumped and dragged them out. Mimi stood amazed at the rescuers' faces. Joy radiated from them. The rescuers continued to pray and worship in the midst of the adversity.
>
> That day she returned to her home moved in her spirit. Mimi talked it over with her husband, Jim. They prayed about it, and conviction overshadowed Mimi. She was convinced that this was what God wanted her to do. "Jimmy gave me the green light," she says. "I knew that the Lord would speak

through my husband. It was time to put our faith into action
and start 'salting' the area."

So, in late February 1985, she joined in a rescue that closed
down a local clinic. When she was first arrested, many members of her church opposed her activities. "You are going to
ruin your testimony!" some said. As Mimi thought about this,
she realized that most Christians actually ruined their testi-
monies by *not* becoming involved in the battle against shed-
ding innocent blood. (deParrie, 1989: 30–31)

For these activists, the compulsion to act is irresistible, even if it must
mean being arrested and going to jail. Their theology not only justifies
such an eventuality—it very nearly demands it. Great heroes of the Bible
did the same—Daniel, Peter, Paul and Silas—and out of their witness
great miracles were wrought. The revivalists have no doubt that any jail
time they may have to do will be at God's behest and for his purposes.
Randy Alcorn says that being jailed is not the issue. The important question is *why* a person is in jail. Citing the examples of John the Baptist,
Jesus, Paul and Peter, John Bunyan, Dietrich Bonhoeffer, and pastors in
the former Soviet Union and contemporary China and the Middle East,
Alcorn reminds the reader that there are *good* reasons to go to jail. For
the abolitionists, abortion is one of those reasons.

Finally, the revivalists, like Paul and Silas of the New Testament, find
their jail time to be yet another opportunity to reach the lost for Jesus.
While incarcerated, groups of people sing hymns and witness to the
other inmates. There are innumerable stories within the rescue movement of prisoners of all kinds (from the prostitute in Wichita to the pro-
choice activist accidentally jailed overnight in a sweeping arrest during
Spring of Life in Buffalo) won to the faith—and the abolitionist cause—
through the witness of jailed rescuers. Moreover, the activists so jailed
provide a rallying point for those remaining on the outside. In Buffalo,
while rescuers were locked up in the county jail, groups of activists stood
daily outside—and several stories below—the barred windows of the
building, singing hymns and shouting encouragement to their compatriots within. In Buffalo, too, I met with an inmate inside the prison who
told me of praying and counseling with the men he had met there. In
short, rescue, like no other tactic of the abolitionist enterprise yet devised,
offers the activist the opportunity to live his or her faith on a continuous,
daily basis and to prove his or her loyalty to the cause and to God in
an undeniable fashion.

With these factors in mind, we can begin to enter the world of the
revivalist abolitionist. The activists who participate in actions such as the
Cherry Hill blockade, the 1991 Hope for the Heartland and Summer of
Mercy campaigns in Wichita, and the 1992 Spring of Life campaign in

Buffalo are of a different breed from those of the first two phases of the post-*Roe* abolitionists. Not only do they differ from the moral crusaders and the social movement activists in their actions, but close examination reveals that they are also distinct in their motivation, rhetoric, and expectations about their chances for success. The revivalist activists find kindred spirits not only among those for whom abortion is a primary motivating issue, but also within segments of the Christian community itself, for whom abortion is merely one of a great many issues that will be dealt with on a spiritual plane, through massive nationwide revival.

As of this writing, the mainstream of the abortion abolition enterprise appears to continue to be of the social movement variety. However, the revivalists bring a new kind of energy into the mixture, and their strategies, tactics, and philosophical underpinnings are unique. Although they are not yet the leaders, they are clearly the most visible in the 1990s.[2] This chapter explores revivalist abolitionists and their theological allies, paying careful attention to the many ways in which they differ from each of the two previous dominant strains. In the process, we will also examine the claims of revival emanating from conservative evangelicals of various Christian denominations, both nationally and worldwide.

WHAT DO THEY MEAN BY REVIVAL?

The momentous nature of what the revivalists expect God to do should not be underestimated. When evangelical conservatives, charismatics, Pentecostals, and charismatic Catholics speak of revival, they do so with the glee of a child waiting for Christmas Day. Indeed, the analogy is not far off, for both believe they have been promised something unique and wonderful, and both fully expect to receive it in due course. The only difference is that the revivalists have no way of knowing just which day is to be Christmas. The revivalists look to their past Christmases for guidance and find cause for great hope. Not only are there biblical promises to lean on (throughout the Old Testament and the New Testament book of Acts), but there are also moments of national history to be recalled. The first Great Awakening occurred before the founding of the American Republic, leading (in their estimation) to the birth of the nation itself. The Second, they believe, led ultimately to the Civil War and the demise of slavery. Other bursts of revivalist impulse have spurred the Missions movement and the settlement of the American West. The coming one, revivalists of all kinds believe, will be just as crucial to the shape and character of the United States in the next millennium; abortion abolitionists in the revival camp believe that a resurgence of moral commitment will result, if not in an end to abortion, at least in a drastic reduction in its daily toll.

We have previously discussed the history of American religious revival from a historical and sociological perspective. Here, because our concern is what the abolitionists believe rather than what the academics do, we will explore the expectations of religious revival as seen through the eyes of the religious. During the 1980s and what has transpired so far in the 1990s, the Christian publishing world has seen an increase in the amount of attention paid to the notion of revival. The anticipation of such an event has been the subject of books, magazine articles, special segments of religious information programs such as "The 700 Club," and commentary by Christian media personalities such as Richard Roberts, Marilyn Hickey, John Osteen, Paul and Jan Crouch, Dr. James Dobson, and others.

In 1983, after decrying the moral, spiritual, and ethical decline of the United States in previous decades, Winkie Pratney wrote of "The Revival to Come":

> And so here we are, left on the brink of the cliff like Ezekiel, listening for the sound of the wind. Do not think God has done yet all He intends to do. Revival is an act of mercy, and if ever the West needed mercy, she needs it now. God has too much of an investment in the West to easily hand her over to the Destroyer; He has yet a destiny for her to fulfill. "I sought for a man," He speaks again to our times, "to stand in the gap." Can He find him in our generation? (1983: 283–284)

As evidenced above, the revivalists are, if possible, even more wedded to the Christian nation narrative than others within the enterprise. While the social movement activists pointed to the narrative as an explanation of the origins of the American nation and a demonstration of how bad things have become, the revivalists see the nation itself as a special work of God. For them, the United States was not just founded by godly people; its very creation was decreed by God Himself, for His own purposes. Hence, the falling away into secularism decried by the movement activists is not merely a rejection of a good gift of God; it is also a violation of His divine plan, a thwarting of His will. Revivalist literature is insistent that the nation was brought into being for a special purpose. The revival that they anticipate is expected to return the United States to its divinely decreed course.

In 1984, William J. Abraham made the following predictions (though with the usual qualifications one uses to predict uncertainties):

> The present moment is a time for celebration and hope. Just when fundamentalism has emerged again as a noisy option, and just when its neo-evangelical offspring is losing its hold on the expression of the evangelical tradition, those evangel-

icals who know the full riches of their history and the winds of the Spirit should entertain hopes of better things to come. Expressing it most boldly, they should be anticipating a coming great revival.

The signs of that revival are already clear. Among a host of groups within and without the mainline churches, there is an urge for renewal that shows no indications of abating. The charismatic movement, despite its faults, has broken down the old denominational barriers, has fostered dreams of better things to come, has retrieved vital elements of the original gospel message, has vastly extended the ministry of the people of God, and has brought fresh vigor and life to a multitude of defeated Christians. . . . Even in the broader culture it is becoming clear that the secularism of the modern world has not delivered the human goods it so confidently promised. Hence there is a greater readiness to look twice at what a revitalized evangelical faith might offer a dying culture. Evangelicals should seize the hour to think, work, and pray for a major new awakening. (Abraham, 1984: 112–113)

Throughout the 1980s and 1990s, the subject of revival surfaced again and again in the Christian media. International events provided grist for the mill of anticipation, as people of faith saw that same faith expressed through revolutionary means in the Philippines and in the dissolution of the Berlin Wall. As Eastern Europe, East Asia, and even communist China began to report significant increases in religious behavior, hope began to build that perhaps there was a revival coming to the United States as well.

Dr. David Yonggi Cho, pastor of the largest Protestant church in the world,[3] writes, in the foreword to a 1995 book on the revival in Pensacola, Florida:

When I was ministering in Seattle, Washington, in 1991, I became deeply concerned about the spiritual decline in America. I began to pray even more earnestly for revival in these United States. . . . Read this book with prayerful anticipation, and let God's Holy Spirit minister to you. God wants His revival fire to spread to you, to your church and to your city. In God's economy, the best is yet to come. (Cho, in Kilpatrick, 1995: vii)

The disintegration of the social fabric that prompts both the desire and the need for revival within the Christian community is everywhere evident in the abolitionist literature, from 1973 until now. Cho's concern noted above for the "spiritual decline" in America is predicated on the same catalog of social catastrophes lamented by the social movement activists and condemned by the general population during the 1980s. However, the distinctive theology of the revivalists leads them to significantly different beliefs about abortion, politics, and action, as we will see in this chapter. For now, it is enough to note that the event that they anticipate is expected to provoke a moral change in the nation as a whole, significant enough to defeat abortion as it was once defeated by legal force during the 1800s.

For the participants, religious revival represents the most fervent prayer of every believer, for it moves toward the fulfillment of Christ's desire that none should perish. When "the Spirit falls," the theological interpretation is that it is an irresistible blessing from God that generates conversion in a manifestly supernatural way. Martyn Lloyd-Jones speaks of revival as "a sense of the majesty of God, of personal sinfulness, of the wonder of salvation through Jesus Christ and a desire that others might know it. . . . people are aware of the presidency of the Holy Spirit over everything and the life of the whole community" (Lloyd-Jones, 1987: 105). He describes its chief characteristics as affecting people of all classes, types, ages, intellects, and temperaments; having a beginning and an end; and producing abiding results.

The attendant features of revival are difficult to understand, particularly for those who are not of a particularly religious sentiment. For those outside the church—and for those inside that part of the church that rejects the notion of the miraculous—it appears as a chaotic, confusing, and inexplicable manifestation of mass hysteria. In recent years, the churches of New Protestantism claim to have experienced moments of large-scale conversion, physical healings, and prophetic utterances. In addition, new or previously forgotten forms of popular religious expression have appeared, such as being "slain in the spirit" and bursting forth with "holy laughter."[4] Pratney, writing of the First Great Awakening, states:

> Crying out and falling down under the Spirit was common in the Wesley-Whitefield revivals. Lady Huntingdon wrote to Whitefield advising him not to remove those who were under the power of the Spirit as it had been done because it seemed to bring a damper on the meeting. "You are making a mistake. Don't be wiser than God. Let them cry; it will do a great deal more than your preaching." . . . Wesley recorded in his journals of July 7, 1739, "He (Whitefield) had an opportunity of informing himself better; no sooner had he begun . . . to invite all sinners to believe in Christ than four persons sunk down close to him almost in the same moment. One of them lay

without sense or motion. A second trembled exceedingly. The third had strong convulsions all over his body but made no noise unless by groans. The fourth, equally convulsed, called upon God with strong cries and tears. From this time I trust we shall allow God to carry on His own work in the way that pleases Him." (Pratney, 1983: 304)

More recently, Kilpatrick describes events at Brownsville Assembly of God in Pensacola, Florida:

As God's manifest presence comes over these individuals, they respond in a variety of ways. It is similar, I believe, to what happens when a human body might hit an electrically charged power—the body often cannot withstand the brilliant force. So it is when a supernatural God manifests Himself on a natural human being: people are sometimes knocked over limp (or slain in the Spirit), some shake uncontrollably, others are rigid and tense. Sometimes people break out into tears or laughter, they dance or sing, they sit or stand. All are touched in accordance to their individual needs and the personal work of the Holy Spirit in their lives. This has been a beautiful part of this move of God. (Kilpatrick, 1995: 84–85)

In addition, the confessional aspects of revival often lead to public destruction of various aspects of one's old life (pornography, alcohol, drugs, and the like), prolonged prayer services (some that continue long into the night), extended worship, and new commitments to evangelism.

In his book, *Revival*, Lloyd-Jones takes great pains to distinguish revival from evangelistic activity. Here, too, it is crucial to our understanding of the revivalist abolitionists that the differences be clear. The religious activities of the social movement abolitionists are best thought of as evangelistic acts. Although they called for repentance, return, and renewal, they put their active faith in the political system. Evangelistic activity seeks to persuade and emphasizes the role of the believer in acting as the agent of that persuasion. (Although it is the Holy Spirit that draws new converts, it is evangelists who confront them.) Evangelism, even if led by the Spirit, is performed chiefly by human agents.

Revival, according to Lloyd-Jones, cannot be produced, explained, or controlled. It is sudden, miraculous, and powerful. While it is a wholly religious event, it is one that holds certain consequences for the secular world as well. For those who might assume (and, perhaps, hope) it will be confined to the interior of the church, Lloyd-Jones's words must be disheartening:

Now, the question we are concerned with at this point is—
why does God do this from time to time? And the answer is
given us very perfectly in these verses that we are looking at
now. The first reason given in verse 24 [of the fourth chapter
of Joshua] is this—"that [in order that] all people of the earth
might know the hand of the Lord, that it is mighty." This then
is the first reason that is given. God does this thing from time
to time, God sends revival, blessing, upon the Church, in order that he may do something with respect to those who are
outside him. He is doing something that is going to arrest the
attention of all the people of the earth. Here, we must always
realise, is the chief reason for ever considering this matter at
all. (Lloyd-Jones, 1987: 119)

Hence, although the aims of revivalists are purely spiritual, they are
intended to have significant and lasting results on the secular world—
primarily that of reducing its population through conversion. Historically, revivals have had that primary effect, converting whole towns and
villages in both of the Great Awakenings, changing people's attitudes
about politics as well as religion, and bringing new spiritual pressures
to bear in the political arena.

This, then, is what would constitute religious revival in the eyes of
those who anticipate it: a serious recommitment of individuals to the
demands of the Christian religion; a publicly discernible wave of conversions from outside the church; a return by the general population to
moral assumptions and paradigms that have fallen from grace in the
public square; and significant social change led by people of faith, resulting in moral and social restoration. The question then remains, how
do they expect to get there? To answer that question and to understand
why the revivalist view of the political landscape differs from that of the
other two groups, the following discussion will compare the paradigm
of the revivalists with that identified by the social movement activists
and noted previously as a "manifesto" for agitation.

THE REVIVALIST PARADIGM

Although they share a common goal (the abolition of abortion) and
draw adherents from some of the same populations, the social movement
activists and the revivalists differ significantly on each point of the paradigm. While they accept the facts of the case as documented by the
social movement activists, the revivalists have a different theory about
them altogether. That theory is what causes one activist to stand for
election as a judge and another to stand for sentencing before one. Moreover, the tensions that arise when the two theories conflict could cause

significant strain within the abolitionist community. In comparing the two groups, this chapter will, it is hoped, identify some of those points of contention to the benefit of both activists and observers and touch on some of the frictions that arise when two conflicting theories of political action are brought together in pursuit of the same goal.

Identifying the Problem

The social movement activists defined the problem of abortion (and all other social ills that they claimed flowed from it) as the result of a spiritual malaise that had gripped the nation in the years after World War II. An essentially godly nation of good and decent people had slowly slipped away from its moral bearings. The problem may be analogized to the disease model of alcoholism, by which the alcoholic knows that his drinking is a problem but doesn't seem able to stop himself. There is a certain sympathy in that model for the person who has fallen victim to the disease, an understanding that, with the right kind of help, the alcoholic can learn to overcome his predisposition to problem drinking and become the kind of person the counselor knows he really wants to be. In the same way, the social movement activists proceed from the notion that the people of America are essentially in agreement with them and will vote with them when asked to. Ralph Reed writes: "Pro-family candidates win at the ballot box because of their views, not in spite of them. They are elected precisely because of who they are and what they stand for. Despite the efforts of some to marginalize religion in the public square, faith is still an asset to most candidates and is considered an admirable character trait to the average voter" (Reed, 1994: 37, emphasis in original).

The revivalists, however, see things in a somewhat different light. The problem of abortion, for the revivalists, is not a general spiritual malaise but the teeming, seething presence of outright sin. The nation has not merely permitted social evils; it has actively courted them. Unlike the disease model, the revivalists' theory of deviant behavior takes a more condemnatory attitude. The alcoholic is not the victim of a disease; he is a drunkard who chooses to drink. The national decline has not been caused by good people doing nothing while rot crept in; it has been caused by the active choices of individual Americans to embrace false gods, bad options, and selfish desires.

This is a move that must be led by God, because the people will not willingly come on their own. In that sense, it is a theory of coercion through conversion rather than of political persuasion. While the "big tent" of the GOP may be a canopy that covers all manner of beliefs and disagreements, the "big tent" of the revivalists is a covering of conviction. Under the revivalist's tent, sinners are transformed instead of coddled, preached to instead of debated with, and expected to depart with a newfound respect for the sanctity of human life. The revivalists, unlike the social movement activists, do not assume that their attitudes are shared by the majority of Americans; to the contrary, they consider themselves a breed apart, a faithful remnant, in the world without being of it. They, like the social movement activists, decry the pro-choice bias of the media, the entertainment world, and academia, but they do not assume that those agents of socialization have not done their work well. Instead, they expect to find themselves on the wrong side of the law and in opposition to general public opinion. They expect things to get worse before they get better.

One of our survey respondents, a 45-year-old contractor from Oregon, speaks of his feelings about the national situation and the requirement to rescue:

> Beginning in the mid-1980s I participated in pickets and prayer vigils at abortion facilities. In 1988 I saw Jerry Falwell present an "Operation Rescue" video on tv and immediately realized the honesty and power of that tactic. I located a group that was beginning to rescue in the Portland area and immediately began to rescue. The resulting arrests, lawsuits, and judgments while somewhat expected still have "shocked" me into a realization of what my country has become.

The meaning of this reaction should be particularly noted by those who would legislate against such actions. The perception of persecution merely solidifies the participants' certainty that they are in the right.

The revivalists' belief that they are significantly different from the general public, coupled with their unwillingness to accept political compromise, has led the social movement abolitionist leadership to worry about the effect this aspect of the enterprise might have on the whole. Reed writes:

> [When the Christian Coalition began to forge an alliance between economic and social conservatives concerning taxes, t]here were also a few attacks from the right. Martin Mawyer, a former Moral Majority operative, blasted the Christian Coalition for becoming "a slave to public opinion polls" and trying to "Christianize the Republican party by Republicanizing the Christian right." Randall Terry, former head of Operation Rescue and an activist in the U.S. Taxpayer party, claimed we were driving "droves of Christians" into the Republican party's "big tent," a tent that was "happily housing child-killers and sodomites." He accused pro-family leaders

of acquiescing to "the whoremongers of child killing, homosexuality, etc., as long as we get to be near the throne." In a
strange twist on Ken Kesey and his Merry Pranksters, Terry
boarded a bus in the fall of 1994 and headed out on a multicity
tour to oppose our new broader agenda, although his jeremiads read more like the book of Revelation than like *The
Electric Kool-Aid Acid Test*. He vowed that God would "spew
out their lukewarm agenda as a rebuke and a sign." (1996:
171)

This division between pragmatists and idealists tends to complicate relations between the leadership and the rank-and-file within the abolition
movement.

Placing the Blame

The social movement activists identified the agents of moral decay
primarily as their opponents on the issues for which they stood, most
clearly that of abortion. America's abortion rate was the fault of those
who had abortions, those who performed them, and those who supported them. The revivalists, on the other hand, reject the passivity of
that explanation, claiming instead that it is the outright and flagrant sin
of God's own people in acquiescing to the legality of abortion that has
called His wrath down on the nation. Terry writes:

> The first thing we need to do is repent . . . of the selfishness
> . . . escapism . . . self-preservation, the if-it-doesn't-affect-me-
> and-mine attitude that has helped destroy America. We Chris-
> tians must accept the fact that America could never have
> decayed so rapidly and so severely without the participation
> (or cultural lack thereof) of the church. . . .
>
> *We* have been unfaithful to the covenant; *we* have not un-
> ashamedly held up God's word to our nation; *we* have wilted
> under fire from the enemies' camp; *we* have surrendered our
> post as watchmen for a tax-exempt mess of pottage; *we* have
> traded the glory of God's look for the similitude of an ox—
> conservative humanism; *we* have loved our reputation more
> than the cross of Christ; *we* have sinned grievously before
> heaven. (Terry, 1993: 159; emphases in original)

This is pure revival preaching. Revival does not proceed in the absence
of this self-abnegation on the part of the church.

To the church, a revival means humiliation, a bitter knowledge of unworthiness and an open humiliating confession of
sin on the part of her ministers and people. It is not the easy
and glorious thing many think it to be, who imagine it fills
the pews and reinstates the church in power and authority. It
comes to scorch before it heals; it comes to condemn ministers
and people for their neglect of the cross, and to call them to
daily renunciation, to an evangelical poverty and to a deep
and daily consecration. That is why a revival has ever been
unpopular with large numbers within the church. Because it
says nothing to them of power such as they have learned to
love, or of ease, or of success; it accuses them of sin; it tells
them that they are dead; it calls them to awake, to renounce
the world and to follow Christ. (James Burns, quoted in Pratney, 1983: 21)

For the revivalist abolitionists, the first order of business is for Christians to stop pretending that they can do nothing to stop abortion. Only
after God's people—both individually and as a body of believers—have
truly repented of the national sin of abortion will conditions be right to
bring about its abolition. In this, they distinguish themselves from the
social movement activists, who demand repentance of the nation as a
whole—not only of believers. Where the social movement activists find
the cause of abortion and its ancillary societal woes to come from the
black hearts of unregenerate sinners, the revivalists take the search for
blame one step closer to home. While they decry the moral dissolution
identified by the social movement activists, they turn the searing light
of revelation inward and place the blame for abortion squarely on the
church itself. This differential location of blame leads, as might be expected, to two different (though uneasily compatible in a pragmatic
sense) paths to the goal.

Prescribing the Solution

In the social movement manifesto, we noted that the proposed way
out of the societal mess was to effect a national return to biblical morality
and traditional values. Revivalists hope for such an outcome but see it
as a futuristic one. For them, Christians must take certain steps before
such a renewal can be made manifest. Where the social movement activists sought to enter the political realm to put the nation back in order,
they did so, in the eyes of the revivalists, without sufficiently straight-
ening their own house. For revivalists, there is no escape from personal
and corporate responsibility on the part of the church; thus, the first steps
toward an end to abortion and a renewal of piety and morality in Amer-

ica cannot be taken in the world of politics. Instead, the people of God must pray, arm themselves spiritually (as recommended in Ephesians 6: 10–20), and act in the most direct way possible to obey God. While they do not reject political participation (indeed, Terry exhorts Christians to enter all forms of public life), they first insist that activists be spiritually prepared.

Perhaps the most popular Scripture verse among revivalists, both within and without the abolitionist activist community, is 2 Chronicles 7:14. After Solomon has completed the temple, God appears to him and says that, when calamity strikes the nation, "if my people, who are called by my name, will humble themselves and pray and seek my face and turn from their wicked ways, then will I hear from heaven and heal their land." It is used as the starting point for concerts of prayer, national days of prayer, and innumerable sermons (particularly on national holidays). The activists we study in this chapter take this verse at its most literal interpretation, focusing on the order in which its components appear and claiming that the desired "healing" of the "land" must be preceded by a resurgence of commitment within the church. History tells them that revivals lead to social change, but 2 Chronicles tells them that nothing happens until the people of God repent and return.

After one has repented, been spiritually strengthened, and heard from God as to what is to be done, the revivalists waste no time in implementing the command they hear. In *Why Does a Nice Guy Like Me Keep Getting Thrown in Jail?* Terry explains the threefold process that he believes will best lead to the abolition of abortion: repentance, resistance, and reformation. Part of the repentance Terry calls for is merely personal and cultural: "If we have failed to do good, we must repent of our sin of omission and show our repentance by doing the works of God. If we have failed to speak God's Word, we must declare it. If we have failed to stand publicly on the Ten Commandments, we must begin doing so. If we have failed to fight in our communities for what is right . . . we must fight. If we have neglected the children and mothers scheduled to go under the abortionist's knife, we must come to their aid" (Terry, 1993: 161).

Some aspects of the repentance are purely political, premised on the notion that the people of God are uniquely situated, both within and outside of government, to affect the state through both their witness and their actions: "If we have neglected the state, if we have not voted, or not aided in the election of godly people to various offices, it's time to enter the fray. The Bible says, 'When the righteous are in authority, the people rejoice: but when the wicked beareth rule, the people mourn' (Prov. 29:2). We are now in mourning because wicked men rule" (Terry, 1993: 161).

The next step Terry outlines is resistance. He warns that the culture will wage a long and protracted war against the abolitionists and their allies, but calls activists to stand firm. Although the revivalists don't plan to be mere observers while others handle the material world of politics, their theory of social action makes it difficult for them to enter the world of electoral politics. Where social movement activists resisted compromise, the revivalists absolutely reject it, which works against them in the political arena. However, Terry's imprecations do not place much emphasis on running for election. Instead, he recommends defending harassed Christians by calling or writing government officials and picketing their workplaces and neighborhoods. When Christians hear of immoral laws or statutes, "whether it's for special sodomite 'rights,' or to make abortion mill pickets illegal," Terry advises direct action and public pressure and protest. "Utilize the media," he says, "as a means of prophesying to your community" (Terry, 1993: 163).

While all of the above activities are legal, they are hardly the type of thing one would find the movement activists engaged in. Picketing, protesting, pressuring individuals—these are the tactics of direct action, and they are used because the revivalists believe that abortion is a direct threat. The social movement activists seek to work through the system as it exists, reforming it here and there as such change becomes politically possible. They spent long years toiling in the fields of the Republican party (and made attempts in the Democratic party but met with little success) in order to gain the recognition they won for the 1992, 1994, and 1996 election seasons. They hope to abolish abortion sometime in the foreseeable future, but in the meantime they tread the traditional path of grass-roots reform. The revivalists, however, don't actually expect to abolish abortion in the foreseeable future, but they aim to stop what they can in the immediate present.

The conflict between these two paradigms of political and social action has led to some friction within the abolitionist enterprise and has the potential to cause more. At the same time, some aspects of the revivalist worldview hold the promise of bringing the two into a vital alliance capable of mobilizing large numbers in significant political actions.

SPEAKING THE LANGUAGE

Before moving on to an examination of the tensions wrought by the presence of the revivalists in what is striving to remain a social movement, it is important to look once again at the issue of language. While the street-level activists overall employ the particular vocabulary noted in Chapter 5, the revivalists and the social movement activists also use different terms both related and unrelated to abortion. While both prefer, for example, "pro-life" to "anti-choice," social movement activists will rarely use terms like "abortuary" or "killing center." Social movement activists speak of "moral" problems and solutions, and revivalists are more likely to employ less politically astute terms like "sin" and "evil."

In addition, the revivalists, not surprisingly, tend to sound like preachers, while the social movement activists, even when employing the presentational style of preachers, still talk a lot like politicians. Note the measured care with which Ralph Reed chooses his words in this paragraph about abortion:

> The reason for religious conservative opposition to abortion is our belief in the sanctity of the individual human being. We believe that every person is created by God with certain inalienable rights, among which is the right to life, and that government is established to protect those rights. In this sense, the abortion issue represents the proper mixture of religion and politics and is consistent with the values of democracy. Both democracy and Christianity are based upon the sanctity of each person. From the Declaration of Independence to the Emancipation Proclamation and the Civil Rights Act of 1964, we have declared those rights and protected them with the rule of law. Protecting innocent life is in the finest tradition of that social justice movement. Straying from the tradition threatens liberalism's intellectual and moral viability as a political philosophy. (Reed, 1996: 81)

Now compare this statement by Randall Terry concerning the same subject:

> One phrase ... has become very real to me: "We pledge our lives, our fortunes, and our sacred honors." If we are going to end this war against children, we must be willing to surrender our lives, our selfish ways, our finances, and our reputations.
>
> Will America be spared the full fury of God's wrath over this bloodshed? Will we be chastened and restored? Or will we be destroyed? The answer to a great degree lies with you and me. Our future depends on our willingness to make the sacrifices necessary to make the rescue movement successful. (Terry, 1988: 26–27)

Essentially, the two statements above represent a sort of answering echo to one another. Both reference the Declaration, but one cites a familiar refrain that is thoroughly acceptable to adherents of what Robert Bellah has identified as America's "civil religion" (Bellah, 1974, 1975,

1978). The other focuses on the less well-known peroration that helps to give the document its revolutionary flavor. Reed bases his argument in the Founding Fathers' rationalization for forming a new nation, while Terry invokes their emotional commitment to the meaning of their actions. Reed speaks of a "proper mixture of religion and politics," while Terry leaves the definite impression that "mixture" is not precisely what he has in mind. Finally, Reed warns of the "threat" to the viability of liberalism, while Terry makes clear exactly what that threat could consist of. Reed's political "threat" is Terry's destruction from "God's wrath."

There are, as well, many purely theological terms sprinkled throughout the revivalist abolition literature that rarely, if ever, appear in the rhetoric of the social movement activists. The revivalists speak the language of Christian conservatism in a way that permits them greater access to those believers than the social movement activists can initially obtain. A great deal of time and energy is expended in the social movement camp to inform and educate Christians about what is going on in the world around them. Some of this activity appears to be aimed at rectifying what is, in some instances, a rather severe lack of concern for worldly issues on the part of the faithful. Particularly in those conservative traditions that have had difficulty in the past with political activity, there is a decided and studied resistance to associating one's self too closely with those agents of socialization that most Americans now rely on for their information about the world of politics. More than most, revivalists distrust the information in mainstream newspapers, on television, and in non-Christian magazines.

In our sample of activists, weekly television watching is low, between six and seven hours, on average. Ninety percent report that they watch less than sixteen hours of television per week, just over two hours per day. Radio listening is greater, but not significantly so, if one considers that Rush Limbaugh alone occupies fifteen hours of radio time every week. On the average, the abolitionist activist in our survey reports listening to between nine and ten hours a week of radio programming, with 44.2% favoring talk radio and an astonishing 49% listening to Christian stations. (Among those who entered the enterprise during the 1990s, the average drops to five hours per week, with 37.5% listening to talk and 31.3% to Christian radio.)

It should be noted that, even on Christian stations that devote little time to talk, most broadcast five-minute programs by politically active Christians, such as Randall Terry, James Dobson, and Charles Colson. Some also carry longer programs in the same vein. Nonetheless, only 49% of activists read a newspaper every day, and 71.2% read a local paper, instead of a national one. Thus, the more political of the social movement activists find themselves at a disadvantage talking to many activists about politics without establishing some kind of background. Make no mistake: the revivalists are not ignorant. They simply prefer to use their intellect, their resources, and their time in what they consider to be more "edifying" pursuits.

When the revivalists approach Christian conservatives of a New Protestant bent, they use the language of those denominations and the assumptions of those theologies. One is unlikely to find the word "tribulation" in social movement literature, unless it is used as a figurative term for "trouble." However, the revivalists use the term in its literal, biblical sense, to mean a time of great distress predicted to occur shortly before, during, or after (depending on one's eschatology) the bodily return of Christ to the earth. Revivalists talk about "praying down strongholds," fighting "spiritual warfare," battling with "demonic oppression," and "atoning for bloodguilt." None of these terms makes them welcome in the political arena, and the social movement activists—though many of them understand them as valid in the same sense as the revivalists do—strenuously avoid bringing them into the public debate. Yet this is the language most easily spoken by Pentecostals, charismatics (Catholic and non-Catholic), and other strongly conservative segments of the Christian population, and they respond to it. Revival-oriented Christians are willing to engage in political action of the social movement style, but it is the revivalist abolitionists who are most capable of telling them why they should.

One problem with the revivalist segment of the enterprise, however, has caused a great deal of difficulty within it. Although Randall Terry is the recognized father and leader of the movement, and although Operation Rescue itself strives to maintain discipline within its ranks, the decentralized nature of the theological theories underlying rescue have led to individual actions condemned by all sectors of the legitimate abolitionist enterprise. Prior to all of its coordinated actions, Operation Rescue requires that potential rescue participants sign a pledge which (with varying wording from place to place) essentially obligates the signee: to remain peaceful; to follow the orders of the on-site leadership; to be polite, passive, and limp when arrested; and to refrain from making any statements, leaving that duty to those appointed by the leadership for that function. However, neither Operation Rescue nor any recognized organization can control all individuals who find abortion an issue of compelling and immediate urgency.

In *The Democratization of American Christianity*, Nathan Hatch explores the decentralized nature of American Protestantism. He observes the populist nature of the awakenings and of the evangelizing of the American frontier. The historical triumph of a religious sentiment that distrusted elites echoes in the enthusiastic choruses, uncredentialed ministries, and individualistic (as opposed to ecclesiastical) interpretations of Scripture that are the hallmarks of the revivalist churches. Hatch writes:

> In the aftermath of the Second Great Awakening, many Americans divorced religious leadership from social position, completing a separation that had been building for a century. They ascribed authority to preachers ill-qualified to stand for public office. In a new nation, premised on equality and struggling to free itself from the past, people were ready to see the hand of God upon a Lorenzo Dow, a Joseph Smith, or a William Miller. They could rejoice that, at last, the weak were confounding the mighty, the last becoming first. (Hatch, 1989: 226)

Within the abortion abolition enterprise, this rooted democratic impulse within the revivalist tradition brings with it certain tensions and drawbacks for political efficacy. The social movement activists recognize and accept the need for order and discipline, not only on the front lines as prescribed by Operation Rescue, but also within the larger enterprise. The revivalists, however, believing themselves to be purely responding to a higher and more important master, will not remain long under the yoke of any governmental authority, even if the reins of the beast are closely held by allies like Ralph Reed, Gary Bauer, or Pat Buchanan. Even if the social movement activists could obtain control over both houses of Congress, the White House, and all other agents of socialization, the revivalists would continue their work until abortion was ended, in law and in fact. This stubborn refusal to behave pragmatically has its uses when the law is against the enterprise as a whole, but when slow gains are being made, it tends to restrain the ability of those trying to make them to sustain the message that they are genuinely interested in dealing fairly with their opponents.

Moreover, there are more troubling aspects to the unrestrained impulse that arises from a decentralized and democratic view of Scriptural interpretation. Although most revivalists, both abolitionist and nonabolitionist, voluntarily submit to the authority of a church, pastor, denomination, or fellowship group of some kind, the individualistic impetus of such a theology, if carried to an extreme, can lead to rogue actions by individuals who use their religious sentiments and their opposition to abortion as a justification for immoral and illegal acts. Without question, this has happened in recent years, for violence aimed at abortion facilities has increased, leading to congressional hearings and to the passage of the Freedom of Access to Clinic Entrances Act. Feminist groups point to the rhetoric of the abolitionist movement as a proximate cause for such violence, but in so doing they both simplify the issue and undermine the potential for movement activists to negotiate some kind of settlement of the debate.

Although groups like NARAL and NOW, and organizations like Planned Parenthood would prefer that abortion be publicly accepted as an unfettered civil right, public opinion polls strongly indicate that the American populace is unlikely to embrace such a theory. If there is to be any compromise on the abortion issue, both sides will have to be willing to move to a consensus position compatible with the desires of the American people.

If the argument over abortion in the political arena is to be in any way brought under control, abolitionist sentiments will have to be addressed in forming a compromise, and the social movement activists are the most likely people within the enterprise to be willing or able to enter into such a discussion. For pro-choice activists to tar all abolitionists with the brush of extremism and terrorism is pragmatically unwise. In the next chapter, we will take up the issues that have generated the actions and events that lead to the image of abolitionists as terrorists, examining instances of explosive violence that have surfaced within the enterprise. Following that, we will assess the role the revivalists have played and what impact they might have in the future.

NOTES

1. As noted in other chapters, among such former pro-choice activists and abortionists are Dr. Bernard Nathanson and Carol Everett. Several others, including former employees of both Dr. George Tiller and Dr. David Gunn, are featured on a video produced by Joe Scheidler's Pro-Life Action League, "Abortion: The Inside Story." The video is a record of one of Scheidler's annual Chicago meetings for former abortion providers, and deals primarily with the abortionist's attitude toward the patient, the safety of clinics, falsification of medical records, and the nature of abortion as a profit-making enterprise.

2. In fact, most of the academic and media focus in this decade has been on these activists. As an example, in her book, *Crusaders; Voices from the Abortion Front*, Marian Faux appears to intend an even-handed treatment of both sides. Yet, the two abolitionists she profiles are Randall Terry and a lower-level operative of Operation Rescue. The other four activists profiled are all pro-choice, though two are dissatisfied with their movement's direction.

3. Yoido Full Gospel Church in Seoul, South Korea, which has over 700,000 members.

4. When a Christian is "slain in the spirit," the theological explanation is that the person has been so overwhelmed by the infilling of the Holy Spirit within him or her that he or she has simply keeled over in submission. Outwardly, people appear to be fainting. "Holy laughter" is a relatively new phenomenon,

associated with a Canadian regional revival known as "the Toronto outpouring." Recently, Richard Roberts, son of evangelist Oral Roberts, publicly affirmed his own such experience on "The 700 Club." It appears to be an uncontrolled hilarity attributed by the person involved to the joy of the Lord and the power of the Holy Spirit.

CHAPTER 7

Tribulation and the New World Coming: Violence, Checks and Balances, and the Big Picture

In the previous chapter, we examined the revivalist segment of the abolitionist enterprise. In this chapter, we discuss the rise of violence in the enterprise and its association with that subgroup and others. However, I will argue here that the perpetrators of violence differ markedly from other abolitionists in important ways. Upon close examination, it becomes clear that the bombers, arsonists, and terrorists who have spotted the abolitionist enterprise display certain character traits that distinguish them from legitimate activists of all phases of the enterprise.

In this chapter, we look at the violence that has surfaced from time to time in the abolitionist enterprise, denying it, in the minds of some, the right to call itself "pro-life." Here we will poke about in the ashes, seeking an explanation. We will not be combing the charred remains of the clinics themselves, like detectives on a hunt for the perpetrators. Instead, we will take it for granted that the actions we examine here—whether or not proven and directly so—can be attributed to individuals whose desire is to abolish abortion. Although in a few cases initial reports hinted that there might be a less political explanation—accident, insurance arson, the madness of a disgruntled employee or relative of same— we shall assume, for the sake of argument, that the destruction of property and life belonging to or associated with the pro-abortion or pro-choice movement stems at least in part from the failure of abortion as an act to receive full acceptance in the public mind. The very existence of an abolitionist sentiment, therefore, makes such tragedies possible. This seems a reasonable concession, even, it is hoped, to the abolitionist. Were abortion as widely accepted a value as the pro-choice community would hope, it is doubtful that such violence would have taken place.

At the same time, however, we note that the presence of violence in association with political issues is neither unique to this enterprise nor universally associated with negative values. Many historical movements upon which we look back today with pride and fondness proceeded in the midst of occasional or even routine acts of violent rebellion. While the United States has a historical record of individual and corporate resistance characterized by nonviolence—the legal reform and passive protest of the women's and civil rights movements—it also has a parallel vein of bloody rebellion that has coursed through the body politic since its very beginnings in violent, matricidal revolution against its mother country.

The revolution of thought and force that brought the nation into being changed the course of history on the continent—and, eventually, in the world. We celebrate that triumph over the tyranny of an external ruler each July 4th. Yet it cannot be overlooked that the militaristic nature of that birth left a psychological justification for violence that the United States has never fully repudiated. Like grim reminders of a suicide attempt, the scars of the Civil War still criss-cross the landscape of national politics, vivid echoes of that bitter and fratricidal conflict. Our histories are written with the blood of patriots and tyrants, and the warlike tendencies that were bred into America in its cradle have never yet been outlived. In this, one of the most violent nations on earth, where guns are more populous than people, and in the late twentieth century, when even children seem capable of cold-blooded murder, it is not surprising that one of the most heated political and social debates that has ever arisen should spark violence, in one form or another. Yet that warlike tendency, historically fed to every schoolchild, can neither justify nor explain the violence itself.

The enabling culture of violence within which the abortion debate stands seems, at this point, at a loss to rein in its consequences. The abolitionist enterprise, surrounded as it is by carnage and mayhem, and steeped in a daily recitation of bloodshed it attributes to the opposition, has bred its own vigilantes. Any collective entity that finds a violent faction within its midst must eventually face and deal with it, if reform is to be successful. The Martin Luther Kings must find a way to credibly reject the violence of the Malcolm Xs. The public cannot be won to a righteous cause by illegitimate action. In this chapter, we search the wreckage to see the damage that violent individuals and groups have wrought on the credibility of the abolitionist enterprise. Then, we will explore the question of what manner of creature might arise from these ashes.

VIOLENCE AND THE FUNDAMENTALIST THEORY

The most important work on violence in the abolitionist enterprise has been done by Blanchard and Prewitt (1993) and Blanchard (1994). They find that abortion-related violence is most often perpetrated by working-class men under forty years of age. These men, as one might expect, are classic "loners," who have few contacts outside their religion. They do, however, believe themselves to have a supportive base within the community. Most importantly, according to these authors, these men are extremely committed to a "fundamentalistic orientation to their religion and culture (Blanchard and Prewitt, 1993: 274). In their assessment, the key factor leading to abortion-related violence is the filtering of those demographic factors, restricted social relationships, and perceived insulation from sanctions through the value system of fundamentalist dualism.

In the following discussion, we ask whether their conclusions implicitly reject another, more likely possibility—that it is the skewed social relationships they observe that are the key dynamic in the equation. In the process, we explore the legacy of abortion-related violence as an aspect of the sentiment from which it springs and ask how it is checked or encouraged by the primary tenets of each of the three branches of abortion abolitionism.

The Big Bang—The Pensacola Trial

The most well-publicized and highly studied individual violent event perpetrated by abolitionists took place in 1984 and constituted what its perpetrators referred to as the "Gideon Project." The Project, the planning and execution of three clinic bombings on Christmas morning of 1984, received widespread publicity and national attention and did a half-million dollars' worth of property damage to the facilities involved. In her book, *Decoding Abortion Rhetoric*, Condit devotes a section to the trial, and Blanchard and Prewitt's *Religious Violence and Abortion: The Gideon Project* (1993) focuses the bulk of its attention on the event, drawing many of its conclusions about the national scene in its light. In his later solo work (1994), Blanchard leaves those conclusions undisturbed.

The perpetrators of the Gideon Project (Matthew Goldsby, Jimmy Simmons, Kathy Simmons, and Kaye Wiggins) hatched their plot after Goldsby and Jimmy Simmons had already successfully planted a pipe bomb in the Ladies Center, an abortion clinic in Pensacola. The bomb did $250,000 worth of damage to the facility, and when their culpability went undetected, the two took it as a sign from God that they were to continue.

Blanchard and Prewitt attribute Goldsby and Simmons's belief that God had blessed their efforts to the Pentecostal belief that God speaks directly to individual believers. According to the authors, the theory of revelation used in the Assemblies of God would support the notion that, since both perpetrators felt they heard the same message from God, and since they were not previously caught, they could assume that it was God's will that they continue. Such a reading, however, opposes the Pentecostal understanding of revelation and, in this case, ignores the bombers' own failure to seek the clarification that Assemblies' doctrine would demand.

Blanchard and Prewitt refer to instances of individual revelation as "a burden laid on my heart" (1993: 45). In one of the texts used during the 1980s for the Christian Broadcasting Network's home-study course, "Living by the Book," J. Rodman Williams clarifies the proper use of such "burdens":

> In addition to the special revelation that is completed with the apostolic witness, God reveals Himself to those who are in the Christian community. This revelation is subordinate or secondary to the special revelation attested to in the Scriptures. . . .
>
> Now, I must strongly emphasize that all such revelation is wholly subordinate to special revelation. Special revelation was given through the Old Testament prophets, Jesus Christ, and the early apostles. This revelation, centered in the Word made flesh, was prepared by the ancient prophets and completed by the early apostles. There is *nothing more to be added*: God's truth has been fully declared. Accordingly, what occurs in revelation within the Christian community is *not* new truth that goes beyond the special revelation (if so, it is spurious and not of God). It is only a deeper appreciation of what has already been revealed, or a disclosure of some message for the contemporary situation that adds nothing essentially to what He has before made known. (Williams, 1988: 44; emphasis in original)

Williams, Assemblies of God literature, and Pentecostal theology in general repeatedly insist that an individual's subordinate revelation must always be "tested," as commanded in 1 Thessalonians 5:21 and 1 John 4:1.

In the note on 1 John 4:1, the editors of the Full Life Study Bible (a study Bible much favored by Pentecostals for its emphasis on the Holy Spirit) write:

4.1 TEST THE SPIRITS. The reason for testing every spirit (i.e., a person moved or inspired by a spirit) is that "many false prophets" will enter the church. This will be especially true as tolerance for unbiblical doctrine increases toward the end of the age. Christians are commanded to test all professed Christian teachers, writers, preachers, and prophets, and in fact any individual who claims his or her work or message comes from the Holy Spirit. Believers may never assume that a ministry or spiritual experience is from God merely because one claims it is. Furthermore, no teaching or doctrine may be accepted as true solely on the basis of success, miracles, or apparent anointing. (Stamps and Adams, 1992: 1980)

Thus, the success of the July bombing was not, according to Pentecostal understandings of subordinate revelation, to be considered a "sign" that the bombers were to continue.

The trial itself became a media event, with demonstrations on both sides of the issue and court testimony and argument during which Matt Goldsby's dysfunctional family history was dissected and abortionists were compared to Nazis. Goldsby and Simmons were found guilty on seven counts each of bombing and conspiracy, while the women were convicted of one count each of conspiracy. Kaye Wiggins and Kathy Simmons were sentenced to five years suspended with probation and a $2,000 fine. Simmons and Goldsby were sentenced to ten years on six counts, to run concurrently; five years suspended with probation on one count; and $353,073.66 in restitution. From their study of this trial and other terroristic events associated with abolitionist sentiments, the authors developed a theory. As noted above, the crux of that theory is the notion of fundamentalist dualism as a motivation for violence.

Defining Fundamentalism

In concluding that fundamentalist dualism is the filter that enables these individuals to turn their antisocial impulses into abortion-related violence, Blanchard and Prewitt attempt to define fundamentalism. Their definitions, however—both of fundamentalism and fundamentalist dualism—are not well drawn or supported by academic or self-imposed descriptions of fundamentalists. For example, the authors state: "as we use the terms, fundamentalism is a subset of the more inclusive group, evangelicals" (1993: 223 n.12). However, when applying that epithet to their violent exemplars, they stretch it to its breaking point, to include "Protestant, Catholic, and Mormon expressions" (p. 230). This mischaracterizes the historical meaning and cultural realities of American fundamentalism, in that most fundamentalists view Mormonism as a cult and reject the dogmatic teachings of Catholicism. Moreover, while the authors stress that the members of the Gideon Project belong to the largest of the classical Pentecostal denominations (Assemblies of God), they ignore the historical fact that Pentecostals were formally rejected from the World's Christian Fundamentals Association in 1928 and themselves broke with fundamentalists in the formation of the National Association of Evangelicals in 1943.

In fact, the very characteristics that Blanchard and Prewitt observe in their sociological and anthropological treatment of the perpetrators of the Gideon Project and their church community are what culturally separate them from fundamentalists. Pentecostals practice a pneumatic or charismatic method of biblical interpretation, which fundamentalists reject;[1] fundamentalists include in their dispensational view of church history an assumption that biblical miracles ceased after the canon was completed—an assumption that essentially denies the very basis of Pentecostalism as a distinct faith. Blanchard and Prewitt strongly imply that the Gideon four's belief in the Holy Spirit inspiration of biblical interpretation and their conception of subordinate revelation led them to believe that God was calling them to plant bombs. Although they interviewed the bombers' pastor and seem, in the narrative portion of the book, to accept his rejection of their unbiblical violence, upon reaching the interpretive section they reinsert "fundamentalist dualism" as the culprit leading to action.

Moreover, in adopting the global view of fundamentalism as used by Martin Marty, Blanchard and Prewitt cast their net so wide as to catch nearly everyone of a conservative bent—whether political, cultural, or theological. In designing an explanatory model, it seems odd to accept a progression that adds people into the filtering process instead of taking them out, yet this is precisely what Blanchard and Prewitt do. In their representation of "the path to anti-abortion violence," the arrows lead from "Social Statuses—Working Class, Age Under 35, Sex: Male," to "Social Relationships—Restricted Relationships, Insulation from Sanctions" to "Values—Fundamentalist Dualism, Authoritarianism, Male Dominance" and finally to "Anti-Abortion Violence." However, they supply no data to support this conclusion, and the specified path remains insufficiently explained.

While this book does not reject—indeed, strenuously argues for—the centrality of faith in the abolitionist mindset, it finds no discernible evidence that fundamentalism (or, more accurately, strict adherence to the traditional teachings of evangelical, charismatic, fundamentalist, and Pentecostal Protestantism; Catholicism; or Mormonism), rather than the severe psychosocial disturbance found in most of Blanchard and Prewitt's subjects, would serve as a trigger for violence. Indeed, it seems more probable that the predisposition to violence can be checked by the proper discipline of individuals within those faith communities. Upon close examination, the case studies offered by Blanchard and Prewitt argue more cogently for a psychosocial explanation for the violence of the perpetrators than a theological one.

Of the twenty-two perpetrators of twenty-eight acts of violence examined by Blanchard and Prewitt in their national survey, nearly all exhibit psychological disturbances that are not shared by the vast majority of their fellow believers. Some have rejected the discipline of a denomination the authors would consider fundamentalist, and a few seem to have no coherent religious pattern at all. A brief survey should clarify the point here.

Peter Burkin, an arsonist, was judged to be guilty but insane. According to Burkin, he wanted to draw public attention to a theory he had developed, holding that the embryo is the seat of the personality. He had previously approached abolitionist activists with this notion but had been essentially rebuffed by them. Although Burkin may or may not hold (or have held) fundamentalist viewpoints (the information is insufficient for such a conclusion), he does not appear to conform to the strictures of any of the fundamentalist denominations.

Don Benny Anderson and Wayne and Matthew Moore, who kidnapped a doctor and his wife in 1983, also do not appear to have been acting as fundamentalists. A Mormon elder convicted of real estate fraud, Anderson left his wife in 1980 and stayed out of the abortion debate "until he received orders from God and the archangel Michael" (Blanchard and Prewitt, 1993: 188). Anderson, then, would be described not as a fundamentalist, or even as a fundamentalist Mormon, but more properly as an apostate.

Joseph Grace presents another exception to the authors' theory of fundamentalist violence. Grace, who set fire to a clinic in Norfolk, Virginia, in 1983, did so as a "symbolic gesture," as he left town, hoping to escape impending atomic attack by the Russians. Blanchard and Prewitt offer no evidence that Grace in any way fits their fundamentalist profile. Indeed, the trend is in this direction rather than toward support for their model. With few exceptions, the individuals profiled were acting individually in their illegal and immoral violent actions and in their everyday faith life as well.

While it is undoubtedly true that a strong motivator like faith can in some cases lead to uncontrolled and dangerous action, it is equally true that in most cases it does not. Indeed, Blanchard and Prewitt virtually concede the point when they say, "The critical point is that these violent crusaders are marginal even in the movement they purport to represent." Not content to make that critical point, they add, "The ambivalence of this relationship is signaled by the fact that the bombers' and arsonists' actions, while somewhat supported, cannot be fully embraced by the public representatives of the anti-abortion movement, if only out of interest in public relations" (Blanchard and Prewitt, 1993: 215). The implication of these statements is that the leaders of the abolitionist movement would embrace violence if they thought they could get away with it, but they realize that they cannot—a conclusion for which the authors offer no evidence, and which their own interviews with leadership in the bombers' church refute.

In their analysis, Blanchard and Prewitt observe that the bombers and arsonists share common traits with rapists, terrorists, and torturers. It would seem intuitively sound to associate clinic bombers with those three criminal groups and to find that a predisposition to such traits might be the triggering factor for violence. In other words, what makes an otherwise law-abiding citizen with a strong issue position into a criminal might well have something to do with the traits they share with criminals. Yet in their conclusions, the authors note that the bombers and arsonists are "uniformly fundamentalist" (though, as noted above, their narratives do not show that uniformity) and state that, "while the vast majority of violent acts in American society appear to be committed by persons who share the same kinds of social statuses and relationships ... abortion-related violence depends on a third factor: those statuses and relationships being filtered through the value system of fundamentalist dualism" (pp. 274–275).

Although they seem to consider it an important observation, what the authors essentially have discovered is that anti-abortion violence is generally carried out by people who oppose abortion and share psychosocial dysfunctions with other members of the violent criminal class. The selection of fundamentalism, rather than mental illness, as the triggering factor seems curious, at best.

It is also necessary to determine what they have defined as fundamentalist dualism. It is worth noting, however, that, in the midst of their discussion of fundamentalism, the authors venture that "[p]erhaps the bombers and arsonists are a unique group in the anti-abortion movement, operating essentially out of motivations that set them apart from the less violent activists in general" (p. 228). Nonetheless, by the time they have concluded the book, they have determined that it is in fact what they have in common with the less violent activists that leads them to be violent.

What, then, is fundamentalist dualism? In their discussion, they find a "general common basis of belief" inherent in all forms of fundamentalism: "Customary beliefs include a personal experience of salvation; verbal inspiration and literal interpretation of scriptures as worded in the King James Version of the Bible; the divinity of Jesus; and the substitutionary atonement" (p. 224).

To begin with the most obvious problem, Blanchard and Prewitt are simply wrong in their claim that fundamentalists adhere to a literal interpretation "as worded in the King James Version." Rather, the fundamentalist position is that the Bible is inerrant in "the original autographs" (Burgess et al., 1988: 324). Indeed, it would come as quite a surprise to many fundamentalists, evangelicals, charismatics, and Pentecostals today to find that they were committing a heresy to be reading the New International Version, the most popular translation ever printed. Specialized study bibles for each of those subgroups have been printed in all recognized biblical translations, without any notable effect on the doctrine of inerrancy.

Moreover, this is a theological definition, and Blanchard and Prewitt seem to require a less precise one in order to place all their subjects under the same umbrella. To do so, they employ the notion of "dualism" as a thought-form inherent in fundamentalism. Yet, upon examination, it becomes clear that their dualism is philosophical in nature, overbroad, and applicable to many other groups in society that have nothing to do with the abortion controversy. As they put it:

> At the heart of fundamentalism in its Protestant, Catholic, and Mormon expressions is a dualistic view of the world.... It divides reality into soul and body, spirit and flesh, good and evil, heaven and earth, God and Satan, male and female. Dualism sees the world and its individuals caught in a cosmic war between good and evil, spirit and body, faith and reason. ... The "real" worlds in this pattern of thought are the ideal worlds of good, God, ideas, and spirituality, rather than the observable physical world.
>
> Fundamentalism also tends to personalize these forces. (Blanchard and Prewitt, 1993: 230–231)

The division of the world into dualistic categories is hardly unique to fundamentalism. Moreover, each of the dualities listed can be found in the Bible itself, which fundamentalists already take to be inerrant. The directly perceivable personal God is universally recognized in evangelical tradition, whether by those of a liberal or a conservative bent on the question of abortion. Few world religions deny the existence of a God to whom one can talk and who occasionally talks back.

It is unclear just how the purported dualistic nature of fundamentalism is linked to abortion-related violence. Despite the authors' assumptions, dualism does not in and of itself carry an assumption that violence is acceptable. Indeed, the historic peace churches draw their own dualistic lines of absolute right and wrong, and within that context violence remains an illegitimate act. Gandhi's use of the concept of passive resistance, by which one forces one's opponent to see the injustice of his own acts, is predicated on the belief that right and wrong are knowable and that there are certain acts that can never be permitted. Yet those assumptions lead not to other-directed violence but to self-abnegation and occasional martyrdom.

In his later work, however, Blanchard offers this curious assertion: "The justification for violence lies in the substitutionary theory of the atonement theology of both Protestants and Catholics" (1994: 45). It is immediately followed by this back-of-the-book footnote: "I do not mean to claim that all or even most fundamentalists are prone to or support violence. I only maintain that the thought pattern encourages violence in the suggestible and in those already prone to violence, especially those that are socially isolated" (p. 139, f18). Yet that is not what the author has stated. Instead, he has said that the *justification* for violence lies in the substitutionary atonement theology—a bedrock teaching of the Christian faith, which does not even serve to divide evangelicals from most Protestants, as Marsden notes (1991: 27). Indeed, it is this atonement that is believed to have *ended* the need for violent punishment. Blanchard continues: "In this theory, the justice of God demands punishment for human sin" (p. 45). The author, however, has missed the point of "substitutionary" entirely. The theory of substitutionary atonement maintains that God sent His Son, Jesus Christ, to atone for those sins Himself; once the sinner accepts that free gift of grace, Blanchard's imagined thirst for revenge is supposed to disappear.

In essence, then, the fundamentalist dualism explanation is unspecified and unclear. The evidence given for it argues against it rather than for it, and the prime characters in Blanchard and Prewitt's book belong to a denomination historically rejected by fundamentalism and engage in practices antithetical to it. However, it is clear that the bombers and arsonists are drawn from a population that rejects abortion, whether for religious reasons or for other reasons. That, unfortunately, is not of much assistance in exploring the controversy.

The question, however, remains. How do the underlying presuppositions of the abolitionist enterprise enhance or repress potential violence, and what might the future hold? The following discussions will examine the place of violence in the worldviews this project has identified, in hopes of addressing that issue.

VIOLENCE OVER TIME AND THE THREE ASPECTS OF ABOLITIONISM

Each of the three aspects of abolitionism relates differently to the question of violence, in both theological and practical terms. In the following section, we look at each type of abolitionist in its theoretical relationship to violent action, exploring the mechanisms and assumptions that might serve to make such action possible or reduce its likelihood.

Violence and Traditional Catholicism: The Moral Crusaders

Although the moral crusaders have moved farther from the spotlight in the enterprise and have been overshadowed by the social movement activists, it should not be assumed that their presence is not felt. The institutions set up during the moral crusade period remain important actors in the debate, with Right-to-Life and affiliated groups among the most active organizations, although their efforts do not draw much public or press attention. Many of those who participate in the enterprise as a social movement do so out of an issue concern motivated by their agreement with the moral crusade positions, notably the demands of the Catholic faith. Moreover, although revival per se is largely a Protestant theological construct, the abolitionist expression of revivalism is shared by Catholics, in such groups as Missionaries for the Preborn and Lambs of Christ, as well as in Operation Rescue. In fact, in our sample of activists, those who have come into the enterprise during the 1990s are 75% Catholic. Taking note of the election results mentioned at the outset of this work, it is no coincidence that the election that saw no pro-life candidates defeated was the same election in which, for the first time in 150 years, Roman Catholics voted Republican in an off-year election.[2] The moral position of the Catholic Church and her adherents has a potentially profound influence on the social movement aspects of the enterprise. Similarly, it is important to understand the traditional positions of the Church that have the potential to incite or suppress violence within the enterprise.

The New Catechism promulgated in 1994 is instructive in this regard. In its summation of the positions mandated by adherence to the fifth commandment, it states that, "From its conception, the child has the right to life. Direct abortion, that is, abortion willed as an end or as a means, is a 'criminal' practice, gravely contrary to the moral law. The Church imposes the canonical penalty of excommunication for this crime against human life." While it is permissible to "render an unjust aggressor unable to inflict harm" and while "[l]egitimate defense is a grave duty for whoever is responsible for the lives of others or the common good," at the same time, "[t]he murder of a human being is gravely contrary to the dignity of the person and the holiness of the Creator" (Catechism, 1994: 558). Thus, the position of the Church is one of defending the unborn from conception, but argues as well for the protection of the lives of those who would perform abortions. Moreover, the bombing or arson of an abortion-providing facility could never fall under the rubric of "legitimate defense," if the sanctity of life of all persons is taken seriously.

It could be argued that the grave nature of abortion brings it within the potential bounds of "just war" theory. However, even if one were to accept the notion that the abortion debate is sufficiently compelling as to fall under those rules, the Church's position on war itself would not permit bombings and arsons. The *Catechism* states plainly that "Because of the evils and injustices that all war brings with it, we must do everything reasonably possible to avoid it." The Church prays: "From famine, pestilence, and war, O Lord, deliver us."

"The Church and human reason assert the permanent validity of the moral law during armed conflicts. Practices deliberately contrary to the law of nations and to its universal principles are crimes" (*Catechism*, 1994: 558–559).

In *The Gospel of Life*, Pope John Paul II states that laws permitting euthanasia and abortion have no legitimate authority, for they are fundamentally opposed to both the well-being of the individual and the greater good of humanity (John Paul II, 1995: 133). From this, it seems that violating such laws would be an imperative for the faithful Catholic believer. Indeed, the Pope makes this duty clear:

> Christians . . . are called upon under grave obligation of conscience not to cooperate formally in practices which, even if permitted by civil legislation, are contrary to God's law. . . . It is never licit to cooperate formally in evil. . . . This cooperation can never be justified either by invoking respect for the freedom of others or by appealing to the fact that civil law permits it or requires it. Each individual in fact has moral responsibility for the acts which he personally performs; no one can be exempted from this responsibility, and on the basis of it everyone will be judged by God himself. (John Paul II, 1995: 136; emphasis in original)

The resistance of which the Pope speaks is of a specific kind, however. "Abortion and euthanasia are thus crimes which no human law can claim to legitimize. There is no obligation in conscience to obey such laws; instead there is a *grave and clear obligation to oppose them by conscientious objection*" (John Paul II, 1995: 133; emphasis in original). The proper response to an unjust law is to refuse to obey it; thus, the Church calls on her followers to refuse to procure, perform, or fund abortion in any of its forms, even if it is permitted by civil law. But can one derive from the obligation of resistance a license to destroy?

In his discourse on the obligations of legislators, the Pope speaks of limits to the means by which "resistance" may be employed. He states that it is permissible for a legislator adamantly opposed to abortion to vote in favor of abortion legislation aimed at limiting the harm done by it, when he or she does not have the opportunity to vote to abolish it. In other words, if a legislator's vote technically upholds abortion rights, yet is more restrictive than a law being replaced or an alternative law being proposed, no violation of conscience is involved in voting for the law that preserves abortion at the lowest possible level (John Paul II, 1995: 134). If the legislator is permitted to countenance a pro-abortion law in order to limit the harm it does, it seems clear that the taxpayer whose revenues support an immoral entity or whose community houses an abortion-providing facility would be compelled to bear witness to the evil of abortion only in ways that do not otherwise violate the moral laws against murder, violence, and war.

What, then, does the Pope recommend that good Catholics do in order to oppose the moral evil of abortion? In *The Gospel of Life*, he advises that all must be committed "to make unconditional respect for human life the foundation of a renewed society" (John Paul II, 1995: 139). To do so requires that the Church and her people work to honor the life of all persons, so that we might see "the establishment of a new culture of life, the fruit of the culture of truth and of love" (John Paul II, 1995: 140).

In *Crossing the Threshold of Hope*, the Pope makes the proper Christian response to the existence of abortion even more clear:

> Therefore, *in firmly rejecting "pro-choice" it is necessary to become courageously "pro-woman," promoting a choice that is truly in favor of women.* It is precisely the woman, in fact, who pays the highest price, not only for her motherhood, but even more for its destruction, for the suppression of the life of the child who has been conceived. The only honest stance, in these cases, *is that of radical solidarity with the woman.* It is not right to leave her alone. The experience of many counseling centers shows that the woman does not want to suppress the life of the child she carries within her. If she is supported in this attitude, and if at the same time she is freed from the intimidation of those around her, then she is even capable of heroism. As I have said, numerous counseling centers are witness to this, as are, in a special way, houses for teenage mothers. It seems, therefore, that society is beginning to develop a more mature attitude in this regard, even if there are still many self-styled "benefactors" who claim to "help" women by liberating them from the prospect of motherhood. (John Paul II, 1994: 206–207; emphases in original)

In essence, then, the position of the Church, properly understood and properly followed, forbids Catholics from engaging in the terroristic acts described by Blanchard and Prewitt. In fact, even the evidence from those authors indicates that it may be in the interest of all concerned for people of strong anti-abortion convictions to be *more* committed to the discipline of a traditionalist denomination or faith community, rather than less. John Malvasi, a Catholic, sentenced for bombing clinics, believed he would not be able to repeat his acts, even though he was not certain that God would disapprove. Rather, he felt he could not do it again because the cardinal had told him not to. It is tempting to wonder whether Malvasi would have done it at all, had he been more closely discipled by his spiritual overseers.

The notion that the moral crusade position tends to suppress rather than exacerbate violence is in part supported by the fact that bombings and arsons did not begin until 1977, according to the statistics kept by the National Abortion Federation. Between 1977 and 1979, twelve such events took place, although Blanchard and Prewitt detail only one—Peter Burkin's failed 1979 attempt to call attention to his theory of the location of personality. Hence, although some of the criminals and terrorists over time have considered themselves to be very religious Catholics, the moral crusade perspective, in and of itself, does not appear to have provided much support for violent activities. Instead, the very heart of the moral crusade response to abortion is to bear witness and to endure, while providing whatever social services can be mustered in providing abortion alternatives.

Although the Church's position is coherent, it is also not widely known. The media's portrayal of Catholics and the Catholic Church, especially in depicting them as being hostile to women and underwriting or tacitly supporting terroristic activities, serves to complicate the task of leadership in clarifying such issues. For the Church to be effective in suppressing rogue elements within the faith community, its leaders must be ready and willing to more precisely articulate the legitimacy of non-violent resistance, while both condemning terroristic acts as violations of the moral law and more effectively advertising its availability as an agent of peace and reconciliation.

Violence and the Political System: The Social Movement Activists

As we will see in the concluding chapter, the social movement activists operate within a curious tension in American society. As religious people, they are called to a less materialist, more compassionate, and other-centered view of human relationships. However, as political activists, they must be capable of moving in a more secular, self-centered, and pragmatic arena. Existing within a political system and hoping to use that system to their advantage, their spiritual concerns must occasionally be set aside—if only temporarily—to accomplish practical goals. In learning to use a secular system, even at times to use it with the pretense of leaving faith concerns out of it, the social movement activists gradually have begun to become more secularized, more accommodationist, and more skilled at striking political deals than was previously the case.

The 1996 Republican platform committee hearings showcased this sophistication, as the majority abolitionists finessed the "tolerance" language previously agreed to by Congressman Henry Hyde of Illinois and presumptive nominee Robert Dole in the plank dealing with abortion. Lee Atwater's "big tent" acquired an "open door" under the guidance of delegates like Congressman Bill McCollum of Florida (head of the Individual Rights subcommittee, which had authority over the issue) and Kay James of Virginia (former head of National Right to Life). The proposed tolerance plank was argued against as being "patronizing" and redundant to the language that had come out of the committee. All amendments seeking to strike the strong abolitionist statements in the plank or to dispense with the issue altogether were voted down after heated debate. Behind the scenes, abolitionist lobbyists such as Ralph Reed, Phyllis Schlafly, and Bay Buchanan consulted with committee members on language, producing the compromise of the "open door" that eventually passed under the stewardship of Kay James. The abolitionists were able to forge an uneasy alliance with pro-choice Republicans with the goal of electing Bob Dole, without relinquishing their hold on their own primary issue. An agreement to publish the minority (pro-choice) statement of the platform plank as an appendix to the platform itself placated those who had threatened a floor fight at the convention. The social movement abolitionists were able to frame an "open door" convention, while retaining power over the issue that mattered the most to them.

Within the Republican party, it is well known that the pro-choice contingent is not as committed as the abolitionists on the abortion issue. Prior to the convention, Bay Buchanan made the case for retaining what she refers to as the "Life" position, by reminding an audience at the Clare Booth Luce Center that you don't abandon your base in the hope of attracting new voters. Indeed, Buchanan well understands that, when one of our survey respondents says, "I feel that this is *the* most important and critical question to ever face the nation," she speaks for a large— and very hard-working—wing of the Republican party. Buchanan warned darkly, "If this party walks away from Life, there will be two parties by the end of the century, and the Republican party won't be one of them." Seasoned in the political process, ever vigilant to the issue, and committed to electing Bob Dole, the abolitionist delegates ensured that Buchanan's prediction would not be tested.

The success of abolitionists in pursuing the political strategy has several potential effects. First, it has the effect of secularizing what might otherwise be an exclusively religious debate, which both assists the enterprise in gaining new adherents and disturbs those in the enterprise who centralize the religious aspect of the issue. As noted previously, Ralph Reed's willingness to bring the forces of the Christian Coalition to bear on economic issues appeared to Randall Terry to be a retreat from his true calling. For those who participate in the social movement sector of the enterprise, the demands of politics and the need of their own leadership to make common cause with less religiously driven activists can sometimes be disheartening. It is important that leadership of a faith-based social movement be able to assure the rank-and-file who are not involved in the day-to-day parry-and-thrust of strategic politics that their concerns are being heard and acted on.

Second, as social movement activists gain adherents by persuading others to agree with them, there is an inevitable moderating effect. Those for whom the issue remains a matter of no compromise are uneasy finding themselves working with less dependable allies who may not agree with them entirely, but at least find their position more comfortable than that of the opposition. While the social movement attracts new activists with its linkage issues, it must also guard against losing sufficient support for the original core issue because, as with most institutions, moderation tends to move downward, with pragmatic elites adjusting their positions to political realities and rank-and-file activists coming around more slowly, if at all.

Again, the 1996 Republican convention provides an interesting case in point. Although certainly a number of important issues were being dealt with in the platform, all the media attention was focused on the abortion plank. The delegates to the convention were largely abolitionist, whether strongly or weakly so, and the abortion plank represented their complete coming of age in the Republican party. At the 1996 convention, the abolitionist effort was able to carry the day, despite direct challenges from pro-choice forces on the platform committee. Their strategic position in this election cycle was unique for four reasons.

This was the first time that a serious challenge had been mounted to the abortion plank since it was first inserted. Second, it was the first time that abolitionists actively controlled the platform committee. Third, the abolitionists were attempting to maintain a platform plank that their presumptive nominee had attempted to change, unlike the Reagan and Bush candidacies, which wholeheartedly endorsed the abortion plank of their platforms. Finally, the social movement abolitionists were able to maintain their agenda both as a majority and as the leadership in a majority party. This last point is not inconsequential. As Newt Gingrich pointed out in his speech to the delegates, a majority party, in order to be a majority party, must be capable of articulating an agenda that satisfies a wide variety of issue positions. In previous conventions, the abortion issue was less contentious, because there were fewer people concerned with the issue who would be likely to disagree with the writers of the plank. This time, the diversity of the party had to be skillfully addressed, and the abolitionists proved themselves equal to that task.

The political orientation of the social movement form of the enterprise has the potential both to reinforce and to restrict a tendency toward violence. In setting themselves up as oppositional to the state, social movement activists run the risk of stirring up antigovernment sentiment of the militia type, if the message they send does not remain clearly rooted in a patriotism that values order. Although the antigovernment sentiments of a Randy Weaver are largely derived from an obsession with conspiracy theory and "fringe" literature, the constant reinforcement of antigovernment sentiment—even by those seeking to become part of that same system—cannot help but have some kind of effect. Perhaps the most serious effect, however, is that the legitimacy of social movement activists falls into question almost the instant they become political players. If they become too accommodationist for pragmatic reasons, they run the risk of losing their most intense support and their best workers. It is for this reason that a Randall Terry, while exhorting Christians to seek elective and appointed office as a service to God, can simultaneously castigate a Ralph Reed for his willingness to seek alliances with those not solely focused on religious issues. Thus, the social movement activist who attacks the establishment as an outsider becomes an insider when the battle is won—and therefore earns the suspicion of those still fighting the wider war.

In some individuals, the psychological investment of fighting the good fight at the grass roots in a social movement, only to find that one's elected or anointed leaders are now willing to make political compromises, may prove too much. Ironically, it is the social movement aspect of the enterprise that most logically might be seen as providing a context for violent rebellion. The patriotism of the Christian nation narrative places heavy emphasis both on the religious roots of that heritage tale and on the nature of the United States as a divinely ordained "miracle nation" (LaHaye, 1987: 65). In the midst of that narrative, the violent moments of history are justified, championed, and in many ways sanctified as necessary and virtuous threads in the tapestry of manifest destiny.

For those who have decided that the government itself has become the enemy, the high view of rebellion promulgated in the Christian nation narrative, coupled with the traditional patriotism common among abolitionists, may well seem a logical rationalization for antistate and illegal action. Moreover, the long history of social movement activity in the United States includes moments of violent resistance (from John Brown at Harper's Ferry to the Stonewall Riot) that, in hindsight, are interpreted by both participants and socializing agents—such as textbooks and television networks—as justified by appeal to a higher value. For those who believe that they are acting in consonance with transcendent and eternal laws, consider themselves loyal to the original intent of the Founding Fathers, and have abandoned hope in the present government, violent rebellion may sometimes appear to be the most honorable option.

At the same time, the characteristics of social movement activism act as a stimulus for the leadership of such activists to contain incipient violence within their followers. As visible political representatives of the abolitionist enterprise, the social movement activists, especially those in leadership positions, have an interest in limiting or eliminating violence whenever possible. Because they seek to obtain the power of the state and maintain their position in it, they must recognize the state's legitimacy to some degree. For those involved in the political aspects of the social movement—becoming convention delegates, candidates, editorialists, and otherwise taking active roles by which the system captures much of their time and energy—violence has little attraction. To retain its legitimacy, the social movement cannot become associated with unacceptable violence in the public mind. Actually perpetrating violent rebellion is a high-investment, low-reward risk on the part of the individual actor. A successful terroristic act effectively eliminates any hope the actor may have had to obtain the sympathy of the wider public or an official position in any government. Terrorism, in its international context, is generally pursued with this understanding. Bombings and hijackings are more often pursued with the goal of forcing a government to perform a particular act (such as releasing a political prisoner) than with the aim of persuading the public to accept a position. To avoid violence, social movement leaders must keep the frustration level relatively low and stay in touch with the grass-roots true believers who can be counted on as the most loyal of working supporters.

Violence and Religion: The Revivalists

The revivalist faction of the abolitionist enterprise carries with it certain risks of violence, but, as with the other two types, it also operates on some assumptions that can serve to suppress potential violence. Indeed, contrary to the assumptions of Blanchard and Prewitt, I will argue here that the revivalists, though among the most serious adherents to what those authors would call "fundamentalist dualism," have the best chance of the three to effect real change in the abortion situation without engaging in terroristic acts. Although the rescuers and the revivalists are the closest to the actual "front lines" of the perimeter of the clinics, both the theology of revivalism and the dictates of revivalist abolitionist leadership argue against the kind of violence assessed by Blanchard and

Prewitt. Whereas there are some who would include everything from public prayer and sidewalk counseling to murder under the heading of "anti-abortion violence," I maintain that there is a significant difference between exercising one's free speech and assembly rights (as in sidewalk counseling, rallies, and literature distribution) and legitimate civil disobedience (sit-ins, passive resistance, and voluntary arrest) on one hand, and illegitimate violent action (arson, bombings, and murder) on the other.

The revivalist enthusiasms that demand action seem intuitively to lead to violence. The image of the abortionist and of abortion in general promulgated throughout the abolitionist literature would seem almost to demand retribution. The language of blood atonement and fiery judgment lends itself to an interpretation that leads to destruction. These elements cannot be denied, and it is important that abolitionist leadership be clear about what is acceptable and what is not. The distinction between God's judgment and man's action must always be made, to the media and the public—and most importantly to the rank-and-file. The revivalist leaders of the enterprise, in their pronouncements, have to recognize that they are acting as preachers and as models. Greater emphasis on the commitment to Christlike behavior that every rescue participant must sign helps to offset the potentially radicalizing effects of spiritual rhetoric that revivalists risk.

However, the activists who participate from a revivalist perspective, for the most part, already speak the language of revival. They believe that the demand for repentance applies first to them, that the battle of abortion is fought through spiritual, not physical, warfare, and that the end of the matter of judgment is in the Lord's hands. Randy Alcorn responds to the hypothetical question "Once You Disobey the Law, Why Not Use Violence?" as follows: "Violence puts human life at risk, and we are there to save lives not endanger them. We want to rescue victims, not create victims. Violence is punitive—we are intervening for the innocent, not doling out punishment for the guilty" (Alcorn, 1990: 207–208). Like any activity that puts people of strong opinions in close proximity, rescuing carries with it a measure of risk for personal violence, but the revivalist mindset dictates that the rescuer do battle with the weapons of Christianity—the Bible, prayer, love, sacrifice, and the help of the Holy Spirit—rather than of man.

When the spiritual nature of the abortion fight is understood, the danger of violence abates. It is when individuals begin to believe themselves capable of mediating the wrath of God that revivalist fire becomes a dangerous torch in the hand of the arsonist. It is a human temptation to strike back when one's opposition is on the attack, or when he is vulnerable. It is the task of those who articulate the meaning and purpose of the revivalist segment of the abolition enterprise to make clear that temptation is to be resisted at all costs.

Finally, aside from the arsonists and bombers, several shootings and murders have been associated with abortion abolitionism. Fortunately, the number is still small enough that we recall the names with relative ease: In March of 1993, Michael Griffin shot and killed Dr. David Gunn in Pensacola, Florida; in August of that year, Rachelle Shannon shot and wounded Dr. George Tiller in Wichita, Kansas; in July of 1994, Paul Hill shot and killed Dr. John Britton and his escort James Barrett in Pensacola, Florida, becoming the first person convicted under the just-passed Freedom of Access to Clinic Entrances Act; and, as noted at the outset of this work, in January of 1995, John Salvi executed two receptionists in Massachusetts. These actions are indefensible, from any Christian perspective, and the future legitimacy of the enterprise hangs heavily on the continued or intensified condemnation of them by legitimate leaders of the movement.

ASSESSING THE EVOLUTION OF THE ENTERPRISE

As we have seen, the abortion abolition enterprise has gone through many changes in its brief life following the *Roe* decision. As circumstances and the political climate changed, the enterprise adapted to each new opportunity or setback in ways that guaranteed its survival. In its initial phase, when adherents were few but the institution of the Catholic Church was available, participants used their resources to the best of their ability to pursue a moral crusade, seeking to drive out what appeared to them to be an anomaly in American political thought. Assuming that all Americans—indeed, all human beings—would agree with them once well-enough educated, the moral crusaders produced literature, formed support institutions, and held their ground until the 1980s.

As time went on, it became clear that *Roe* was not going to be easily reversed; in fact, American culture was fast adapting to the availability of legal abortion and seemed largely undisturbed by it. Conservative Protestants began to develop their own political consciousness toward the end of the 1970s and allied themselves with the moral crusaders once they discovered the issue of abortion. Moreover, their theological and political assumptions took the enterprise in new and profitable directions, helping to elect a president and expanding the political base of the enterprise itself. Despite public pronouncements to the contrary, Reagan and his administration proved unwilling to hand the abolitionists the favors they thought they had earned. While remaining within the Reagan camp, the abolitionists once again adjusted their strategy, working in other federal, state, and local elections to fill positions from the grass roots and running as convention delegates, city councilors, and school board members themselves.

With the rise of grass-roots Christian activism in the 1980s, the social movement was able to tap into a large constituency of loyalists and potential allies, enough to field Pat Robertson as a candidate in the 1988 Republican primaries. After his defeat, they merely adjusted the strategy again, learning to run their own local candidates, working to get George Bush elected, and making the Catholic/Protestant truce official in the form of the Christian Coalition alliance of pro-life Catholics, conservative Protestants, and Orthodox Jews. The social movement strategy, while somewhat successful in the long run, was incomplete as a recruiting tool. The political focus of the enterprise during the 1980s was designed to attract voters, candidates, and grass-roots support. The real battle, however, would be won or lost in individual hearts and on the concrete aprons of abortion clinics nationwide. The enterprise as a social movement, able to seek legislation and influence policy in faraway Washington, could not address the problem of the aborting woman and her child in Cherry Hill, New Jersey.

Into the breach stepped Randall Terry and Operation Rescue, and a new energy revitalized the enterprise as a whole. The revivalists could actually demonstrate that their efforts paid off—they had women and children to prove their case. They had entire days when abortion appointments went unmet. They had changed lives and saved babies. In addition, the revivalists, willing to pay the ultimate legal price for their belief in the sanctity of life, visibly going to jail to stop abortion, provided the enterprise with new heroes and fresh commitment. Moreover, they were newly involved; rescue didn't take social movement activists out of commission. The political work could be done while other activists did the street-level activism that kept the issue alive in the public mind.

At the present moment, all three elements of the enterprise discussed here remain active and vital. To restrict an analysis of the enterprise to any one of them would be to do a disservice to all. The following chapter will explore the possible future directions the enterprise might take and propose a new way of looking at faith-based political action that will enable us to discuss it in a more complete fashion than has previously been possible in the academic world. It is hoped that this approach will help academics and laypeople alike move beyond the stereotypes that are often applied to religious people, and conservatively religious people in particular. It seeks in some small way to explain the interactions we have so often observed between an ostensibly secular state and people whose apparent goal is to demolish that state for a theocracy of their own making. It is offered in the hope that its observations will aid us all not only to understand the abortion issue, but to comprehend—and perhaps even anticipate—the actions of people of faith when they move into the political arena.

NOTES

1. The Pentecostal method of biblical interpretation proceeds from what is called the "pneumatic" assumption that the interpreter is reliant on the illumination of the Holy Spirit for his understanding of the text. This assumption derives from the Pentecostal epistemology, which sees knowledge "not as a cognitive recognition of a set of precepts but as a relationship with the One who has established the precepts by which we live." It is only in relationship to God and through the fellowship of the Holy Spirit that the believer can rightly interpret the text (Burgess et al., 1988: 382).

2. The Democratic party would do well to consider the effect its abortion position has on traditional Catholics. One of our survey respondents, a 33-year-old Catholic Hispanic, identified herself as a Democrat, did not feel that the speakers at the 1992 Republican convention represented "people like me," and had previously voted for Anderson, Mondale, and Dukakis. However, in 1992, she voted for George Bush. Economically and politically a Democrat, this respondent is alienated within her party on cultural issues.

CHAPTER 8

A New Creature: The Future of the Enterprise and a Reinterpretation of Faith-Based Political Action

As with all issues in active development, any predictions as to the future of the abortion abolition enterprise are speculative, at best. For that reason, it is best to avoid making specific prognostications and attend more closely to generalized trends to get some sense of what might be expected for the future. It seems unlikely that any of the groups discussed here will disappear any time in the near future, particularly the social movement activists, whose recent successes have put them more centrally in the mainstream of the political process. Since politics is such a volatile and dynamic process, groups that arise to address political issues rarely disappear completely. More often, they blend into other groups concerned with similar issues or simply decline over time as the public becomes less and less willing to listen to their argument. The presence of millions of Roman Catholics, evangelicals, Pentecostals, charismatics, and fundamentalists in the body politic, however, argues against the notion that groups like the Christian Coalition will lose steam or withdraw from the fray any time soon. The following discussion is intended to draw the reader's attention to potential trends and shifts in the enterprise that may prove interesting and important in the future.

AFTER THE 1996 ELECTIONS

Although it may be tempting for their opposition to hope that, after President Clinton's resounding defeat of his challengers, the abolitionists are through, it would be more than premature to write the epitaph of the abortion abolition enterprise just yet. One election has little meaning in the larger cultural picture, unless it shows signs of establishing a lasting trend. Certainly, for abolitionists the 1996 results seemed disheartening, leaving as they did the most pro-choice president ever still in the White House, despite his many personal and professional scandals. For those to whom character was an important trait for a president to have (and who defined that character in terms of personal trustworthiness rather than political performance), the morning-after hangover following the election was bad indeed.

As with all things, however, a little time and perspective tell a different story. The electorate, though reelecting President Clinton, also reelected his nemesis, the Republican Congress. And most of those who are considered to be abolitionists on the Hill remained in place. (One notable exception was Representative Robert K. Dornan, who also ran against Dole in the primary. In the congressional election, he was defeated by a progressive, pro-choice Latina, although the election is, as of this writing, still being legally contested by Dornan, who accuses Loretta Sanchez of several varieties of voter fraud.) The important chairmanships, and the all-important speakership of the House, have remained solidly abolitionist, and Congress wasted little time before reintroducing the Partial-Birth Abortion Ban Bill in its original form (i.e., no political concessions to the president's position) once revelations had emerged concerning the false nature of previous pro-choice testimony about the procedure.

Moreover, it would be difficult to consider the 1996 election a true test of the abolitionists' power, considering the final choice that was to be made. Although Clinton was certainly pro-choice, Senator Dole was considered by the abolitionists as a significantly less reliable spokesman for the pro-life position. As for Jack Kemp, abolitionists have nothing but warm feelings for him, but his disappointingly deferential performance in the presence of Al Gore during their only debate merely reinforced the abolitionists' feeling that, after all their work and all their investment, they had once again been abandoned by the "establishment" forces of the Republican party. Those feelings sank all the lower after former-all-star Kemp clearly dropped the ball by not forcefully pursuing the issue of partial-birth abortion (a practice most Americans find repugnant at the least).

In looking at the 1996 election from the abolitionist perspective, we find little reason for activists to have held much hope for the Dole candidacy, except to remove Clinton from office (which is why so many of them voted for him after all; if there was anyone to vote for, it was Dole—but that "choice" seemed hollow, at best). The candidate himself attempted to introduce moderating language into the party platform to appease the pro-choice minority at the convention; if he wouldn't stand up for the position within his own party, how was anyone to believe he would stand up against the Democrats? Kemp, though well known as 100% pro-life (Clinton's press people called him an "extremist"), leaned so heavily on the 15% tax cut, which everyone in the nation was being told would not work, that abolitionists (particularly of the revivalist type) feared that he had abandoned principle for worldly pragmatism—a definite minus when you are playing to an audience of idealists.

Many now argue that it was Dole's inconsistency that defeated him, in that he could never develop a clear pro-family message for the voters once the convention had closed. Indeed, on many small issues, it was the president who stole the family issue—with heavy emphasis on the Family and Medical Leave Act, ending "drive-by deliveries" (the practice of sending women home twenty-four hours after they have given birth), advocating school uniforms, and the like. Even on an issue on which Clinton was clearly vulnerable—the drug problem—Dole was unable to articulate a strong and effective message down to the last ninety-six marathon hours of his campaign. Though Clinton clearly won the election, it should not be forgotten that nearly half of the eligible electorate stayed home.

Following the defeat, abolitionists remain optimistic and active, noting that the complexion of Washington politics—for all the hope of change on both sides—has remained essentially the same. Though distracted somewhat by the growing public attention to gay rights and media expressions of pro-homosexual sentiment (the Hawaii gay marriage decision and the very public—and extraordinarily hyped—coming out of television's "Ellen"), the traditional family lobby has not backed away from its rock-solid commitment to the sanctity of unborn life. Indeed, the re-installation of President Clinton seems merely to have served as yet another wake-up call for the enterprise—something its members have come to expect over the years. The abortion abolitionists are as active as ever, though perhaps less attention is paid to them than in the past. But it would be foolish to assume that less press actually means less presence.

Moreover, in the past few years, the effort has moved once again into formerly uncharted waters, taking advantage of the newest technologies. Ralph Reed's Christian Coalition presence at the Republican convention featured a network of hundreds of cellular phones to keep the faithful in touch with one another. The Internet has a number of groups dedicated to discussing the subject of abortion, on both sides of the issue, and even those general discussion groups that are not centrally concerned with it find themselves, from time to time, in the midst of heated discussion concerning the latest developments in the abortion wars. Although it is quite common for moderators to declare a temporary cease-fire when the subject gets too heated, nothing seems to be able to stop the incendiary subject of abortion from re-surfacing again and again, in one newsgroup after another.

There is also reason to expect not shrinkage but growth in the movement in the years to come. The abolitionists in Congress and the Senate are not going away, nor are the abolitionist governors, mayors, and other state and local officials. Moreover, as discussed below, there are a number of new areas from which abolitionists are emerging that could buttress the enterprise and keep it vital well into the twenty-first century.

FORMING NEW ALLIANCES AND HOPING FOR GROWTH

There are interesting signs of possible new allies for the existing coalition of abolitionists. Increasingly, conservative African Americans have been making their voices heard in both the religious community (Bishop Wellington Boone, Dr. Harold Carter, Tony Evans, Ben Kinchlow, Earl Jackson) and the political arena (Congressman J. C. Watts, Kay James, Starr Parker). In fact, the only African-American candidate for the presidency in 1996 in either major party was abolitionist commentator and former UN ambassador Alan Keyes. These voices remain overwhelmed both by the white dominance of the abolitionist movement and the pro-choice official voice of the African-American population, but they are growing in number, and theirs is every bit as strident as any other abolitionist message. Indeed, Keyes's speeches on the issue of abortion draw deeply from the well of African-American history, reminding his hearers that he, too, would once have been considered a nonperson.

In recent years, several major denominations—most notably the Southern Baptist Conference—have issued statements on or made official moves toward racial reconciliation. The recognition of historical wrongs and the new ecumenism blossoming in white and black conservative churches holds great promise for overcoming the previous walls of separation that have prevented the races from full cooperation in matters of moral politics. Moreover, the overtures made by white church groups and the Christian Coalition toward those whose churches have been victimized by arson in the past few years are also helping to heal that rift. Politically, and especially concerning the abolition issue, this represents a growth opportunity, because black Christians are well established as among the most morally conservative of all American religious groups. In addition, several large national movements in conservative Protestantism, such as Promise Keepers, stress racial equality as a bedrock tenet of their teachings.[1]

Despite the distaste many abolitionists harbor for his other messages, the opposition to abortion displayed by Louis Farrakhan in the name of the Black Muslim religion, coupled with the growing number of such believers, especially among the largely nonvoting poor, could provide a rich source of new participation. The recent "Million Man March" did not mention abortion, but it is no secret that Farrakhan and the Nation of Islam do not share the pro-choice sentiments of many of the speakers in attendance, believing abortion to be a genocidal plot perpetrated by white elites against the African race. An African-American evangelical minister, a leader in the Buffalo Spring of Life operation, spoke to me of his experiences speaking on abortion in inner-city high schools. Black Muslims, he told me, are against abortion but don't feel that the current efforts are doing much good. He reported that one young man came up to him after a talk and told him, "When you people get serious about this, then you call us." The minister told me, "My fear is, if we don't bring in the Martin Luther Kings now, if we don't find alliances with the peace-orientated [sic] of them [Black Muslims], we'll have to deal with the Malcolm X's when they get fed up."

There is also a growing Jewish voice in conservative circles, with traditional outlets like *Commentary* magazine being joined by new visibility for the Jewish Policy Center, a conservative think tank in Washington, D.C. *First Things*, the abolitionist magazine edited by Richard John Neuhaus, has seen an increase in articles addressing Jewish concerns, and new media figures, such as Michael Medved and Don Feder, address a constituency not previously attended to much on the American scene—culturally conservative Jews. The willingness of conservative Protestants, such as Pat Robertson and Jerry Falwell, to enthusiastically support the nation of Israel has also helped to build bridges to the American Jewish community. Although some of the new faces in Jewish conservatism, such as Dennis Praeger, are not entirely abolitionist, they are disturbed by what they see as a cavalier attitude about life-taking in the pro-choice movement. Whether these visible figureheads carry with them any sizable constituency has yet to be seen, but any inroads Christian cultural conservatives could make within the Jewish community would bode well for the enterprise's potential for growth.

Though not explicitly explored in the text due to the overwhelmingly Christian nature of the enterprise, there are other faiths represented in very small numbers in the survey sample (12.5% in total), all of which have come into the movement since 1990. A 43-year-old Wiccan from Oregon writes of his experience in the movement as one of cooperation: "In alliance with Christians I and others picketed at a feminist mill (suffered harassment, etc.!!) [This group] is a project of our coven." However, not every non-Christian has been so welcomed. A 38-year-old Krishna priest says, "I send donations to our local chapter in Colorado. I, with my wife, have attended 2–3 national Right-to-Life conferences to see how members of our faith and others (Hindus) could participate. Although warmly greeted, there was little scope for our participation as a religious organization; thus, our activity has been limited to our own internal educational processes." Yet, when religious barriers can be overcome, a number of fruitful avenues might be explored in the future by the enterprise, as many world religions not currently participating in the effort have doctrinal or traditional opposition to abortion.

Eventually, the abolitionist movement will have to go beyond the walls of any church, temple, or synagogue if there is ever to be a cease-fire in the war over abortion. Some abolitionist sympathizers, such as Nat Hentoff of the *Village Voice,* have the potential to breach those walls, with a well-articulated abolitionist message based not in religious rhetoric but, as will be discussed below, in the shared language of our civil religion. If alliances are to be made that can bring the abortion debate beyond the religious realm and into the wider arena of morality and ethics, abolitionists will have to bring to the debate an argument that, like the pro-choice argument, is rooted in shared secular values as well as religious ones. If abortion, as appears likely, remains a constitutionally protected right, the abolitionists' best chance of reducing its usage is to encourage a national debate that asks serious questions as to when that right is more honored in the breach than in the observance. A vigorous discussion of the ethical ramifications and responsibilities may at least begin a dialogue leading to some kind of cease-fire.

At present, such arguments are largely made by religious legal analysts, such as John Whitehead of the Rutherford Institute and Jay Sekulow of the American Center for Law and Justice, and by Alan Keyes. Keyes, in particular, is careful to link his abolitionism to the Declaration and the Constitution, arguing against the current Supreme Court interpretation and for greater emphasis on the primacy of the Declaration as a guiding force. For those who believe that "life" inheres at some point earlier than birth, the slavery parallel and the equal protection argument can be compelling. One survey respondent, a 55-year-old independent voter (who voted for Carter in 1976, John Anderson in 1980, Mondale in 1984, and Bush in 1988 and 1992), responds to "why did you join a pro-life group" with these words: "Because I believe in the U.S. Constitution: All are created equal. We will destroy ourselves if we don't treat all as equals." If abolitionists pursue alliances in the secular realm, they could find other acceptable messengers for a less theological debate. Such arguments, properly presented and divorced from the religious or emotional content usually found in abortion debates, could potentially prove persuasive.

It should also be remembered that abolitionists do not march in lock-step on other issues. If the linkage issues of the social movement can be set aside temporarily in pursuit of abortion abolition, there are a number of areas of politics out of which abortion opponents might come. Despite the official position of the National Organization for Women, Feminists for Life argue that abortion is not necessarily a fundamental component of feminism. One of our survey respondents, a 32-year-old female social worker from Ohio, speaks of her feminist sentiments: "I've been a feminist and pro-life as long as I've realized they were issues (mid-teens). I shied away from women's groups because they were all pro-abortion. I called the president of [an abortion abolition group] in 1982 and got involved. At the time I was non-Christian. Believed in a God but practiced a la carte religion—a little reincarnation, some bio-rhythms, astral projection—stuff like that. Was 'born-again' November 2nd, 1984. True Christianity does not conflict with true feminism."

Moreover, other life issues normally associated with "liberal" political positions are also reconcilable with an abolitionist position, as they are for this respondent, a 31-year-old female Episcopalian social worker:

> From the beginning of my pro-life work, I've been committed to the Consistent Ethic of life, so therefore am interested in helping people see the connections between different forms of violence in our society (e.g.—war, poverty, abortion, capital punishment). I've been arrested at a nuclear weapons storage facility and participated in "pray-ins"/sit-ins at abortion facilities. I've been involved in starting local chapters of several national groups and have been a board member of [group], a Consistent Ethic of Life group. I see all this as closely connected to my work as a geriatric social worker and end-of-life issues in general. LIFE is of primary importance, and I aim to fight for it wherever it is threatened.

Finally, though perhaps the least likely avenue for growth, there is the possibility of gaining adherents from within the Democratic party, particularly when the more nurturant aspects of the enterprise are stressed. Former Pennsylvania governor Robert Casey (denied a speaking role in the 1992 Democratic convention) argues that the natural home of abolitionist sentiment is the Democratic party, with its tradition of concern for the downtrodden. In a 1992 speech at the Notre Dame law school, he pleaded with his party to consider the abolitionist position in light of its other concerns. He said:

> This is my message to my party in 1992.
> Just as we fought so hard and so well for the rights of the workers of America, for the dignity and human rights of mi-

norities, for women and children and families. For the poor.
The disabled. The dispossessed.

Just as we fought for all of these, the time has come as well
to fight to protect the most vulnerable, the most defenseless,
the most powerless members of our human family.

The Democrats of 1992 are heirs to an historic legacy that
wraps a protective embrace around those who have no means
to protect themselves. The time has come for the Democratic
Party to protect what should be a natural constituency—our
unborn children.

Just feel the power and passion of these words:

> "What happens to the mind of a person, and the
> moral fabric of a nation that accepts the aborting
> of the life of a baby without a pang of conscience?
> What kind of a person, what kind of a society, will
> we have 20 years hence if life can be taken so ca-
> sually?"

Jesse Helms didn't say that. Jesse Jackson did. In 1977. Four
years after *Roe v. Wade*. . . . [F]or the past 25 years, too many
Democrats in this country have had a bad feeling in their
hearts and in their souls about the national Democratic
Party. Because the Democratic Party broke its historic compact with mainstream America when it volunteered itself as
the party of abortion on demand. . . . On the fundamental issue of abortion, the national Democratic Party doesn't speak
for me. Nor does it speak for millions of pro-life Democrats.
(Casey, 1992)

Casey is not entirely alone in his party, though it often seems that
way. Other pro-life Democrats have never been as vocal, either as Casey
or as abolitionist Republicans have been. In fact, the highest ranking pro-
life Democrat in Congress now rarely makes his dissent known and is
one of President Clinton's most loyal point men on nearly every other
issue. If that Democrat, David Bonior of Michigan, were so inclined, he
might be able to make some room in the party for those who agree with
him on the issue of abortion. Ralph Reed is fond of stating that the
Christian Coalition has no party of its own and makes no partisan en-
dorsements; if Casey's "millions" would make themselves known, both
the Christian Coalition and the Democratic Party would have the opportunity to live up to their own rhetoric of inclusion.

MORAL CRUSADERS, SOCIAL MOVEMENT ACTIVISTS, REVIVAL, AND THE FUTURE

As the recent reforms of the national welfare system play out, those who entered the enterprise as moral crusaders may find themselves more necessary than ever in the abortion abolition enterprise. In a fallen world where messages of promiscuity abound, the compassion and the self-lessness expressed by a Mother Teresa will always be an asset in caring for those who find themselves in a crisis pregnancy. The hands-on emphasis of ministry to the soul that Catholicism views as a duty lends itself well to that portion of the abolitionist enterprise that provides the support promised by the rhetoric of the social movement and prayed for by the revivalists.

The Christian compassion and other-directedness characteristic of Catholic charity makes those believers particularly suited to the support roles that are vital to the enterprise. The abolitionist mindset does not deny that there are problem pregnancies, but to fully serve both the unborn child and his crisis-ridden mother, the enterprise must provide a compassionate and realistic alternative. The Catholic Church and her followers concerned about the abortion issue bring with them a tradition that embraces and nurtures life, even in the most difficult of circumstances. Father Damien's leper colony on Molokai, Mother Teresa's nuns in the streets of Calcutta—such examples demonstrate the highest and best expression of ministering to "the least of these" and sharing in their suffering. Without the continued participation of the moral crusaders, the abortion abolition enterprise would become merely another effort to lobby the government, and much of its heart would be lost. It does not seem, however, that the Church or the Pope will change the stand against abortion within the foreseeable future, and there will always be servants of the Church to pray, witness, and work against abortion.

At the same time, neither of the other two groups would survive long in the political arena without the leadership of the social movement activists. As they gain more influence in the halls of government, social movement activists will press for legislation that not only will restrict abortion itself, but will also seek wider recognition of and support for abortion alternatives and agencies that provide them. Already, bills have been passed to lift racial restrictions on adoption, making more children available to those who wish to adopt them. Adoption as an alternative to abortion becomes a more attractive proposition when the birth-mother feels secure in the placement process.

It seems likely that social movement conservatives will petition their allies in Congress to repeal or negate the Freedom of Access to Clinic Entrances Act, at least insofar as it addresses nonviolent protest. Other possibly fruitful avenues for future legislation include reinstating President Bush's international policies concerning Planned Parenthood, fetal tissue testing, abortion for military personnel, and RU-486; enacting restrictive legislation addressing health, safety, and licensing regulations for abortion clinics; and pushing again for a Human Life Amendment to the Constitution, as well as continuing the fight to pass a veto-proof ban on partial-birth abortion. The amendment process itself has the potential to set in motion a protracted national debate, in which those currently on the sidelines could be motivated to ask serious and important questions about the national availability of abortion.

To truly abolish abortion will require a changing of hearts more than of minds or even of laws, and for this the revivalists were made. Their Spirit-led demonstrations of conscience, if pursued in the form of nonviolent civil disobedience, carry with them the greatest potential for change. Changed laws may dissuade some from having abortions but do not solve the attitude that abolitionists see as the problem. Changed circumstances—in the form of greater availability of abortion alternatives and private charity—succeed only until the next misfortune comes. It is only when individuals turn away from the action they have a legal right to take—for spiritual, ethical, or moral reasons—that long-term transformation can be achieved.

There is also some indication that the revivalists may be experiencing the very thing they predicted. No longer just a whisper, "revival" is becoming a murmur in conservative Protestant churches, especially Pentecostal and charismatic ones. Whether that murmur has the potential to become a nationwide shout has yet to be seen, but the documented cases of protracted instances of local and regional revival have recently been growing. Revivals have been reported in Wheaton, Illinois; Brownwood, Fort Worth, and Corinth, Texas; and at Colorado Christian University, Iowa State University, and other colleges across the nation. In addition, in Pensacola, Florida, the Brownsville Assembly of God Church is still experiencing a revival that began on Father's Day of 1995, with 42,000 reported conversions to date. If, as revivalist abolitionists maintain, the spiritual transformation wrought by revival is translatable into cultural change, Pensacola, with its sorry history of the worst forms of anti-abortion violence, might be the first place to look for enduring success for the revivalist abolitionists.

In the long run, however, no single aspect of the abortion abolition enterprise will carry the day; instead, it is the triune nature of the enterprise and its ability to adapt that will sustain it. Each of the three aspects has a different focus, and each has a distinct role to which it is most suited in the multipronged fight to abolish abortion. From a spiritual perspective, the revivalists and the moral crusaders provide the prayer support that the social movement activists believe they need to operate in an otherwise hostile environment. From a political standpoint, the social movement activists use their influence to enable the other two groups to continue their activities without interference and to enact legislation that facilitates their success. From a social welfare perspective, the moral crusaders provide the caretaking facilities and personal attention demanded by an enterprise that works with people in crisis. In the eyes of the public, the revivalists challenge the complacency of those who would do nothing, prompting the internal transformations that eventually lead to social change. The revivalists speak to the troubled spirit, the social movement activists engage the material world of concrete politics, and the moral crusaders tend to the wounded soul.

The persistence of the abortion abolition enterprise has been made possible first by the deep religious commitments of those who first entered into it. Second, in later years, participants were able to attract new constituencies and form alliances around other issues that the enterprise felt were closely linked to abortion. In recent years, it has been both energized and endangered by the participation of still other groups with divergent understandings of the place of faith in society and the right relationship of the citizen to the state. In the past, the enterprise has brought together faith systems that once had nothing but fear and contempt for one another. It fused Catholic and Protestant, fundamentalist and Pentecostal. In the name of the unborn, abolitionists have been able—albeit sometimes slowly—to overcome divisions that once seemed unbridgeable. Few movements in American history have managed to endure so visibly for so long with so little apparent success, and it is a testament to the seriousness with which they hold their position that the abolitionists are still a vital part of the political scene.

As the enterprise moves toward its third decade, its ability to adapt to the needs and beliefs of those who would join it will likely be tested again. In essence, the continued success of the abortion enterprise lies in its ability to balance disparate elements within it, as well as to reach out to others who may differ from them on all subjects but this one. As in the past, old suspicions will have to be put to rest if new groups are to be brought into the enterprise. The dynamic history of this enterprise, however, demonstrates that nothing is impossible in a debate that is both deeply personal and unavoidably public.

I have made every effort here to refrain from making any pronouncements as to the merits of the argument itself, but the tenacity with which abolitionists persevere and the passion with which they act should give all of us pause. If, as they argue, abortion is a matter of the gravest importance, with the most serious consequences to all involved, then the debate must go beyond rights and law. It must reach past the characterizations of pro-abortion and anti-choice, of baby-killers and woman-haters. At present, Americans are deeply divided and ambiguous about the matter of abortion. While favoring the retention of *Roe*, they hesitate to endorse an unfettered right throughout gestation and for any reason. The questions concerning when and how abortion crosses a visceral line that disturbs the body politic are important ones, and abolitionists at least encourage us to examine those issues. If this national debate is to proceed, all Americans—abolitionists, pro-choicers, conservatives, liberals, Democrats, Republicans, and others—are better served by clear pictures of the issues and the individuals involved. To that end, this chapter suggests a new way of looking at faith-based political action.

I have sought, in a variety of ways, to explore the abortion abolition movement during the past three decades, largely through the eyes of its participants. In so doing, it is hoped that some of the observations made here may be of use to academics in understanding a group of people who are, quite frankly, largely unknown to them. The academic world, largely pro-choice, has found abortion abolitionists difficult to understand, intractably illogical, and hostile to women's rights.

Abortion abolitionists, however, understand women's interests and human rights differently than most academics do, and, within their thought systems, they have legitimate and logical reasons for doing so. The discounting of these deeply held primary beliefs as secondary to political concerns has not helped us to understand faith-based politics or its participants. As we have explored the aspects of the enterprise over time, certain elements are enduring, and it is these to which we must attend in finding a comprehensive way of understanding the actions and attitudes of faith-based activists. Here we will use what we have learned to move toward a new approach to the study of faith-based political movements that will, it is hoped, begin a process of equalizing the academic image of such entities with the visions and realities of those who participate in them.

THE MILITARY MODEL OF FAITH-BASED POLITICS

Whereas Olson's theory of collective behavior begins from an economic model of cost-benefit analysis, the approach I propose for understanding the dynamics of faith-based collective action instead employs a militaristic one. Just as certain strains lead to hostility between those who have otherwise peacefully coexisted, so are there moments in history when people of intensive faith-based commitments feel themselves so out of harmony with the world in which they live that they feel there is no option but to engage the opposition, even when their own traditions would dictate stasis.

For people of deep religious faith, the first loyalty is to God. The very nature of theology, the very essence of the concept of an all-encompassing God, demands that the life of faith take precedence over all other considerations. A creator God, an immanent being that gives meaning and purpose to the life of the individual and the community, cannot be made the servant of the state, no matter what the nature of that state may be. For its part, the state must have the loyalty of its citizens to arise, to survive, and to retain its legitimacy in any lasting form. At times, the interests of the state conflict with the mission of the church. When such conflicts occur, the true nature of church and state as oppositional entities becomes clear.

When the demands of the state conflict with the commandments of the faith, history has shown that people of faith are capable of incredible feats of resistance. From its earliest days, Christianity survived as a minority religion through the willingness of its followers to stand against the state, even when the penalty was death. Martyrdom and self-sacrifice in the name of faith are found throughout the history of every world religion, and every religion honors those who have refused to renounce their God even when the state put them to death merely for that refusal. The depth of faith as a motivation transcends political concerns, cultural realities, and self-preservation instincts.

Despite Jefferson's hoped-for "wall of separation" between the church and the state, in practice Americans over time developed what Robert Bellah (1967) has termed a "civil religion." This theology of the state has permitted the United States to move beyond its beginnings as a "Christian Republic" into a more secular state, without abandoning its underlying moral principles. It is the shared mythology of patriotism that allows the president to end his speeches with "God bless America" without leaving the impression of deep religiosity, the Supreme Court to open with prayer without incurring the wrath of atheists, and the coinage to bear the phrase "In God We Trust." It is a hybrid of religious and governmental language that starts in religion and ends in legislation. Yet it is more than mere language; in modern America, it is the conceptual location in which the vast majority of Americans do their everyday business.

The state as it exists today is one of great religiosity and small ethics. We are both the most churched and the least moral nation in the industrialized world. Our faith tends to be institutional, inherited, and ill-informed. Yet we can hardly go a full week without an elected representative invoking the blessing or curse of the Almighty for one reason or another. I wrote part of this book during the 1996 political convention season, and all parties seemed to have spent their previous few months in church; God and country are never so close to one another as when politicians are trying to speak to real people. This is a politically astute approach to a population of which the vast majority call themselves "religious." The politicians, however, whose second (and sometimes first) language is civil religion, know the hollowness of those statistics. Seldom do they go beyond the patriotic generalities that appeal to the Deity and actually address why He might want to listen. Rarely do they speak of the desperate need for prayer recognized by the Founding Fathers or ask publicly for it. And almost never do they specify the name of the Lord they would press into their service.

Most Americans claim to be religious, but the content of their faith is vast and varied. Millions worship Jesus, and some find God to be a force within themselves, but all those individuals, with their diverse understandings, are addressed by the civil religion. Although the root of the religion is Christianity, it is sufficiently diluted as to be palatable to everyone. The pervasive presence of civil religion leads to a confusion for those whose religion is deeply meaningful and whose language is put to service in civil religion. It is this confusion that leads to the conflicts that arise from time to time between people of faith and the state of which they are citizens.

For the people we have studied here, the central reality of life lies in one's relationship to God, not to the state. The civil religion, by its use of the references and rhetoric of actual religion (specifically Christianity), draws believers not merely into loyalty to the state, but as well into a false sense that the interests of the state are in harmony with the interests of their faith. When the state asserts its secularity against the faithful, this illusion of harmony is damaged and challenged. When the demands of secularity appear to violate the precepts of what they believe to be a faith-based law of the civil religion (such as the inalienable right to life), they do not initially reject the state. Instead, they seek to reassert their understanding of those precepts, believing themselves in harmony with the national tradition.

$$\text{State} \ \Big|\ \begin{array}{c} \text{Demilitarized Zone} \\ \text{of Civil Religion} \end{array}\ \Big|\ \text{Church}$$

The rhetorical cushion of civil religion has served to provide something of a buffer zone between the antagonistic points of church and state, enabling those committed to their faith to participate as full and equal citizens, rooting their social desire and their drive to community service in deeply held religious beliefs, without seeking to enforce specific tenets of that faith as law. For the first two centuries of the nation's existence, the civil religion both preserved and strengthened church, state, and a truce between the two.

In recent years, however, in the eyes of conservatively religious people and especially those who perceive the Bible to be the primary means through which one understands life, the state crossed the demilitarized zone numerous times, seemingly in an attempt to drive those whose civic participation was informed by serious faith out of the political arena entirely. As people who believe that their faith makes them good citizens, religious conservatives find it difficult to understand why the trappings even of civil religion seem to be increasingly excluded from the public square. When the state began to enforce its own values against those of religiously motivated citizens—especially when the areas of conflict involved personal life and the education of children—the soldiers of the church felt themselves under attack and therefore began to fight back.

Whether and when the lines of demarcation have been crossed seems to be largely in the eye of the beholder. For religious people, *Roe* is a moment of unacceptable incursion to those who were aware of its importance, while secularists assume that the state was merely carrying out its ordinary duty as mediator of the Constitution. The confusion merely highlights the obfuscatory nature of the civil religion. The studied ambiguity in which the state and the church interact led both sides to believe that interpreting the meaning and place of abortion was within their purview. For the religious, the state's decision to pronounce abortion permissible usurps the authority of the church; for secularists, the church's desire to control the debate on a legal question seems presumptuous.

As we have seen, the first mobilization following *Roe* was of Catholics, and by the proposed model this can be explained by the traditional closeness between the political world and the Church, particularly coming just out of the 1960s, which saw a great politicization of the clergy, of which the laity were aware. Having long been engaged in social welfare issues and Democratic politics, Catholics were well positioned within the civil religion milieu to recognize the societal import of the *Roe* decision. Having never compromised on the issue of abortion and having recently completed a protracted discussion within the Church on birth control issues, the Catholic faithful were keenly aware of the disequilibrium between the vision they held of the civil religion state and the reality the Supreme Court had made clear. America's civil religion had, for them, become corrupt by this decision and had to be righted. Thus, right-to-life groups were set up and spiritual pressures were brought to bear. Yet, despite the willingness of the Church leadership to cross the demilitarized zone to lobby the state, parishioners by and large stayed in their comfort zone of the Church, praying and waiting for God to act.

At the same time, the Catholics' potential allies of other faiths were almost entirely inured in their own churches, blissfully ignorant of what had just taken place. Secure that they could remain "in the world" without being "of" it, conservative evangelicals, fundamentalists, and others were largely untouched by the transformation of civil religion assumptions that so bothered the Catholics. Individually, and as a faith community, those who would become the next wave of activists would not find the American abortion situation to be an intolerable strain for years.

The proposed model asserts that each person of faith, and by extension each faith community, lives in a nation that is at once sacred and secular. G. K. Chesterton called America "a nation with the soul of a church." For religious people, who believe that faith is the first allegiance, it is the soul of the nation that should be preeminent, its moral base that should dictate its policy. For secular people, who read the establishment clause as a bar to any faith expression in public life, it is the nation itself that matters most, its pragmatic needs that must be satisfied. People of faith employ civil religion and its rhetoric to justify more religious and quasireligious forms in government, while ordinary civil patriots use them to exhort citizens to greater loyalty to the republic. The civil religion allows for a compromise between the two, by which patriotism can appear more Godly and God more patriotic than either side would otherwise grant the other.

When the state, the church, and the civil religion are functioning normally, this harmony serves both state and church. Good Christians march loyally off to war in the service of a nation that asks its allegiance, and do so under a flag said to fly over a nation that is "under God." Powerful impulses toward charity, compassion, and self-sacrifice are turned not just to the community but to public service. In return, the state recognizes the value of the church and grants it tax exemptions and other special benefits that help it to do its work more directly.

However, when an event takes place or a new element is introduced that disturbs the equilibrium between the two, the civil religion is the milieu in which the two opposing forces seek compromise. When that becomes impossible, a choice of allegiances must be made. For every individual and for every church, this point of departure may come at a different time, but I argue here that it comes when the demands of faith and government are no longer felt to be reconcilable. When enough individuals in one faith reach that point and share that discomfort with each other, a faith-based political campaign is born.

From observations of the abolition enterprise, it seems that several elements must be in place for this feeling of disequilibrium to manifest itself sufficiently to prompt action:

1. The individual believer must have a significant concern about the issue or event.

2. The individual believer must have a strong sense of the linkage between the issue/event and his or her faith.

3. The individual believer must come to believe that the civil religion cannot provide an acceptable compromise.

4. The individual believer must believe that there is something that can be done.

In the abortion abolition enterprise, activists speak of what I have here termed a "second conversion," and I argue that it is that defining moment that both signals the advent of intolerable disequilibrium and drives the activist into the political arena. All four of the above elements must be present before an individual finds the need to move beyond his or her chosen area of action and further toward opposing the secular state. A person who has concern but does not connect the issue to his or her faith is unlikely to become a faith-based activist, and even one who does see that connection will first attempt to live at peace with the compromise that civil religion affords. If the state is seen as all-powerful and the individual sees no hope of change, it is unlikely that he or she will seek the avenue of activism. All three groups of activists we have studied here have demonstrated these precursive beliefs prior to becoming part of the abortion abolition enterprise.

Once the individual has become alert to the importance of the issue, there seems to be a tendency to seek out others who are likely to agree with the religious precepts and persuadable to action for the cause. Abolitionists are largely self-recruiting, and they seek others within their own circle of social, political, and religious compatriots as they begin to cast about for something they can do. As individuals persuade others in their faith community to join the cause, the larger church units of sect, denomination, convention, or international assembly become actively involved for the same reasons. In some cases, as with the Catholics, the underlying principles are never in question, and the leadership either spearheads the effort or welcomes it as a grass-roots development. In other cases, particularly in single churches, the connections between faith and issue must be explicated from doctrine, tradition, belief, or dogma. In still other cases, the basis for the faith position is unclear from the first, and more time must be spent on persuasion before individuals are activated. In yet others, individuals who have come to the beliefs noted above find themselves seeking new churches that, in their eyes, will prove more loyal to both the issue and the faith.

Taking the case of the abolitionists, we can see that the traditional Catholic position was well entrenched in those who would become activists and that they understood that opposition to abortion as a fundamental tenet of the faith. Moreover, when the Supreme Court itself pronounced their moral position to be irrelevant to the civil religion, it was clear that the former demilitarized zone had become enemy territory. What to do about the problem, however, remained unclear for quite a while, although it was always evident that there was something to do. Persuading others, praying, and building organizations for later use occupied the abolitionists from 1973 until the end of the decade. Their position was largely defensive. The first wave of activists held the line against a complete defeat until reinforcements arrived.

As the 1980s approached and conservative Protestants were activated by what was, in their eyes, an intolerable interference in their educational system, they discovered what seemed to them the appalling abortion situation, apparently for the first time. Because it is a more directly linked issue to the faith, abolition overtook the conservative Protestant movement. As individuals and as faith groups, evangelicals, fundamentalists, charismatics, and other socially conservative believers felt the disconnect between what they believed the state to be and what it was, and reacted accordingly. Moving into the demilitarized zone and using the rhetoric of civil religion, the social movement activists sought to reassert what they believed the underlying civil religion norms to be, both on abortion and on other social and moral issues.

When we examine the revivalist abolitionists, however, the picture changes slightly. Whereas the initial activists of the moral crusade largely stayed within the church, engaging the state in a defensive mode, and the social movement activists used the civil religion territory to their advantage, the revivalists discarded civil religion and remained rhetorically within their church mode. Arguing for allegiance to the church rather than the state, the revivalists essentially ignored the civil religion. In doing so, they abandoned the hope of finding allies in the demilitarized zone, but they essentially flew over it to make direct attacks on the legitimacy of the state.

Once faith-based activists begin to enter the world of politics, they find themselves operating more and more in the realm of civil religion, and moving closer to a direct attack on the state itself. In the case of the abolitionists, as we have seen, the faithful found themselves in a battle they had no experience of and realized the need to find other allies and to use the terminology of civil religion to legitimize their attempts to push the state out of their territory. As they did so, they found other aspects of the political realm that displeased them, and they sought to drive the totality of those anti-faith elements out.

When faith-based activists move into the political arena, using both ordinary religious rhetoric and the language of civil religion, others who either believe the civil religion to be more civil than religion or who see it that way on particular issues react. If that reaction fails to take into account the legitimacy of the religious voice in the civil religion zone, people of faith become more convinced of the righteousness of their cause. Persecution solidifies conviction, and the battle becomes more intractable than ever. Compromise is possible when all parties are willing to recognize the legitimacy of each other's most deeply held beliefs. When that recognition is not forthcoming, the debate is no longer a debate, no longer possible in the neutral zone of the civil religion, and no longer winnable for either side. The war is engaged, and there is no end in sight.

Despite its apparent pessimism for a negotiated outcome, the military model is useful for several reasons. First and foremost, it takes into account the prime factor that activists cite for their own motivation—faith. It also allows us to discuss the entire history of the enterprise without denying the importance of any particular phase and without claiming one to be more legitimate than the others. Finally, it is felt that the military model comes closer to explaining the intensity of feeling involved and the volatility of the conflict than any other approach has been able to do. James Davison Hunter has written of "culture wars" and has described the antagonisms of our moral culture, but the notion has not been treated explicitly as an explanatory model.

It should always be understood that, in ordinary times, the essential desire of both sides is to be left alone as the sovereign of its own territory. The church, though constantly proselytizing to win new adherents to itself, desires to be left to practice its faith without interference from the state. The state, though needing all people, including the religious, for its legitimacy, prefers not to engage the church and prefers that its peculiar tenets be left out of law. The civil religion allows both to take place in the public square, without either entity being made subordinate to the other.

In applying this model to other matters of faith concerns that intersect the political realm, certain potential developments become evident. Because each issue of faith-based politics exists on both sides of the church-state wall and in the demilitarized zone of civil religion, they may be seen as separate armies that form alliances when it becomes convenient. Thus, the actors who oppose abortion may or may not pick up allies to assist them when they also turn their attention to gay rights. The interaction between the soldiers of church and state may occasionally be peaceful and cooperative. However, because we have developed a shared understanding of this civil religion that co-mingles faith-speech with nationalism and civic duty, it is inevitable that some issues that cling closely to both will bring the two into conflict (as when the state permits previously illegal activity to blossom, without due regard for the sentiments of the faithful, or when the faithful seek to implement their own doctrine, having been falsely led to believe, through a prevalence of civil religion rhetoric, that it is a matter of universal understanding).

It should not be assumed that this dynamic is exclusive to those of what might be called a "conservative" mindset, though they have been the most active segment of the faith community in recent years. However, it should be noted that the antislavery and civil rights movements arose when the faith concerns of individuals made it clear that the difference between a nation where "all men are created equal" and one where Dred Scott could be sent back to his master, no better than a piece of property, were too intolerable to continue. Indeed, Lincoln's Second Inaugural has been described as "perhaps the greatest speech in American history precisely because, with singular eloquence and at a moment of unparalleled national trauma, it spoke to the entire country in an idiom that the entire country could understand" (Weigel, 1994: 85). This idiom is the civil religion, and Lincoln was perhaps its most skillful practitioner.

The question of why some faiths engage in this behavior and some do not is irrelevant. Throughout history, all faiths have attempted to assert themselves against the state, and all states have, to one degree or another, sought to define some spheres of action as apart from the influence of religious prescriptions. This can be observed in the abolition movements against both slavery and abortion, both the civil rights and women's movements, and both the temperance and labor movements. The presence of faith as a motivational factor for social change has ever been more observed than wanting. The abortion issue, however, perhaps more than any other, has afforded us an opportunity to observe the remarkable antagonisms that can arise when the church and the state are intractably opposed. It is hoped that this approach to understanding that conflict will help other scholars to interpret the dynamics of this issue and other faith-based political campaigns, both on the present scene and in the future.

NOTE

1. The brainchild of Colorado football coach Bill McCartney, Promise Keepers is a men's support organization that holds stadium rallies for the purpose of bringing men together to learn how to be better husbands, fathers, and Christians. The sixth of the seven promises of a Promise Keeper is: "A Promise Keeper is committed to reach beyond any racial and denominational barriers to demonstrate the power of biblical unity" (back cover, *Man of His Word* NIV New Testament, published by the International Bible Society for Promise Keepers).

Appendix: The Data and the Survey

The initial data used for this project consisted of available material in each of the following categories: primary documents from within the enterprise; primary documents from the pro-choice movement; secondary scholarly analyses of the two; and secondary popular analyses of the two. In addition, activists within the abortion abolition enterprise were surveyed via mailed questionnaire, with follow-up interviews conducted for a regionally diversified sample.

DOCUMENTARY ANALYSIS

Because of the nature of the documents available, activity and development over time were studied primarily through the newsletters of particular groups and secondary observational documents generated during those periods (such as newspaper and magazine articles, and the academic and popular analyses available). Brochures, posters, handouts, and other such documents, being generally haphazardly generated and undated, were not considered as useful in determining the historical development of the enterprise. In cases where no primary data are available, secondary analyses from within the movement were utilized to get an overall picture of the state of the enterprise. However, documents that appear repeatedly, even when dating is impossible, have been used to assess rhetorical strategies and to provide exemplars of the overall linguistic strategy of the enterprise. Citations from these documents, however, are only used as representative of the enterprise as a whole when they are found in more than one document and in more than one region. A number of rhetorical devices, statistics, and stories appear in documents nationwide, and these are considered to be useful in gauging the overall development of the enterprise as a whole. For example, the "Is this a Choice? Or is this a CHILD?" poster used in advertisements for National Right to Life appears ubiquitously in the literature. The "American War Casualties" graphic generated by the Minnesota Citizens Concerned for Life (used to demonstrate that more Americans have been killed through abortion in the years since *Roe v. Wade* than in all the military actions engaged in by the United States, combined) has had a similar evolution. While these documents were initially published by a particular group, they have become representative of the literature of the enterprise as a whole.

After the documentary data were thus divided and examined, the primary documentary material from within the abolitionist enterprise was selected out for further examination, while secondary analyses and primary documents from other sources were utilized as background material.

THE SURVEY

One of the difficulties of surveying the abortion abolition enterprise is that there are no dependable figures that can be used to assess the size of the true population. Therefore, the investigator first gathered the names and addresses of as many issue-oriented groups as possible, from the appendices of abolitionist books, the Encyclopaedia of Associations, pamphlets handed out at issue-oriented events, e-mail lists, and other wide-ranging sources. From this, a list of five hundred organizations emerged, of which fifty were randomly selected to be approached to provide survey participants.

Each organization was sent ten questionnaires and asked to distribute them to members of the organization for the members to return. The organizations also received an optional response form asking the leader to indicate whether the organization would be participating. In addition, each organization was sent a postcard two months after the initial mailing, as a reminder to have members return the questionnaires. The surveys were mailed in September of 1992, and the last response coded was received in May of 1993. This generated 104 responses, for a return rate of 21%. However, it is felt that the breadth of the returned responses (representing twenty-nine states in all nine designated national regions) somewhat makes up for the rather low response rate. In addition, in this case the self-selection bias generally apparent in return-mail surveys works to our advantage, since our interest here is in those who are most interested in the issue. The responses were rendered anonymous during the encoding process in order to ensure complete confidentiality.

The survey itself was designed to generate an accurate picture of the current committed membership of the abortion abolition enterprise in the United States today. The survey asks a number of questions regarding actions taken by the participants, whether they would take such action again, and whether, if they have not done so before, they would consider taking the action. These questions were included to give the project some ability to predict the possible future directions the enterprise might take.

In addition, several unstructured, background interviews were conducted in Wichita, Kansas, during the Summer of Mercy Campaign of Operation Rescue and Hope for the Heartland campaign of associated Kansas pro-life groups in 1991. Such interviews were also conducted in 1992 in Buffalo, New York, surrounding Operation Rescue's activity there. Many of the Buffalo interviews were conducted with leaders in the movement and provide an interesting measure by which to gauge the degree to which leadership and membership interests, attitudes, and opinions converge.

The questionnaire contains inquiries concerning the participants' opinions of individuals, groups, and agencies whose rhetoric tends to focus on the moral questions involved (or rejects same). The personal narratives and interviews provided by participants were also used to deepen the analysis and allow for a greater understanding of these opinions and attitudes.

Questions of age, race, gender, educational level, marital status, family size, religion and denomination, political affiliation, and voting behavior were used to explore diversity within the movement, while several questions address the hierarchy of groups, asking participants how many people are in their group, whether they have a leadership role, and how long they have been active on the issue. In addition, space is provided for personal narratives regarding the individual's experience as an activist, which allow us to get some sense of the development over time of hierarchy and structure in particular groups, without resorting exclusively to official statements by group leaders or to the literature produced by the groups themselves.

Questions of diversity and group development were also addressed in some detail in individual interviews. Background interviews conducted in Wichita and Buffalo were pursued in an informal manner, prior to the development and finalization of the questionnaire, largely due to the immediacy of developments regarding collective activity on the abortion issue. It was felt that the Summer of Mercy campaign and the Spring of Life event were significant developments in abortion abolition activism, which required immediate attention.

While much of the data regarding recent revivalist sentiment came from the literature provided from the groups themselves, some of the questions on the survey were also designed to get at the extent to which enterprise participants echo that rhetoric or show evidence of familiarity with those assumptions. The individual's perceptions of the importance of religion in his or her own life, the frequency with which church is attended and prayer performed, and the details of the participant's attitude toward other aspects of religion are important indicators of the degree to which the assumptions of revivalism are likely to be accepted. In addition, the personal narratives and interviews provided important information concerning the levels of revivalism present in the enterprise.

OTHER CONSIDERATIONS AND CONCERNS

Included in the survey are various questions designed to provide an accurate overall picture of the current status of the enterprise. Several economic questions and general social attitude questions are included to help us assess the degree to which activists differ from the general population in their opinions, attitudes, and experiences. To aid the predictive capacity of the survey in exploring the possible future directions the enterprise might take, one section of the questionnaire asks a number of questions regarding actions the participants have taken in the past, and whether they would be willing to take those same actions or others in the future.

In addition to information culled from the documents and the questionnaire, the interviews offered an opportunity to explore the respondents' expectations for the future. While the bulk of futuristic responses were focused on the potential for the movement itself, several respondents chose to add predictions regarding the moral and ethical future of the United States, the American economy in general, developments in public education, historical and theological theories, and eschatological concerns.

As with all self-administered surveys, it is always possible that the respondents are simply lying. However, the correspondence between the literature and the responses of the activists, coupled with the length of the questionnaire and the voluntary nature of its return, somewhat reassure this researcher that the responses are genuine. As mentioned before, the response rate turned out to be low; therefore, the information generated by the survey should be qualified with that in mind.

It should also be noted that this is an issue in active development from one day to the next. As with any viable political issue, our ability to make statements about it must be qualified by our understanding that the political and social atmosphere is in flux. While this is unfortunate, it is only to be expected on an issue that has been controversial for an extended period of time and that shows no signs of being definitively settled. While it would be academically convenient if the political and social culture would cooperate in settling the question so that a definitive historical document could be written on a closed question, there is little likelihood that this will take place. Every effort has been made to make this work as up-to-date as possible, but it should be remembered that politics is an inexact science at best, and social science can only offer predictions and analyses based on the information available at the time of writing.

Bibliography

WORKS CITED

Abraham, William J. (1984). *The Coming Great Revival: Recovering the Full Evangelical Tradition*. San Francisco: Harper & Row.

Ahlstrom, Sydney E. (1972). *A Religious History of the American People*. New Haven, CT: Yale University Press.

Alcorn, Randy C. (1990). *Is Rescuing Right? Breaking the Law to Save the Unborn*. Downer's Grove, IL: InterVarsity Press.

Beisel, Nicola. (1990). "Class, Culture, and Campaigns Against Vice in Three American Cities, 1872–1892." *American Sociological Review* 55: 44–62.

Bellah, Robert. (1974). "Civil Religion in America." In Russel E. Richey and Donald G. Jones, eds., *American Civil Religion*. New York: Harper & Row.

———. (1975). *Broken Covenant: American Civil Religion in Time of Trial*. New York: Seabury Press.

———. (1978). "Religion and Legitimation in the American Republic: Civil Religion." *Society* 15: 16–23 (May).

Blanchard, Dallas A. (1994). *The Anti-Abortion Movement and the Rise of the Religious Right*. New York: Twayne.

Blanchard, Dallas A., and Terry J. Prewitt. (1993). *Religious Violence and Abortion: The Gideon Project*. Gainesville: University Press of Florida.

Bloom, Harold. (1992). *The American Religion: The Emergence of the Post-Christian Nation*. New York: Simon & Schuster.

Bright, William R. (1986). "Nothing as Important as Our Love for Him." In Richie Martin, ed., *Judgment in the Gate*. Westchester, IL: Crossway.

Burgess, Stanley M., Gary B. McGee, and Patrick H. Alexander, eds. (1988). *Dictionary of Pentecostal and Charismatic Movements*. Grand Rapids, MI: Regency Reference Library/Zondervan.

Carroll, Peter N., and David W. Noble. (1977). *The Free and the Unfree: A New History of the United States*. New York: Penguin.

Casey, Robert P. (1992). "The Politics of Abortion." Address given at Notre Dame Law School, April 2; reprinted in *Human Life Review* 18(3): 35–46 (Summer).

Catechism of the Catholic Church. (1994). Mahwah, NJ: Paulist Press.

Cohn, Carol. (1987). "Sex and Death in the Rational World of Defense Intellectuals." *SIGNS: Journal of Women in Culture and Society* 12(4).

Colson, Charles, with Ellen Santilli Vaughn. (1987). *Kingdoms in Conflict*. New York: William Morrow/Zondervan.

Condit, Celeste Michelle. (1990). *Decoding Abortion Rhetoric: Communicating Social Change*. Urbana and Chicago: University of Illinois Press.

Craig, Barbara Hinkson, and David M. O'Brien. (1993). *Abortion and American Politics*. Chatham, NJ: Chatham House.

Cunningham, Lawrence S. (1987). *The Catholic Faith: An Introduction*. Mahwah, NJ: Paulist Press.

Curro, Ellen. (1990). *Caring Enough to Help: Counseling at a Crisis Pregnancy Center*. Grand Rapids, MI: Baker Book House.

Davis, John Jefferson. (1984). *Abortion and the Christian: What Every Believer Should Know*. Phillipsburg, NJ: Presbyterian and Reformed Publishing CO.

deParrie, Paul. (1989). *The Rescuers*. Brentwood, TN: Wolgemuth & Hyatt.

Diamond, Sara. (1989). *Spiritual Warfare: The Politics of the Christian Right*. Boston: South End Press.

Dobson, James, and Gary L. Bauer. (1990). *Children at Risk: The Battle for the Hearts and Minds of Our Kids*. Dallas: Word Publishing.

Doner, Colonel V. (1988). *The Samaritan Strategy: A New Agenda for Christian Activism*. Brentwood, TN: Wolgemuth & Hyatt.

Donovan, Charles, and Robert Marshall. (1991). *Blessed Are the Barren: The Social Policy of Planned Parenthood*. San Francisco: Ignatius Press.

Everett, Carol. (1991). *The Scarlet Lady: Confessions of a Successful Abortionist*. Brentwood, TN: Wolgemuth & Hyatt.

Falwell, Jerry. (1986). *If I Should Die Before I Wake*. Nashville, TN: Thomas Nelson.

Faux, Marian. (1990). *Crusaders: Voices from the Abortion Front*. New York: Birch Lane Press.

Ferree, Myra Marx, and Beth B. Hess. (1985). *Controversy and Coalition: The New Feminist Movement*. Boston: Twayne.

Finke, Roger, and Rodney Stark. (1992). *The Churching of America 1776–1990: Winners and Losers in Our Religious Economy*. New Brunswick, NJ: Rutgers University Press.

Fletcher, Joseph. (1954). *Morals and Medicine*. Princeton, NJ: Princeton University Press.

———. (1966). *Situation Ethics: The New Morality*. Philadelphia: Westminster Press.

Glendon, Mary Ann. (1987). *Abortion and Divorce in Western Law*. Cambridge, MA: Harvard University Press.

Goen, C. C. (1985). *Broken Churches, Broken Nation: Denominational Schisms and the Coming of the American Civil War*. Macon, GA: Mercer University Press.

Grant, George. (1991). *Third Time Around: A History of the Pro-Life Movement from the First Century to the Present*. Brentwood, TN: Wolgemuth & Hyatt.

Grunlan, Stephen A., and Marvin K. Mayers. (1979). *Cultural Anthropology: A Christian Perspective*. Grand Rapids, MI: Zondervan.

Gusfield, Joseph R. (1963). *Symbolic Crusade: Status Politics and the American Temperance Movement*. Urbana: University of Illinois Press.

Hadden, Jeffrey K., and Anson Shupe. (1988). *Televangelism, Power and Politics on God's Frontier*. New York: Henry Holt.

Hatch, Nathan O. (1989). *The Democratization of American Christianity*. New Haven, CT: Yale University Press.

Heffernan, B. (circa 1973). "Feminists for Life." Pamphlet.

Hertzke, Alan D. (1988). *Representing God in Washington: The Role of Religious Lobbies in the American Polity*. Knoxville: University of Tennessee Press.

Hunter, James Davison. (1991). *Culture Wars: The Struggle to Define America*. New York: Basic Books.

———. (1994). *Before the Shooting Begins: Searching for Democracy in America's Culture War*. New York: Free Press.

Jaggar, Alison. (1989). "Love and Knowledge: Emotion in Feminist Epistemology." In Alison Jaggar and Susan Bordo, eds., *Gender/Body/Knowledge: Feminist Constructions of Being and Knowing*. New Brunswick, NJ: Rutgers University Press, pp. 145–71.

James, Kay Coles. (1992). *Never Forget*. Grand Rapids, MI: Zondervan.

John Paul II, His Holiness Pope. (1994). *Crossing the Threshold of Hope*. New York: Knopf.

———. (1995). *The Gospel of Life (Evangelium Vitae): The Encyclical Letter on Abortion, Euthanasia, and the Death Penalty in Today's World*. New York: Times Books, a division of Random House.

Kennedy, D. James. (1985). "Myths and Realities." In John W. Whitehead, ed. *Arresting Abortion: Practical Ways to Save Unborn Children*. Westchester, IL: Crossway, pp. 18–31.

Kilpatrick, John. (1995). *Feast of Fire: The Father's Day Outpouring*. Pensacola, FL: In Times Like These Publications.

Koop, C. Everett, and Francis A. Schaeffer. (1979). *Whatever Happened to the Human Race?* Westchester, IL: Crossway.

Kreeft, Peter. (1992). *Back to Virtue: Traditional Moral Wisdom for Modern Moral Confusion*. San Francisco: Ignatius Press.

LaHaye, Tim. (1987). *Faith of Our Founding Fathers*. Brentwood, TN: Wolgemuth & Hyatt.

Lawler, Philip F. (1992). *Operation Rescue: A Challenge to the Nation's Conscience*. Huntington, IN: Our Sunday Visitor Books.

Lloyd-Jones, Martyn. (1987). *Revival*. Westchester, IL: Crossway.

Luker, Kristin. (1984). *Abortion and the Politics of Motherhood*. Berkeley: University of California Press.

Marsden, George M. (1991). *Understanding Fundamentalism and Evangelicalism*. Grand Rapids, MI: Eerdmans.

Marshall, Peter, and David Manuel. (1977). *The Light and the Glory*. Old Tappan, NJ: Fleming H. Revell.

Marty, Martin E. (1984). *Pilgrims in Their Own Land: 500 Years of Religion in America*. New York: Penguin.

Marx, Paul. (1971). *The Death Peddlers: War on the Unborn*. Collegeville, MN: St. Johns University Press.

Miravelle, Mark I. (1993). *Mary: Coredemptrix, Mediatrix, Advocate*. Santa Barbara, CA: Queenship.

Olasky, Marvin. (1988). *The Press and Abortion, 1838–1988*. Hillsdale, NJ: Lawrence Erlbaum Associates.

———. (1992). *Abortion Rites: A Social History of Abortion in America*. Wheaton, IL: Crossway.

Olson, Mancur. (1965). *The Logic of Collective Action*. Cambridge, MA: Harvard University Press.

Pierard, Richard V. (1983). "Reagan and the Evangelicals: The Making of a Love Affair." *The Christian Century*, December 21–28: 1183.

Pierson, Ann. (1991). *52 Simple Things You Can Do to Be Pro-Life*. Minneapolis, MN: Bethany House.

Pratney, Winkie. (1983). *Revival: Principles to Change the World*. Springdale, PA: Whitaker House.

Quindlen, Anna. (1990). "A Time to Choose." Reprinted in *The Human Life Review* 16(2): 117–18 (Spring).

Reed, Ralph. (1994). *Politically Incorrect: The Emerging Faith Factor in American Politics*. Dallas: Word Publishers.

———. (1996). *Active Faith: How Christians Are Changing the Soul of American Politics*. New York: Free Press.

Robertson, Pat. (1986). *America's Date with Destiny*. Nashville, TN: Thomas Nelson.

Schlafly, Phyllis. (1981). "The Conservative, Pro-family Movement Nominated, Elected Ronald Reagan." *Conservative Digest* 7(1): 20–21.

Scholl, John P. (1973). *A New Catechism of the Catholic Faith*. Des Plaines, IL: FARE.

Sloan, Don, with Paula Hartz. (1992). *Abortion: A Doctor's Perspective/A Woman's Dilemma*. New York: Donald I. Fine.

Smelser, Neil. (1963). *Theory of Collective Behavior*. New York: Free Press.

Smith, F. LaGard. (1990). *When Choice Becomes God*. Eugene, OR: Harvest House.

Snow, David A., and Robert D. Benford. (1992). "Master Frames and Cycles of Protest." In Aldon D. Morris and Carol McClurg Mueller, eds., *Frontiers in Social Movement Theory*. New Haven, CT: Yale University Press.

Snow, David A., E. Burke Rochford, Jr., Steven K. Worden, and Robert D. Benford. (1986). "Frame Alignment Process, Micromobilization, and Movement Participation." *American Sociological Review* 51: 464–81.

Sproul, R. C. (1990). *Abortion: A Rational Look at an Emotional Issue*. Colorado Springs, CO: NavPress.

Staggenborg, Suzanne. (1989). "Organizational and Environmental Influences on the Development of the Pro-Choice Movement." *Social Forces* 68(1): 204–40 (September).

Stamps, Donald C., and J. Wesley Adams. (1992). *The Full Life Study Bible, New International Version*. Grand Rapids, MI: Zondervan.

Stewart, Charles J., Craig Allen Smith, and Robert E. Denton, Jr. (1989). *Persuasion and Social Movements*. Prospect Heights, IL: Waveland Press.

Straub, Gerard T. (1988). *Salvation for Sale: An Insider's View of Pat Robertson.* Buffalo, NY: Prometheus.

Stravinskas, Rev. Peter M. J., ed. (1991). *Our Sunday Visitor's Catholic Encyclopedia.* Huntington, IN: Our Sunday Visitor.

Terry, Randall. (1988). *Operation Rescue.* Springdale, PA: Whitaker House.

———. (1993). *Why Does a Nice Guy Like Me Keep Getting Thrown in Jail?* Lafayette, LA, and Windsor, NY: Huntington House and Resistance Press.

Turner, Ralph, and Lewis Killian. (1972). *Collective Behavior.* 2nd ed. Englewood Cliffs, NJ: Prentice-Hall.

Weigel, George. (1994). "Talking the Talk: Christian Conviction and Democratic Etiquette." In Michael Cromartie, ed., *Disciples and Democracy: Religious Conservatives and the Future of American Politics.* Grand Rapids, MI: Eerdmans.

Williams, Glanville. (1968). *Sanctity of Life and the Criminal Law.* New York: Knopf.

Williams, J. Rodman. (1988). *Renewal Theology: God, the World and Redemption.* Grand Rapids, MI: Academie Books.

Wilson, John. (1973). *Introduction to Social Movements.* New York: Basic Books.

Wuthnow, Robert. (1988). *The Restructuring of American Religion: Society and Faith Since World War II.* Princeton, NJ: Princeton University Press.

Young, Perry Deane. (1982). *God's Bullies: Native Reflections on Preachers and Politics.* New York: Holt, Rinehart, & Winston.

Zald, Mayer N. (1992). "Looking Backward to Look Forward: Reflections on the Past and Future of the Resource Mobilization Research Program." In Aldon D. Morris and Carol McClurg Mueller, eds., *Frontiers in Social Movement Theory.* New Haven, CT: Yale University Press.

FOR FURTHER READING

Abercrombie, Nicholas, Stephen Hill, and Bryan S. Turner. (1994). *Penguin Dictionary of Sociology.* 4th ed. New York: Penguin Books.

Abram, M. B. (1976). "Governor Carter's Religion." *The Nation,* September 25, pp. 261–62.

Alcorn, Randy C. (1992). *Pro-Life Answers to Pro-Choice Arguments.* Portland, OR: Multnomah Press.

Ammerman, Nancy. (1982). "Comment: Operationalizing Evangelicalism: An Amendment." *Sociological Analysis* 43(2): 170–71.

Andrusko, Dave. (1992a). "Supreme Court Reaffirms Abortion on Demand in Casey." *National Right to Life News* 19(12): 1+ (July 21).

———. (1992b). "Republican Platform Remains Strongly Pro-life." *National Right to Life News* 19(13): 18 (August 25).

Ankerberg, John, and John Weldon. (1989). *When Does Life Begin?* Brentwood, TN: Wolgemuth & Hyatt.

Avant, John, Malcolm McDow, and Alvin Reid, eds. (1996). *Revival! The Story of the Current Awakening in Brownwood, Ft. Worth, Wheaton, and Beyond.* Nashville, TN: Broadman & Holman.

Babcock, Charles R. (1987). "Charity Begins at Home . . . and Ends at Campaign Headquarters: Robertson's Fund-Raising Blends Ministry and Politics." *The Washington Post National Weekly Edition,* November 16, pp. 12–13.

Bajema, Clifford E. (1974). *Abortion and the Meaning of Personhood*. Grand Rapids, MI: Baker Book House.

Baker, Don. (1985). *Beyond Choice: The Abortion Story No One Is Telling*. Portland, OR: Multnomah Press.

Bangs, Carl. (1972). "Deceptive Statistics." *Christian Century* 89: 852–53.

Barna, George. (1991). *What Americans Believe: An Annual Survey of Values and Religious Views in the United States*. Ventura, CA: Regal Books.

Barrett, L. (1979). "Politicizing the World: Jerry Falwell's Patriotic Rallies." *Time*, October 1, 1979, pp. 62+.

Bauer, Gary L. (1996). *Our Hopes, Our Dreams: A Vision for America*. Colorado Springs, CO: Focus on the Family Publishing.

Beck, David W., ed. (1991). *Opening the American Mind: The Integration of Biblical Truth in the Curriculum of the University*. Grand Rapids, MI: Baker Book House.

Beckwith, Francis J., and Norman L. Geisler. (1991). *Matters of Life and Death: Calm Answers to Tough Questions About Abortion and Euthanasia*. Grand Rapids, MI: Baker Book House.

Bell, Daniel. (1955). *The New American Right*. New York: Criterion Books.

———. (1963). *The Radical Right*. Garden City, NY: Doubleday.

Bellah, Robert, Richard Madsen, William M. Sullivan, Ann Swindler, and Steven M. Tipton. (1985). *Habits of the Heart: Individualism and Commitment in American Life*. New York: Harper & Row.

Benson, P. L., and D. L. Williams. (1986). *Religion on Capitol Hill: Myths and Realities*. New York: Oxford University Press.

Bibby, R., and M. Brinkerhoff. (1973). "The Circulation of the Saints: A Study of People Who Join Conservative Churches." *Journal for the Scientific Study of Religion* 12: 273–82.

Bokenkotter, Thomas. (1977). *A Concise History of the Catholic Church*. New York: Image Books, Doubleday.

Bowers, James R., and Ellen M. Dran. (1991). "Adoption as the Solution to Abortion: Who Supports It?" Paper presented at the Midwest Political Science Association annual meeting, Chicago, Illinois.

Boyd, M. (1976) "Does God Have a Candidate?" *The Progressive*, November, pp. 25–27.

Bright, William R., interview. (1987). "Yoking Politics and Proclamation: Can It Be Done?" *Christianity Today*, September, pp. 20–22.

Brown, Les. (1953). *Television: The Business Behind the Box*. New York: Harcourt, Brace, Jovanovich.

Brudney, Jeffrey L., and Gary W. Copeland. (1984). "Evangelicals as a Political Force: Reagan and the 1980 Religious Vote." *Social Science Quarterly* 65(4): 1072–79.

Callahan, Daniel. (1970). *Abortion: Law, Choice, and Morality*. New York: Macmillan.

Cannon, David. (1985). "Abortion and Infanticide: Is There a Difference?" *Policy Review* 32: 12–13+ (Spring).

Carter, James Earl. (1976). "Politics and Religion." *America*, August 7, p. 40.

Case, Shirley Jackson. (1975). *The Social Origins of Christianity*. New York: Cooper Square.

Christian, S. Rickly. (1985). *The Woodland Hills Tragedy*. Westchester, IL: Crossway.

Clarke, Alan. (1987). "Moral Protest, Status Defense, and the Anti-abortion Campaign," *British Journal of Sociology* 38: 235–53 (June).

Cleghorn, J. S. (1986). "Respect for Life: Research Notes on Cardinal Bernardin's 'Seamless Garment,'" *Review of Religious Research* 28: 129–41.

Coleman, Evelyn. (1991). "Black Women Fight Silence on Abortion." *Utne Reader* (March/April), reprinted from *Southern Exposure*, Summer 1990.

Connery, John. (1977). *Abortion: The Development of the Roman Catholic Perspective*. Chicago: Loyola University Press.

Conover, Pamela Johnston. (1983a). "The Mobilization of the New Right: A Test of Various Explanations." *Western Political Quarterly* 36: 632–49.

———. (1983b). *Feminism and the New Right: Conflict over the American Family*. New York: Praeger.

Conway, Flo, and Jim Siegelman. (1984). *Holy Terror: The Fundamentalist War on America's Freedoms in Religion, Politics, and Our Private Lives*. New York: Dell Publishing Co.

Crawford, Alan. (1980). *Thunder on the Right: The Politics of Resentment*. New York: Pantheon.

Danforth, John C. (1994). *Resurrection: The Confirmation of Clarence Thomas*. New York: Viking Penguin.

Davis, Angela Y. (1983). *Women, Race, and Class*. New York: Vintage.

Dayton, Donald W., and Robert K. Johnston. (1991). *The Variety of American Evangelicalism*. Downer's Grove, IL: InterVarsity Press.

DeCoursey, Drew. (1992). *Lifting the Veil of Choice: Defending Life*. Huntington, IN: Our Sunday Visitor.

DeCoursey, Drew, and Mary Pride. (1988). *Unholy Sacrifices of the New Age*. Westchester, IL: Crossway.

Destro, Robert A. (1975). "Abortion and the Constitution: The Need for a Life-Protection Amendment." *California Law Review* 63: 1303.

Doner, Colonel V. (1988). *The Samaritan Strategy: A New Agenda for Christian Activism*. Brentwood, TN: Wolgemuth & Hyatt.

Donovan, John B. (1988). *Pat Robertson: The Authorized Biography*. New York: Macmillan.

Dugan, Robert P., Jr. (1991). *Winning the New Civil War*. Portland, OR: Multnomah Press.

Dunn, Charles W., ed. (1984). *American Political Theology*. New York: Praeger.

Ellerin, Milton, and Elisha H. Kesten. (1981). "The New Right: What Is It?" *Social Policy* 11(5): 54–62 (March/April).

Ellis, S. (1978). "Active in Politics: Concerned Christian Citizens for Political Action in Whatcom County, Washington." *Christianity Today*, March 24, pp. 50–51.

Ethridge, F. M., and J. R. Feagin. (1979). "Varieties of Fundamentalism: A Conceptual Analysis of Two Protestant Denominations." *Sociological Quarterly* 20: 37–48.

Evans, Debra. (1989). *Without Moral Limits: Women, Reproduction, and the New Medical Technology*. Westchester, IL: Crossway.

Exley, Richard. (1989). *Abortion: Pro-life by Conviction, Pro-choice by Default*. Tulsa, OK: Honor Books.

Falik, Marilyn. (1983). *Ideology and Abortion Policy Politics*. New York: Praeger.

Falwell, Jerry, ed. (1982). *Judgment Without Justice: The Dred Scott and Roe Vs. Wade Decisions*. Lynchburg, VA: Old-Time Gospel Hour.

Farmer, David Hugh. (1992). *The Oxford Dictionary of Saints*. 3rd ed. New York: Oxford University Press.

Feder, Don. (1993). *A Jewish Conservative Looks at Pagan America*. Lafayette, LA: Huntington House.

Fernandez, James. (1979). "On the Notion of Religious Movement," *Social Research* 46(1): 36–62 (Spring).

Finch, Phillip. (1983). *God, Guts, and Guns*. New York: Putnam.

Flake, Carol. (1984). *Redemptorama: Culture, Politics, and the New Evangelicalism*. Garden City, NY: Anchor Doubleday.

Flanagan, Geraldine Lux. (1962). *The First Nine Months of Life*. New York: Simon & Schuster.

Fletcher, Joseph. (1974). *The Ethics of Genetic Control: Ending Reproductive Roulette*. New York: Anchor.

Fore, William F. (1987). *Television and Religion: The Shaping of Faith, Values, and Culture*. Minneapolis: Augsburg Publishing House.

Forster, Arnold, and Benjamin R. Epstein. (1976). *Danger on the Right*. New York: Praeger.

Foss, Daniel. (1972). *Freak Culture: Lifestyle and Politics*. New York: E. P. Dutton.

Fowler, Robert B. (1985). *Religion and Politics in America*. Metuchen, NJ: Scarecrow.

Foy, Felicia A., and Rose M. Avato. (1986). *A Concise Guide to the Catholic Church II*. Huntington, IN: Our Sunday Visitor.

Francke, Linda Bird. (1978). *The Ambivalence of Abortion*. New York: Random House.

Francome, Colin. (1984). *Abortion Freedom*. London: George Allen & Unwin.

Furniss, Norman F. (1954). *The Fundamentalism Controversy*. New Haven, CT: Yale University Press.

Gallup, George, Jr., and Jim Castelli. (1989). *The People's Religion: American Faith in the 90's*. New York: Macmillan.

Ginsberg, Benjamin, and Martin Shefter. (1985). "A Critical Realignment? The New Politics, the Reconstructed Right, and the 1984 Election." In Michael Nelson, ed., *The Elections of 1984*. Washington, DC: CQ Press, pp. 1–26.

Glendon, Mary Ann. (1989). *The Transformation of Family Law: State, Law, and Family in the US and Western Europe*. Chicago: University of Chicago Press.

Glenn, Gary D. (1988). "Rhetoric and Religion in the 1984 Campaign," *Political Communication and Persuasion* 5(1).

Glessner, Thomas A. (1990). *Achieving an Abortion-Free America by 2001*. Portland, OR: Multnomah Press.

Glock, Charles Y., and Robert N. Bellah, eds. (1976). *The New Religious Consciousness*. Berkeley: University of California Press.

Glock, Charles, and Rodney Stark. (1968). *American Piety: The Nature of Religious Commitment*. Berkeley: University of California Press.

Goppel, A. (1974). "Political Dealings and Christian Belief." *Political Studies* 25: 195–214.

Gorman, Michael J. (1982). *Abortion and the Early Church.* Downer's Grove, IL: InterVarsity Press.

Granberg, Donald. (1978). "Pro-life or Reflection of Conservative Ideology? An Analysis of Opposition to Legalized Abortion." *Sociology and Social Research* 62: 414–29.

Grant, George. (1988). *Grand Illusions: The Legacy of Planned Parenthood.* Brentwood, TN: Wolgemuth & Hyatt.

———. (1991). *The Quick and the Dead: RU-486 and the New Chemical Warfare Against Your Family.* Wheaton, IL: Crossway.

———. (1994). *The Family Under Siege: What the New Social Engineers Have in Mind for You and Your Children.* Minneapolis, MN: Bethany House.

———. (1996). *Immaculate Deception: The Shifting Agenda of Planned Parenthood.* Chicago, IL: Northfield.

Gritsch, Eric W. (1982). *Born-Againism: Perspectives on a Movement.* Philadelphia: Fortress Press.

Grunlan, Stephen A. (1984). *Marriage and the Family: A Christian Perspective.* Grand Rapids, MI: Zondervan.

Gulotta, Joe. (1992). *Pro-life Christians: Heroes for the Pre-born.* Rockford, IL: Tan Books.

Guth, James L. (1983). "Politics of the Christian Right." In Allan J. Cigler and Burdett A. Loomis, eds., *Interest Group Politics.* Washington, DC: CQ Press.

Guth, James L., Ted G. Jelen, Lyman A. Kellstedt, Corwin E. Smidt, and Kenneth D. Wald. (1988). "The Politics of Religion in America: Issues for Investigation." *American Politics Quarterly* 16(3): 357–97 (July).

Hadden, Jeffrey K. (1969). *The Gathering Storm in the Churches.* Garden City, NY: Doubleday.

Hadden, Jeffrey K., and Charles E. Swann. (1981). *Prime-Time Preachers.* Reading, MA: Addison-Wesley.

Hammond, John L. (1979). *The Politics of Benevolence: Revival, Religion, and American Voting Behavior.* Norwood, NJ: Ablex.

Hammond, Phillip E. (1985). "The Curious Path of Conservative Protestantism." *Annals of the American Academy of Political and Social Science,* July, pp. 53–62.

Harrell, David E., Jr. (1987). *Pat Robertson: A Personal, Religious, and Political Portrait.* New York: Harper & Row.

Harrison, Michael I., and Bernard Laserwitz. (1982). "Do Denominations Matter?" *The American Journal of Sociology* 88(2): 356–77 (September).

Hart, Roderick P. (1977). *The Political Pulpit.* West Lafayette, IN: Purdue University Press.

Hartsock, Nancy. (1983). *Money, Sex, and Power.* New York: Longman.

Heldenbrand, Richard L. (1989). *Christianity and New Evangelical Philosophies.* Winona Lake, IN: Self-published.

Hershey, Marjorie Randon, and Darrell M. West. (1983). "Single Issue Politics: Prolife Groups and the 1980 Senate Campaign." In Allan J. Cigler and Burdett A. Loomis, eds. *Interest Group Politics.* Washington, DC: CQ Press.

Hertz, Sue. (1991). *Caught in the Crossfire: A Year on Abortions' Front Line*. Engle-wood Cliffs, NJ: Prentice-Hall.

Hibbs, Douglas A. (1982). "President Reagan's Mandate for the 1980 Elections: A Shift to the Right?" *American Political Quarterly* 10(4): 387–420.

Hill, Samuel S., and Dennis E. Owen. (1982). *The New Religious Political Right in America*. Nashville, TN: Abingdon Press.

Himmelstein, Jerome L., and James A. McCrae, Jr. (1984). "Social Conservatism, New Republicans, and the 1980 Election." *Public Opinion Quarterly* 48: 592–605.

Hirschman, A. O. (1977). *The Passion and the Interests: Political Arguments for Capitalism Before Its Triumph*. Princeton, NJ: Princeton University Press.

Hitchcock, James. (1981). "Church, State and Moral Values: The Limits of American Pluralism." *Law and Contemporary Problems* 44(2): 3–22 (Spring).

Hooper, Manny. (1987). *The Effect of Revivals on the World Missionary Movement: 1727 to Present*. Pasadena, CA: Fuller Theological Seminary.

———. (1989). *Worldwide Evangelical Awakenings and Revivals, 1700 Onwards and the Completion of the Great Commission*. Pasadena, CA: Fuller Theological Seminary.

"House Panel Approves Bill: Make Clinic Sit-Ins Federal Crime, Administration Urges." (1993). *National Right to Life News* 20(6): 13–14.

Hunter, James Davison. (1981). "Operationalizing Evangelicalism: A Review, Critique, and Proposal." *Sociological Analysis* 42(4): 363–72.

———. (1983). *American Evangelicalism: Conservative Religion and the Quandary of Modernity*. New Brunswick, NJ: Rutgers University Press.

———. (1987). *Evangelicalism: The Coming Generation*. Chicago: University of Chicago Press.

Issel, William. (1985). *Social Change in the United States, 1945–1983*. New York: Schocken.

Johnson, Stephen D., and Joseph B. Tamney. (1988). "Factors Related to Inconsistent Life-Views." *Review of Religious Research* 30(1): 40–46 (September).

Johnston, Michael. (1982). "The 'New Christian Right' in American Politics." *Political Quarterly* 53(2): 181–99 (April-June).

Jones, D. Gareth. (1985). *Brave New People*. Grand Rapids, MI: Eerdmans.

Judges, Donald P. (1993). *Hard Choices, Lost Voices: How the Abortion Conflict Has Divided America, Distorted Constitutional Rights, and Damaged the Courts*. Chicago: Ivan R. Dee.

Jung, Patricia Beattie, and Thomas A. Shannon, eds. (1988). *Abortion and Catholicism: The American Debate*. New York: Crossroads.

Kater, John L., Jr. (1982). *Christians on the Right: The Moral Majority in Perspective*. New York: Seabury Press.

Kelley, Dean. (1972). *Why Conservative Churches Are Growing*. New York: Harper & Row.

———. (1984). "Why Conservative Churches Are Still Growing." In Patrick H. McNamara, ed., *Religion: North American Style*. Belmont, CA: Wadsworth.

Kelly, George Armstrong. (1982). "Faith, Freedom, and Disenchantment: Politics and the American Religious Consciousness." *Daedelus* 111(1): 127–48 (Winter).

Kennedy, D. James. (1985). "Myths and Realities." In John W. Whitehead, ed. *Arresting Abortion: Practical Ways to Save Unborn Children*. Westchester, IL: Crossway, pp. 18–31.

Keynes, Edward, with Randall K. Miller. (1989). *The Court v. Congress: Prayer, Busing, and Abortion*. Durham, NC: Duke University Press.

Kilpatrick, John M. (1996). Speech at Lake Shafer Christian Center, Monticello, IN (August 17).

King, Desmond. (1987). *The New Right: Politics, Markets, and Citizenship*. Chicago: Dorsey Press.

Klatch, Rebecca A. (1987). *Women of the New Right*. Philadelphia: Temple University Press.

Kosmin, Barry A., and Seymour P. Lachman. (1993). *One Nation Under God: Religion in Contemporary Society*. New York: Harmony Books.

Kuklinski, James H., and Darrel M. West. (1981). "Economic Expectations and Voting Behavior in United States House and Senate Elections." *American Political Science Review* 75: 436–47.

Ladd, Everett Carll. (1990). *Abortion: The Nation Responds*. New York: W. W. Norton.

Lader, Lawrence. (1966). *Abortion*. Boston: Beacon Press.

———. (1973). *Abortion II: Making the Revolution*. Boston: Beacon Press.

Lang, Kurt, and Gladys Lang. (1961). *Collective Dynamics*. New York: Thomas Y. Crowell.

Lenski, G. (1963). *The Religious Factor*. New York: Doubleday.

Liebman, Robert C., and Robert Wuthnow, eds. (1983). *The New Christian Right*. New York: Aldine.

Lienesch, Michael. (1982). "Right-Wing Religion: Christian Conservatism as a Political Movement." *Political Science Quarterly* 97: 403–25.

Lindstrom, Dr. Paul D. (1988). *4 Days in May . . . Storming the Gates of Hell*. Arlington Heights, IL: Christian Liberty Press.

Lipset, Seymour Martin, and Earl Raab. (1981). "The Election and the Evangelicals." *Commentary* 71: 25–31.

Little, Rev. Daniel J. (1987). *The Right and Responsibility to Rescue*. San Francisco: Christian Resource Network.

Lorentzen, L. J. (1980). "Evangelical Life Style Concerns Expressed in Political Action." *Social Analysis* 41: 144–54.

Lovejoy, David S. (1969). *Religious Enthusiasm and the Great Awakening*. Englewood Cliffs, NJ: Prentice-Hall.

Lovenduski, Joni, and Joyce Outshoorn, eds. (1986). *The New Politics of Abortion*. London: Sage.

Macaluso, Theodore F., and John Wanat. (1979). "Voting Turnout and Religiosity." *Polity* 12(1): 158–69 (Fall).

Macedo, Stephen. (1987). *The New Right v. the Constitution*. Washington, DC: Cato Institute.

MacNair, Rachel, Mare Krane Derr, and Linda Naranjo-Huebl, eds. (1995). *Prolife Feminism: Yesterday and Today*. New York: Sulzburger & Graham.

Maloy, Kate, and Maggie Patterson. (1992). *Birth or Abortion? Private Struggles in a Political World*. New York: Plenum.

Mannion, Michael T. (1986). *Abortion and Healing: A Cry to Be Whole*. Kansas City, MO: Sheed & Ward.

Margolis, Michael, and Kevin Neary. (1980). "Pressure Politics Revisited: The Anti-abortion Campaign." *Policy Studies Journal* 8: 698–716.

Marsden, George M. (1980). *Fundamentalism and American Culture: The Shaping of 20th-Century Evangelicalism 1870–1925*. New York: Oxford University Press.

Marshall, Peter, and David Manuel. (1986). *From Sea to Shining Sea*. Old Tappan, NJ: Fleming H. Revell.

Martin, Jane. (1993). *Keely and Du*. New York: Samuel French.

Marty, Martin E. (1976). *A Nation of Behavers*. Chicago: University of Chicago Press.

———. (1992). "Fundamentals of Fundamentalism." In Lawrence Kaplan, *Fundamentalism in Comparative Perspective*. Amherst: University of Massachusetts Press.

Marty, Martin E., and R. Scott Appleby. (1992). *The Glory and the Power: The Fundamentalist Challenge to the Modern World*. Boston: Beacon.

Marx, Gary T. (1967). "Religion: Opiate or Inspiration of Civil Rights Militancy Among Negroes." *American Sociological Review* 32: 64–72 (February).

McCarthy, John D. (1977). "Resource Mobilization and Social Movements: A Partial Theory." *American Journal of Sociology* 82: 1212–41.

———. (1987). "Pro-Life and Pro-Choice Mobilization: Infrastructure Deficits and New Technologies." In Mayer N. Zald and John D. McCarthy, eds., *Social Movements in an Organizational Society*. New Brunswick, NJ: Transaction Books, pp. 49–66.

McCarthy, John D., and Mark Wolfson. (1992). "Consensus Movements, Conflict Movements, and the Cooptation of Civic and State Infrastructures." In Aldon D. Morris and Carol McClurg Mueller, eds., *Frontiers in Social Movement Theory*. New Haven, CT: Yale University Press.

McDowell, Josh, and Don Stewart. (1989). *Handbook of Today's Religions*. San Bernardino, CA: Here's Life Publishers.

Medved, Michael. (1992). *Hollywood vs. America: Popular Culture and the War on Traditional Values*. New York: HarperCollins/Zondervan.

Mehl, Roger. (1970). *The Sociology of Protestantism*. London: SCM Press.

Melton, J. Gordon, ed. (1991). *The Encyclopedia of American Religions: A Comprehensive Study of the Major Religious Groups in the United States and Canada*, vol. I. Tarrytown, NY: Triumph.

Menendez, Albert J. (1976). "Will Evangelicals Swing the Election?" *Christianity Today*, June 18, pp. 20–22.

Miller, Arthur H., and Martin P. Wattenberg. (1984). "Politics from the Pulpit: Religiosity and the 1980 Elections." *Public Opinion Quarterly* 48: 301–17.

Miller, T., and T. Rush. (1976). "God and the GOP in Kansas City." *Christianity Today*, September 10, pp. 59–60.

Moen, Matthew C. (1984). "School Prayer and the Politics of Lifestyle Concern." *Social Science Quarterly* 64(4): 1065–71 (December).

———. (1992). *The Transformation of the Christian Right*. Tuscaloosa: University of Alabama Press.

Mohr, James. (1978). *Abortion in America*. New York: Oxford University Press.

Mol, Hans J. (1976). *Identity and the Sacred: A Sketch for a New Social Scientific Theory of Religion*. New York: Free Press.

Morris, Charles R. (1984). *A Time of Passion: America, 1960–1980*. New York: Harper & Row.

Morrow, Lance. (1992). "The US Campaign: Family Values." *Time* 140(9): 22–27 (August 31).

Mueller, Carol. (1981). "Belief Constraint and Belief Consensus: Toward an Analysis of Social Movement Ideologies—A Research Note." *Social Forces* 60(1): 182–87 (September).

———. (1983). "In Search of a Constituency for the 'New Religious Right,'" *Public Opinion Quarterly* 47(2): 213–29 (Summer).

———. (1992). "Building Social Movement Theory." In Aldon D. Morris and Carol McClurg Mueller, eds., *Frontiers in Social Movement Theory*. New Haven, Connecticut: Yale University Press.

Myers, Nancy. (1993). "Hitting a New Low in Bias." *National Right to Life News* 20(6): 4–8 (March 30).

Nash, Ronald H. (1987). *Evangelicals in America: Who They Are, What They Believe*. Nashville, TN: Abingdon.

Nathanson, Bernard. (1979). *Aborting America*. Garden City, NY: Doubleday.

Nice, David C. (1988). "Abortion Clinic Bombings As Political Violence." *American Journal of Political Science* 32: 178–95.

Nolan, Kathleen. (1988). "Genug ist genug: A Fetus Is Not a Kidney." *The Hastings Center Report* 18: 13–19.

Noonan, John T. (1965). *Contraception: A History of Its Treatment by the Catholic Theologians and Canonists*. Cambridge, MA: Harvard University Press.

———. (1970). *The Morality of Abortion*. Cambridge, MA: Harvard University Press.

———. (1979). *A Private Choice: Abortion in America in the Seventies*. New York: Free Press.

North, Gary. (1989). *When Justice Is Aborted: Biblical Standards for Non-Violent Resistance*. Fort Worth, TX: Dominion Press.

"NRLC Condemns Shooting of Abortionist Dr. Gunn." (1993). *National Right to Life News* 20(6): 1 (March 30).

Olasky, Marvin. (1988). *Prodigal Press: The Anti-Christian Bias of the American News Media*. Westchester, IL: Crossway Books.

Page, Ann L., and Donald A. Clelland. (1978). "The Kanawha County Textbook Controversy: A Study of the Politics of Life Style Concern." *Social Forces* 57(1): 265–81.

Paige, Connie. (1983). *The Right to Lifers: Who They Are, How They Operate, Where They Get Their Money*. New York: Summit.

Patel, Kent, Denny Pilant, and Gary Rose. (1982). "Born-Again Christians in the Bible Belt: A Study in Religion, Politics, and Ideology." *American Politics Quarterly* 10(2): 255–72 (April).

Piven, Frances Fox, and Richard A. Cloward. (1992). "Normalizing Collective Protest." In Aldon D. Morris and Carol McClurg Mueller, eds., *Frontiers in Social Movement Theory*. New Haven, CT: Yale University Press.

Powell, John. (1981). *Abortion: The Silent Holocaust*. Allen, TX: Argus Communications.

Quebedeax, Richard. (1978). *The Worldly Evangelicals*. New York: Harper & Row.
———. (1983). *The New Charismatics II*. New York: Harper & Row.
Reardon, David C. (1987). *Aborted Women, Silent No More: 20 Women Share Their Personal Journeys from the Tragedy of Abortion to Restored Wholeness*. Westchester, IL: Crossway.
Reichley, A. James. (1985). *Religion in American Public Life*. Washington, DC: Brookings Institution.
Reisser, Teri, and Paul Reisser. (1989). *Help for the Post-Abortion Woman*. Grand Rapids, MI: Zondervan.
Robertson, Pat. (1972). *Shout It from the Housetops*. Plainfield, NJ: Logo International.
———. (1990). *The New Millennium*. Dallas: Word Publishing.
Rodman, Hyman, Betty Sarvis, and Joy Walker Bonar. (1987). *The Abortion Question*. New York: Columbia University Press.
Roof, Wade Clark, and William McKinney. (1985). "Denominational America and the New Religious Pluralism." *Annals of the American Academy of Political and Social Science* 480: 24–38 (July).
Rosen, Harold, ed. (1954). *Therapeutic Abortion: Medical, Psychiatric, Legal, Anthropological, and Religious Considerations*. New York: Julian Press.
Rosten, Leo. (1975). *Religions of America: Ferment and Faith in an Age of Crisis*. New York: Simon & Schuster.
Rothenberg, S., and F. Newport. (1984). *The Evangelical Voter*. Washington, DC: Institute for Government and Politics.
Rowland, Robyn, ed. (1984). *Women Who Do and Women Who Don't Join the Women's Movement*. Boston: Routledge & Kegan Paul.
Saltenberger, Ann. (1983). *Every Woman Has a Right to Know the Dangers of Legal Abortion*. Glassboro, NJ: Air-Plus Enterprises.
Sandeen, Ernest. (1967). "Toward a Historical Interpretation of Fundamentalism." *Church History* 36: 66–83.
———. (1970a). "Fundamentalism and American Identity." *The Annals* 387: 56–65.
———. (1970b). *The Roots of Fundamentalism*. Chicago: University of Chicago Press.
Schaeffer, Francis A. (1981). *A Christian Manifesto*. Westchester, IL: Crossway.
Schlafly, Phyllis. (1984). *Child Abuse in the Classroom*. Excerpts from official transcript of proceedings before the U.S. Department of Education in the Matter of Proposed Regulations to Implement the Protection of Pupil Rights Amendment, Section 439 of the GEPA, also known as the Hatch Amendment. Alton, IL: Pere Marquette Press.
Schultze, Quentin J. (1991). *Televangelism and American Culture: The Business of Popular Religion*. Grand Rapids, MI: Baker Book House.
Shaver, Jessica. (1995). *Gianna: Aborted . . . And Lived to Tell About It*. Colorado Springs, CO: Focus on the Family Publishing.
Shibley, David. (1989). *A Force in the Earth: The Charismatic Renewal and World Evangelism*. Altamonte Springs, FL: Creation House.
Shriver, P. L. (1985). "Religion's Very Public Presence." *Annals of the American Academy of Political and Social Science* 480: 142–43 (July).
Shupe, Anson, and William Stacey. (1983). "The Moral Majority Constituency."

In Robert C. Liebman and Robert Wuthnow, eds., *The New Christian Right*. New York: Aldine.

Sider, Ronald J. (1987). *Completely Pro-Life: Building a Consistent Stance on Abortion, the Family, Nuclear Weapons, the Poor*. Downer's Grove, IL: InterVarsity Press.

Skoglund, Elizabeth R. (1989). *Life on the Line*. Wheaton, IL: Tyndale House.

Slann, Martin, and Susan Duffy, eds. (1990). *Morality and Conviction in American Politics: A Reader*. Englewood Cliffs, NJ: Prentice-Hall.

Smidt, Corwin. (1989). " 'Praise the Lord' Politics: A Comparative Analysis of the Social Characteristics and Political Views of American Evangelical and Charismatic Christians." *Sociological Analysis* 50: 53–72.

Snyder, David, and Charles Tilly. (1972). "Hardship and Collective Violence in France, 1830–1960." *American Sociological Review* 37.

Sommers, Christina Hoff. (1994). *Who Stole Feminism: How Women Have Betrayed Women*. New York: Simon & Schuster.

Spero, Rabbi Aryeh. (1989). "Therefore Choose Life: How the Great Faiths View Abortion." *Policy Review* 48: 38–44 (Spring).

Staggenborg, Suzanne. (1987). "Life-Style Preferences and Social Movement Recruitment: Illustrations from the Abortion Conflict." *Social Science Quarterly* 68: 779–97.

———. (1991). *The Pro-Choice Movement: Organization and Activism in the Abortion Conflict*. New York: Oxford University Press.

Stedman, M. S., Jr. (1964). *Religion and Politics in America*. New York: Harcourt, Brace, & World.

Swan, George Steven. (1973). "Untitled Article by George Steven Swan." *The Sisterlife Journal* 2(1): 1–4.

Swindoll, Charles R. (1990). *Sanctity of Life: The Inescapable Issue*. Dallas: Word Publishing.

Tarrow, Sidney. (1992). "Mentalities, Political Cultures, and Collective Action Frames: Constructing Meanings Through Action." In Aldon D. Morris and Carol McClurg Mueller, eds., *Frontiers in Social Movement Theory*. New Haven, CT: Yale University Press.

Tatalovich, Raymond, and Byron W. Daynes. (1981). *The Politics of Abortion: A Study of Community Conflict in Public Policymaking*. New York: Praeger.

Terry, Randall. (1990). *Accessory to Murder: The Enemies, Allies, and Accomplices To the Death of Our Culture*. Brentwood, TN: Wolgemuth & Hyatt.

"This Week." (1994). *National Review* 46: 12 (December).

Thompson, Kenneth W. (1986). "Religion and Politics in the United States: An Overview." *Annals of the American Academy of Political and Social Science* 483: 12–24 (January).

Tribe, Laurence H. (1990). *Abortion: The Clash of Absolutes*. New York: W. W. Norton.

Turner, Ralph. (1969). "The Theme of Contemporary Social Movement." *British Journal of Sociology* 20: 390–405.

Viguerie, Richard. (1980). *The New Right: We're Ready to Lead*. Falls Church, VA: Viguerie Co.

Wald, Kenneth. (1987). *Religion and Politics in the United States*. New York: St. Martin's.

Wald, Kenneth, Dennis E. Owen, and Samuel S. Hill. (1988). "Churches As Po-
    litical Communities." *American Political Science Review* 82: 531–48.
Wallis, Jim. (1995). *The Soul of Politics: Beyond "Religious Right and Secular Left."*
    New York: Harcourt Brace & Co.
Wallis, Roy. (1979). *Salvation and Protest: Studies of Social and Religious Movements.*
    New York: St. Martin's.
Walter, Jess. (1995). *Every Knee Shall Bow: The Truth and Tragedy of Ruby Ridge and
    the Randy Weaver Family.* New York: HarperCollins.
Warner, R. S. (1979). "Theoretical Barriers to Understanding Evangelical Chris-
    tianity." *Sociological Analysis* 40: 1–9.
Wennberg, Robert N. (1985). *Life in the Balance: Exploring the Abortion Controversy.*
    Grand Rapids, MI: Eerdmans.
Whitehead, John W., ed. (1985). *Arresting Abortion: Practical Ways to Save Unborn
    Children.* Westchester, IL: Crossway.
Wilcox, Clyde. (1986). "Fundamentalists and Politics: An Analysis of the Effects
    of Differing Operational Definitions." *Journal of Politics* 48: 1041–51.
———. (1987a). "Religious Attitudes and Anti-Feminism: An Analysis of the
    Ohio Moral Majority." *Women and Politics* 7: 59–77.
———. (1987b). "Religious Orientations and Political Attitudes: Variations
    Within the New Christian Right." *American Politics Quarterly* 15: 274–96.
———. (1987c). "America's Radical Right Revisited: A Comparison of the Activ-
    ists in the Christian Right in Two Decades." *Sociological Analysis* 48: 46–
    75.
———. (1988). "Political Action Committees of the New Christian Right: A Lon-
    gitudinal Analysis." *Journal for the Scientific Study of Religion* 27(1): 60–71.
———. (1989a). "Feminism and Anti-Feminism Among Evangelical Women."
    Western Political Quarterly 42(1): 147–60 (March).
———. (1989b). "The Fundamentalist Voter: Politicized Religious Identity and
    Political Identity and Behavior." *Review of Religious Research* 31: 54–67.
Will, Jeffry, and Rhys Williams. (1986). "Political Ideology and Political Action
    in the New Christian Right." *Sociological Analysis* 47: 160–168.
Wilson, John. (1978). *Religion in American Society: The Effective Presence.* Engle-
    wood Cliffs, NJ: Prentice-Hall.
Wuthnow, Robert. (1989). *The Struggle for America's Soul: Evangelicals, Liberals, and
    Secularism.* Grand Rapids, MI: Eerdmans.
Young, Curt. (1983). *The Least of These.* Chicago: Moody Press.
Zald, Mayer N., and Roberta Ash. (1966). "Social Movements: Growth, Decay,
    and Change." *Social Forces* 44: 327–40.
Zald, Mayer N., and Michael Berger. (1978). "Social Movements in Organizations:
    Coup d'Etat, Insurgency, and Mass Movement." *American Journal of Soci-
    ology* 83: 823–60.

Index

About the Author

KERRY N. JACOBY, Ph.D., is a political science and American Studies specialist who currently makes her home in West Lafayette, Indiana, with her husband and two children.

ISBN 0-275-96044-7

90000>

EAN

9 780275 960445

HARDCOVER BAR CODE